THE POLITICS

OF

MULTIRACIALISM

The

POLITICS

of

MULTIRACIALISM

Challenging Racial Thinking

Edited by

Heather M. Dalmage

State University of New York Press

Published by
STATE UNIVERSITY OF NEW YORK PRESS, ALBANY

© 2004 State University of New York

For information, address the State University of New York Press,
90 State Street, Suite 700, Albany, NY 12207

Production, Laurie Searl
Marketing, Michael Campochiaro

Library of Congress Cataloging-in-Publication Data

The politics of multiracialism : challenging racial thinking / edited by Heather M.
Dalmage.
    p. cm.
    Includes bibliographical references and index.
    ISBN 0-7914-6153-X (acid-free paper)—ISBN 0-7914-6154-8 (pbk.: acid-free paper)
    1. United States—Race relations.   2. Racially mixed people—Race identity—
United States.   3. Race awareness—United States.   4. Ethnicity—United States.
5. Racism—United States.   6. Racially mixed people—United States—Social
conditions.   7. Social movements—United States.   I. Dalmage, Heather M., 1965–

E184.A1P655 2004
305.8'05073—dc22   2004043454

10 9 8 7 6 5 4 3 2 1

To my beautiful children,

Mahalia and Owen

CONTENTS

ACKNOWLEDGMENTS

This book would not have been possible without the engaging insights (and unending patience) of the contributing authors. I would like to particularly thank Barbara Katz Rothman who continues to provide mentorship and friendship. The early support of Clarence Wood and Terry Johnson at the Human Relations Foundation of Chicago, Lucreticia Bailey at the Chicago Council on Urban Affairs, and the Institute for Metropolitan Affairs and the Center for New Deal Studies at Roosevelt University were central to making this book a reality. The Mansfield Institute for Social Justice and the St. Clair Drake Center for African American Studies have also provided necessary resources to complete this project.

I would like to thank a few individuals who helped in various ways to bring this book to completion: Anna Stange, Lionel G. Trepanier, DaShelle Frazier, Lutricia Johnson, Cedtrice Baker, Bertha Cousins, Emilia Anton, Jason Cook, Andy Lowry. A special thanks to Dorothy Trepanier for carefully reading the entire text in very short time. Thanks also to the anonymous reviewers who gave detailed and helpful criticism. To the editors at SUNY Press, thanks. Ronald Helfrich saw the potential of this project and Nancy Ellegate guided it through to completion. In addition, thanks, as always, to everyone in my family for their unending support. Thanks to Philip for his continued friendship, support, and love. Thanks to my baby-girl, Mahalia for asking so many questions. Owen, I am looking forward to your insights.

INTRODUCTION

Heather M. Dalmage

"Almighty God created the races White, Black, Yellow, Malay, and Red, and he placed them on separate continents. The fact that he separated the races shows that he did not intend them to mix."[1] With these words Judge Bazile sentenced Mildred and Richard Loving, an interracial couple from Virginia, to one year in prison in 1950. The crime—marrying across race lines. His ruling reflects the history of racial formation in the United States. Calling upon a mixture of religious and scientific mythology, the judge used his power on behalf of the state to strengthen racial categories and white supremacy. After living in exile in Washington, D.C., for nearly seventeen years, the Lovings finally had their case heard before the Supreme Court. Buttressed by the strength of the civil rights movement in 1967, more than 240 years since the first codified antimiscegenation law,[2] the United States Supreme Court declared intermarriage legal in every state.[3] Given the legal green light, multiracial families began to form, leading to what Maria Root has called the "biracial babyboom."[4] Of course, intermixing has occurred throughout history, but this would mark the first time that U.S. law would honor each partner as racially equal in the marriage contract. The Loving decision created the legal, if not the social, space for the growth of multiracial family organizations and other forms of multiracial expression, which eventually became collectively known as the Multiracial Movement.

1

Cynthia Nakashima defines the Multiracial Movement broadly as "the emergence of community organizations, campus groups, magazines and newsletters, academic research and writing, university courses, creative expression, and political activism—all created and done by mixed-race individuals and members of interracial families, with the purpose of voicing their own experiences, opinions, issues and interests."[5] Because multiracial people, and often their families, are visible indicators that the color line has been breached they "will very likely be forced to participate in the dialogue at some level."[6] Thus, the movement extends beyond those who are active in multiracial organizations and overt politics. It includes all members of multiracial families; even those who want to opt out of racial discussions. For instance, when identifying themselves and others they may claim to be color-blind (culture matters not race), they may claim membership in a single racial community (my dad may be white, but I'm black and that's that), they may advocate for recognition of a multiracial identity (I have the right to identify how I choose). In each of these examples a particular racial ideology and racial politics is being forwarded. This anthology will focus on the political issues and interests conveyed through the broadly defined Multiracial Movement by exploring the origins, discourse, and social justice outcomes. The goal of this anthology is to both better understand racial thinking that may ultimately reproduce the hegemonic racial discourse and to posit a counterhegemonic "multiracial politics grounded in historical and material realities."[7]

A BRIEF HISTORY OF THE MOVEMENT

While the Multiracial Movement has its origins in the civil rights movement, many of the six dozen or so multiracial family organizations that currently exist across the United States were developing socially, ideologically, and politically during the conservative Reagan years. By the 1990s, conservative politicians became a force behind the Multiracial Movement.[8] Four other factors intersected to create the current momentum of the Multiracial Movement: the increased academic and popular literature on the topic of multiracialism; the question of racial categories on Census 2000; the debates surrounding race and adoption; and the popularity of celebrities such as Tiger Woods and Mariah Cary.

Multiracial family organizations began to sprout up in the late 1970s as places where parents could gain support and learn how to guide their multiracial children in a racially divided and racist society. I-Pride (Interracial/Intercultural Pride), the "oldest existing multiracial group in the U.S.," was founded in February 1979 in the San Francisco Bay area to address the issue of racial classification and identity of multiracial children.[9] For instance, I-Pride was particularly active in the school system and by the early 1980s, its newsletters were reporting the victories of having an "interracial" category added by some schools. While I-Pride became politically involved early in the 1980s, most organizations were coming together for social support. A year after the founding of I-Pride, the Biracial Family Network (BFN) in Chicago was developed. One of the founders of BFN explained, "My son was really the reason I wanted to start an organization. I had heard about I-Pride in California so I wrote to them and they gave me tips on how to get the group started. In September 1980 there were six women, each was a mother of biracial children, and we've evolved since."[10] From the early 1980s, then, communication was developing among multiracial family members and between multiracial organizations. The Association of MultiEthnic Americans (AMEA) was founded in 1988 as an umbrella organization for multiracial organizations across the country. A year later, AMEA president Carlos Fernandez forwarded a proposal to the chair of the Subcommittee on the Census and Population. In the cover letter Fernandez wrote:

> We would propose that all federal forms, including the Census, add the category "multiethnic/interracial" and permit those who check this box to check all other boxes that apply. . . . We realize it is probably too late to add a new category to the 1990 census form. However, it is not too late to amend the rules governing the tallying of race/ethnicity on the 1990 census form to allow individuals the opportunity to designate more than one ethnic/racial category to accurately reflect the fullness of their heritage.[11]

The BFN in Chicago was a primary affiliate to AMEA, and thus became decidedly political. Like other multiracial family organizations across the country, what had began as a group of mothers meeting to discuss the narrowness of racial categories, community, kinship, and racism was now becoming an organization with a political agenda that would challenge the discussion of race in the United States.[12]

The development of multiracial organizations in the 1980s was occurring in a political climate overwhelmingly defined by the backlash against and retreat from group rights legislation, and programs and a movement toward racial color blindness. Omi and Winant point out that under Reagan history was rewritten "to suggest that discrimination against racial minorities had been drastically curbed."[13] Local, state, and federal agencies driven by neoconservative agendas were actively questioning the relevance of race-based policies.[14] Conservatives both within and outside the Multiracial Movement seized the opportunity to posit race as a human construction void of material outcomes. The logic that followed was that race-based programs in an otherwise equal society are nothing short of reverse racism.

The advocacy of color blindness by conservatives in the Multiracial Movement extends to issues of adoption, affirmative action, and beyond, and is part of a larger societal movement away from group-based policies.

Throughout the 1990s, civil rights gains were being repealed with regularity. Not coincidentally, these years were also marked by an increasing public visibility and awareness of multiracialism. The reversal of civil rights gains and the visibility of multiracialism merged in 1997 when conservative Republican Newt Gingrich voiced his support for a multiracial category.[15] His support was embraced by many in the Multiracial Movement, for a few others it was a wake-up call.[16] Multiracial organizations have continued to link arms with conservative organizations such as Ward Connerly's American Civil Rights Institute, an organization dedicated to dismantling group-based protections. For instance, at the "Multiracial Leadership Round Table 2000 Census: A Discussion About Our Choices," Connerly was inducted into the 2000 Racial Harmony Hall of Fame. The award was created by the conservative multiracial organization, A Place For Us Ministry for Interracial Couples.[17] It was the support by Newt Gingrich, however, that proved to be a turning point for the most politically influential organization in the Multiracial Movement: AMEA began, at this time, to outwardly express concern about accepting support from and aligning itself with conservatives. Long-standing tensions within the movement erupted into a full-fledged cleavage.

Broadly speaking, each side is ultimately interested in the same outcome, that is, official recognition of multiracial people. However, the political means for reaching that end differ. On the one side are those who align themselves with conservatives and believe that the Multiracial Movement needs to focus on removing the concept of race either through the introduction of a multiracial category or by advocating for color-blind agendas; on the other side are those who align themselves with liberals and believe that multiracial people should be a "protected" group. Within each of these sides additional splits and tensions have arisen.[18]

As the movement continued to develop and transform in the 1990s it began to find voice in academic literature, popular literature, census debates, and pop culture icons. The introduction of discussions of multiracialism, hybridity, and racial mixing occurred amidst existing discussions of authenticity, community boundaries, identity politics, the social construction of race, and postmodern fragmentation. These discussions have prompted race theorists to more clearly delineate connections between community boundaries, identities, and politics.[19] Moreover, a number of autobiographies written by members of multiracial families have been widely read,[20] including James McBride's The Color of Water, which spent a number of weeks on the New York Times bestseller list. Collectively these books began a process of rearticulating traditional understandings of race both inside and outside the academy. Individuals have been invited to think about race as a social construction, something created in the context of human interaction not human biology.

The question of racial classification further invited a rethinking of race and strengthened the Multiracial Movement. The struggle on behalf of "our children" has prompted many parents (mostly white) of multiracial children to challenge traditional categories.[21] In an attempt to count the U.S. population the Office of Management and Budget (OMB) created the 2000 Census Advisory Board which was charged with debating and ultimately informing the OMB about how it should approach questions of race on the census. For the first time in history the advisory board included a representative from the Multiracial Movement; then-president of AMEA Ramona Douglass. Tensions developed between the Multiracial Movement and other groups represented on the board. Traditional civil rights organizations such as the National Council of LaRaza, the NAACP, the Urban League, and the National Congress of American Indians were already struggling against conservative political ideologies and the reversal of civil rights gains when the 2000 census debates erupted. These organizations spoke out publicly and sharply against a multiracial category, and at times worked together against the addition of a multiracial category. Concern for the further erosion of civil rights gains was central to the opposition.

As the advisory board was embroiled in debates about the meaning of racial categorization, process of tabulation, and the possible addition of a multiracial category, Tiger Woods was tearing up the fairways and had just won his first Professional Golf Association (PGA) tournament. His claims to a multiracial, "Cablanasian" identity caught the attention of the nation. Although cleavages existed, the Multiracial Movement rode the wave of Tiger's multiracial stardom to further strengthen its demands for a reconsidering of racial classification on the census.

Despite the political differences among the politically active individuals in the Multiracial Movement, signs appeared that a sense of community was developing among many members of multiracial families. These signs included the growth of local multiracial organizations, and the increasing number of books, magazines, newspaper articles, television specials, websites, conferences, and newsletters. Like all social movements that "create collective identity, collective subjectivity, by offering their adherents a different view of themselves and their world," the Multiracial Movement began to shape and transform collective multiracial identities.[22] The task of *The Politics of Multiracialism* is to analyze what this transformation means within the current racial politics. The chapters that follow will collectively show that the outcome desired by both the conservative and liberal multiracial agendas is official multiracial recognition and that such an agenda is undermining struggles for liberation currently being waged against white supremacy and racial injustice.

POTENTIAL AND PITFALLS: DISCOURSE OF THE MOVEMENT

The Multiracial Movement has expanded the way many individuals in the United States think about race. First, notions of race as biological and essential, which had been challenged through the civil rights movement, have been further disrupted through the ways in which members of multiracial families have framed their lived experiences. Second, the Multiracial Movement has expanded racial language, at times allowing for a more sophisticated understanding of race and racism. Primarily, a language is being created that is challenging notions of authenticity and the lines that divide racial communities, while acknowledging individual and racial differences in a positive light.[23] At the same time the movement can be credited with these advances in racial thinking, the movement is also being complicit with white supremacy as seen through claims to color blindness and by the acknowledgment of racial divisions without the acknowledgment of racial hierarchies.

For most of our history, the United States has created and functioned with an essentialist vision of race, a vision that paints race as historical, natural, static, biological, universal, and immutable. The civil rights movement forced a rethinking, a rearticulation of race.[24] For instance, when Martin Luther King Jr. pointed out that people should be judged by the content of their character and not the color of their skin, he was disrupting biological and essentialist notions of race. He was asserting a belief that racial essentialism is a surrender of human agency to the constraints imposed by racist categories. Unfortunately, disrupting essentialist notions of race, including myths of white purity and the one-drop rule does not create a more progressive and just society. In fact, the undoing of racial essentialism, and the acceptance of race as a social construction, has in many ways set the stage for a further entrenchment of white supremacy in the United States. As Howard Winant points out, "[I]t is now often *conservatives* who argue that race is an illusion."[25] Conservatives have taken King's words and ideas and have used them in a struggle to undo civil rights protections. If race is understood as an illusion, then the power and inequality embedded in the construction of race are ignored.

DuBois asserted that she or "he who ignores or seeks to override the race idea in human history ignores and overrides the central thought of all history."[26] Race must be understood as constructed within a history of injustice and inequality that continues to shape lives. Positing race as a social construction without further analyzing the ways race is entrenched and embedded and, indeed, the very foundation of the society (social institutions and individual consciousness) is nothing short of dismissing the concept of race and by extension racism. Some individuals in the Multiracial Movement who claim to understand race as a social construction make the leap to suggest that since it is a human creation, then humans can uncreate race and racism by ignoring race. For example, this idea can be heard loudly within the movement around the demand to remove race from adoption laws.[27] In short, the argument is: "If we collectively don't 'do' race, then race won't exist." Such an understanding of race requires a bit of amnesia, a bit of social naiveté and a bit of unfounded optimism. Likewise, such an understanding of race dismisses white supremacy and the centrality of power to the construction of race.

The ignoring of the power relations inherent in the U.S. racial hierarchy is not new. In the early 1960s, for instance, whites were claiming that because many blacks chose to *separate* themselves from whites, whites should not be culpable for *segregation* in society. In 1963 Malcolm X responded to these claims by noting that racial separation and racial segregation are not the same. Separation is a choice, while segregation occurs in the context of inequality and imposition. In his statement, "It's only segregated when it's controlled by someone from the outside," Malcolm X was making the power relations clear, segregation was about the use of power to maintain an unjust system.[28] A movement that ignores power relations will likely work in ways that reinforce white supremacy and undermine those struggling for liberation. For instance, AMEA makes claims that in a racist society civil rights legislation is necessary, yet within the same breath they demand recognition of multiracial people and families as a protected group. Consider a statement made in an open letter by Levonne Gaddy, the current president of AMEA:

> The systematic and institutionalized discrimination against multiracial individuals, interracial couples, and multiracial families must continue to be challenged. With compassion and sensitivity for those who have fought civil rights battles before us, I will stand strong for multiracial people and insist on the same consideration that has been given to other groups before us.[29]

Within the Multiracial Movement many claim a liberal political location and point to the multiracial "us" as the victims of discrimination by the monoracial "them." The inference is that multiracial people and families need protection from all "monoracial" groups, regardless of where the groups are situated in the U.S. racial hierarchy. As such, an agenda for a separate "protected" group will reproduce white supremacy in society by reifying yet another category without calling into question white supremacy.

Analyzing the context and discourse of the movement can help us to draw valuable lessons as we dream of social transformation and forge political alliances. By understanding the pitfalls of the movement individuals can rethink the movement's political location in the U.S. racial landscape. The lessons provided through the Multiracial Movement can help to create a racial agenda able to push the boundaries of racial thinking within traditional racial communities and forward a more progressive struggle toward liberation in a white-dominated nation.

CHAPTER OVERVIEWS

Race is both deeply personal and strongly political. Each of the authors in this anthology has in-depth knowledge of the Multiracial Movement. Some have been actively involved in multiracial organizations, others have spent much time and energy researching and theorizing multiracialism, most come from multiracial families. These authors have carefully documented and theorized the pitfalls and lessons of the Multiracial Movement.

In part I, *The Context of the Multiracial Movement*, the authors make clear that the Multiracial Movement has its origins in historical battles over the meaning of race in society. The authors will show that while race is socially constructed, those in the movement must be mindful of the historical, political, economic, and social reasons race has been constructed to mean what it means. In this first section multiracialism is tied to three powerful and historical phenomena: the construction of family, white supremacy, and the civil rights movement.

In chapter 1, "All in the Family: The Familial Roots of Racial Divisions," Kimberly McClain DaCosta looks at the ways in which "family" has been invoked both historically and politically to maintain white supremacy and divisive racial categories. Kinship networks, regulated through laws and customs, have created a racialized society in which multiracial families have been called unnatural and unlawful. DaCosta points out that the civil rights movement created the political space necessary to successfully challenge anti-miscegenation laws, which ultimately allowed for the development of a Multiracial Movement. And yet, the movement itself is struggling to reify a multiracial category, an action that will undermine the very successes of the civil rights movement that laid the groundwork for the existence of a Multiracial Movement. DaCosta contends that the desire to create a multiracial category is about the desire to create acceptable kinship networks—something long denied to these families. DaCosta writes, "I argue there are two related historical processes of significance here: I dub them 'the racialization of the family' (the racial premises buried in our understandings of family, in which genetic/phenotypic sharing is coded to signify cultural sharing, intimacy, and caring) and 'the familization of race' (the ways in which members of the same racial group feel a kin-like connection and how that familial understanding is used politically). These two processes for the context in which 'multiracial' becomes a distinctive social identity in the United States, and are the subtext of multiracial politics." While a multiracial category will not lead to greater social justice in society, the demand for such a category becomes clearer.

In chapter 2, "Defending the Creation of Whiteness: White Supremacy and the Threat of International Sexuality," Abby L. Ferber posits the central role white supremacist movements have played in the construction of the Multiracial Movement. In this chapter Ferber questions the logic of a Multiracial Movement that vies for a separate category rather than struggle against all manifestations of white supremacy. By analyzing the most overt forms of white supremacy—white supremacist organizations, Ferber is able to clearly delineate the way in which white supremacy in reinforced through the maintenance of the color line. Ferber notes that within white supremacist discourse interracial sexuality is the "ultimate abomination, because it is a transgression of the boundaries between what are constructed as distinct races. It is a particular threat to the construction of whiteness based on purity, and represents a threat to not only whiteness, but white males especially." Given the historical treatment of multiracial families and people in a white supremacist system, the Multiracial Movement should foremost be concerned with subverting white supremacy.

While Ferber analyzes explicit forms of white supremacy and DaCosta analyzes the historical construction of race and family, in chapter 3, "Racial Redistricting: Expanding the Boundaries of Whiteness," Charles A. Gallagher explores, through in-depth interviews and focus groups with white college students, the boundaries of racial acceptability in white familial relations. Gallagher argues that the Multiracial Movement must acknowledge the "racial redistricting" taking place in the United States in which the whiteness is expanding to include multiracial Asians and light-skinned Latinos. He writes, "[A]s whites and other nonblack groups inhabit common racial ground, the stigma once associated with interracial relationships between these groups is diminishing." The shifting boundaries of whiteness have "important implications" for the Multiracial Movement and, if not careful, the movement will exacerbate antiblack sentiment in the United States.

In chapter 4, "Linking the Civil Rights and Multiracial Movements," Kim M. Williams asserts that the Multiracial Movement is part of a "larger cycle of protest, one initiated by the civil rights movement." Based in her in-depth research in multiracial organizations across the country, Williams notes that the Multiracial Movement is not necessarily "changing" race in the United States, but rather continuing a trajectory laid out through civil rights struggles. Williams analyzes the characteristics, ideological framework, tactics, and goals of the Multiracial Movement. She argues that leaders of this movement have utilized the language and legacy of the civil rights movement: "By arguing that the recognition of multiracial people is the 'next logical step in civil rights'" they "have shrewdly drawn on the symbolism of the civil rights movement, and in the process cast themselves as more progressive than the so-called progressives (i.e., the civil rights lobby)." Ultimately, Williams maps the Multiracial Movement as a legacy of the civil rights movement.

The second section of the book, *Discourses of the Multiracial Movement*, is concerned with the libratory potential and limitations of the discourse of the Multiracial Movement. Each of the authors in this section will look at the discourse underlying the claims made by the Multiracial Movement, including academic writing, the use of media images, the expansion of multiracial advocacy on the Web, and racial discourses within multiracial families. Authors will specifically address ideas such as racial essentialism, the social construction of race, race as an illusion, racial categories, and color-blind language, which have shaped and defined the political location of the movement in a nonprogressive manner.

In chapter 5, "Beyond Pathology and Cheerleading: Insurgency, Dissolution, and Complicity in the Multiracial Idea," Rainier Spencer suggests that in the realm of theory, the multiracial idea can provide a path toward the dismantling of racial essentialism. Unfortunately, when applied to our political structures, primarily through the struggle for a multiracial category on the census, the multiracial idea undermines oppressed racial groups in their struggle for liberation. Once the multiracial idea is applied to the creation of census categories and other practical applications, the multiracial idea loses its corrosive, subversive, and theoretical energy. The outcome is a complicity with the idea of race as a biological construct and the undermining of the struggles of oppressed racial groups. Spencer points out that "in addition to the problem of further cementing in place the idea of racial groups, a federal multiracial category could in no sense serve legitimately as the signifier of a group that has suffered historical, government-sanctioned oppression. Its very adoption would belittle those people whose tremendous sufferings were the rationale for the federal categories in the first place." He suggests that rather than expending energy fighting for official recognition and the practical application of the multiracial idea, advocates should be fighting for the destruction of all racial categories and the pervasive racism grounded in the categories. Spencer concludes that while "there is a frustration among those who feel that current monoracial categories do not fit their self-identification needs, the manner in which that frustration is directed—the call for a federal multiracial category—is wrongheaded to say the least. It would be better to devote our energies toward challenging and dismantling the myth of white purity that is the parent of the multiracial myth. . . . As we await the next round of arguments over a federal multiracial category, we must maintain our goal of debunking the idea of biological race, while ensuring that we do not undermine civil rights compliance monitoring in the process."

In chapter 6, "Deconstructing Tiger Woods: The Promise and Pitfalls of Multiracial Identity," Kerry Ann Rockquemore highlights the myriad ways multiracial people identify. Through her analysis of celebrity multiracial people, she explores why and how the Multiracial Movement claims some multiracial celebrities, but not all. Central to her analysis is the Multiracial Movement's glorification of Tiger Woods. Rockquemore argues that the attention given to Woods helps to explain what the Multiracial Movement envisions as the "authentic" multiracial identity. She writes, "[M]any movement activists assume that individuals who have parents of different races understand their racial identity exclusively as a border identity." A border identity, is a "blending of all an individual's racial backgrounds . . . and represents a break with the paradigmatic reliance on the one-drop rule to understand the multiracial experience." Rockquemore suggests that activists in the Multiracial Movement have a narrow and limited understanding of the varying ways multiracial people identify.

Similar to Rockquemore's concern that the movement is defining *multiracial* in narrow and confining ways, in chapter 7, "Multirace.com: Multiracial Cyberspace," Erica Chito Childs explores the creation of boundaries in the multiracial community through a content analysis of two large multiracial activist websites. Through a content analysis of the websites and interviews with the editors of these sites, Childs suggests that far from creating an inclusive multiracial community, these websites actually shun those who do not accede to an acceptable vision of multiracialism. Further, these sites promote contradictory ideologies that include: color blindness, antiblack sentiment, and notions of authentic multiracialness. While the Multiracial Movement is advocating for a recognition of multiraciality in society, at the same time, the cyberspaces from which the discourse is being created and controlled reflects a very limited understanding of race that ultimately reproduces white supremacy.

In chapter 8, " 'I Prefer to Speak of Culture' : White Mothers of Interracial Children," Terri A. Karis explores, through in-depth interviews, why many white mothers of multiracial children get trapped in color-blind ideologies. She notes that "despite their increasing racial awareness, white women often prefer the language of culture to race, and color-blind interpretations to those that take race into account, particularly when they are discussing family dynamics." Karis explains that the women are facing several competing social constraints, including a patriarchal society in which women are the primary caretaker and a racist society where they are not seen as having an authentic voice when addressing race and racism with their children of color. If married, these women might defer race discussions and race education to their spouse of color. Other white women claim a desire to learn black history *for the sake of the children.* Finally, in an attempt to counter negative racial stereotypes about interracially married white women, they downplay the significance of race in their family relations and struggle to maintain "middle-class respectability as 'good (white) girls.' " Thus these women often attach their identity to their children, they begin to identify racially as mothers of multiracial children, rather than interracially married white women. Karis writes, "Focusing on one's role as a mother may help to emphasize, and reinstate, a white woman's respectability." Moreover, such a shift removes the immediate pressure these women might experience to name their whiteness. Karis concludes that understanding the ways white women in multiracial families define themselves racially can help forge a space for individuals to move beyond narrow color-blind constructions of race. "As we become aware and name the ways in which race impacts our lives, even within our most intimate relationships, we extend the possibilities for conscious choices, authentic moments of connection, and strategies that move away from normative whiteness toward social justice." Through this chapter Karis is helping to uncover the attraction many white women may feel to the conservative politics of the Multiracial Movement, particularly those calling on a color-blind agenda and the removal of race from legislation, programs, and policies.

The third section of the book, *Lessons from the Multiracial Movement,* provides several ideas about how those in the Multiracial Movement and other interested parties, can begin to examine and address multiracial politics in a more progressive and transformative manner. Each author in this section suggests that progressive politics must be first and foremost concerned with larger social relations that make the Multiracial Movement relevant. Couched in a history of group-based racial discrimination, a white supremacist society will not be challenged by moving the discourse to the level of the individual, that is, individual rights, racism as an individual pathology, claims to rugged individualism, or falling into the trap of postmodern fragmentation through which community building and solidarity are painted as impossibilities. In each of the following chapters, the authors explain their vision of a more progressive Multiracial Movement.

In chapter 9, "Model Minority? The Struggle for Identity among Multiracial Japanese Americans," Rebecca Chiyoko King-O'Riain addresses the importance of understanding the specific historical context of group formation as a way to understand the confluences of a progressive Multiracial Movement. Her analysis points to a weakness in the Multiracial Movement, that is, the lack of attention to the experiences of multiracials beyond black and white. King-O'Riain addresses the specific factors (demography, immigration, historical construction of race in Japan, and gender dynamics) that have made it possible and desirable for multiracial Japanese Americans to work from *within* the Japanese American community.

In chapter 10, "Transracial Adoption: Refocusing Upstream," Barbara Katz Rothman addresses a major concern of many multiracial families: transracial adoption. Most multiracial family organizations have at some point advocated the removal of race considerations in the process of adoption. Rothman suggests that by focusing on color-blind adoptions, the Multiracial Movement has lost sight of the fact that transracial adoption is itself an outcome of larger institutional inequalities and injustices that have pushed so many children of color into the child welfare system. Rothman writes:

> Transracial adoption is a Band-Aid solution where far more radical solutions are immediately needed. . . . Adoption is the result of some very bad things going on upstream, policies that push women into having babies that they cannot raise. . . . A lot of adoption is about poverty: a lack of access to contraception and abortion; a lack of access to the resources to raise children. And a lot of what poverty is about in America is racism.

Through her personal experiences of adopting and raising Victoria, an African American child, Rothman addresses the complexity of race on a personal level and the injustices of race (as it intersects with gender) on the societal level. She concludes by stating, "Transracial adoption—as a problem, or as a solution, as an issue that troubles us—does not resolve at an individual level. Victoria and I are at the bottom of a long strange funnel. . . . The solutions will not be found down here at the bottom where we are all doing the best we can. No, if you want to understand, help, or prevent transracial adoption you're going to have to refocus upstream." Focusing on individuals and individual families, she argues, will not create a more just world. Individuals concerned with social justice must understand larger social relations of inequality and injustice that continue to shape individual lives, and thus must "refocus upstream."

In chapter 11, "Protecting Racial Comfort: Protecting White Privilege," Heather Dalmage explores the construction of racial identities of whites who belong to multiracial family organizations. Based on in-depth interviews with seventeen white members of multiracial families she argues that the desire and demand for racial comfort largely explains why whites are disproportionately represented in multiracial family organizations. Drawing on arguments of color blindness, meritocracy, and individualism, many of these whites use their interracial relationship to cling to white privilege. Others who may belong to multiracial organizations struggle to create antiracist identities. These individuals may belong to the organizations, but rarely attend meetings and events, instead spending their time and energy working alongside people of color. Ultimately, Dalmage argues that understanding the desire for racial comfort by whites can help us understand and challenge the less progressive ideologies found in the Multiracial Movement.

Finally, in chapter 12, "Ideology of the Multiracial Movement: Dismantling the Color Line and Disguising White Supremacy?" Eileen T. Walsh addresses the need for the Multiracial Movement to account for race, gender, and class as "mutually constructed and supported hierarchies." She argues that these constructs will not be undone through a color-blind agenda. "Disappearing race from the vocabularies and consciousness of academics, policy makers, and the citizenry prior to dismantling the structures of inequality that persist not only puts the cart before the horse, it also serves to render white privilege invisible—a most dangerous proposition with a long legacy." Ultimately, Walsh suggests that social justice must be central to the goals of the Multiracial Movement or the movement will work on behalf of white supremacy.

NOTES

1. Quoted in D. Hollis, "A Legacy of Loving," in *New People* (1991): 2, 9–12.

2. For a discussion of the history of antimiscegenation laws see J. A. Rogers, *Sex and Race, Volume II* (St. Petersburg, FL: Helga Rogers, 1942), 155. Rogers quotes The Henning Statues of Virginia: "September 17, 1630. Hugh Davis to be soundly whipped before an assembly of Negroes and others for abusing himself to the dishonor of God and the shame of Christians by defiling his body in lying with a Negro." Note that no mention is made of what happened to the woman in this instance. Moreover, drawing on religious ideology, as Judge Bazile did in 1950, the courts were used to uphold white supremacy through the myth of "white purity."

3. W. E. B. DuBois, *The Philadelphia Negro: A Social Study* (Philadelphia: University of Pennsylvania Press, 1899/1996).

4. Maria P. P. Root, "Within, Between, and Beyond Race," in *Racially Mixed People in America*, ed. Maria P. P. Root (Thousand Oaks, CA: Sage, 1992), 3.

5. Cynthia Nakashima, "Voices from the Movement: Approaches to Multiraciality," in *The Multiracial Experience*, ed. Maria P. P. Root (Thousand Oaks, CA: Sage, 1996), 80.

6. Ibid., 82.

7. Michael Eric Dyson, "Keynote Address," *Color Lines in the 21st Century Conference* (Chicago: Roosevelt University, 1998).

8. See Heather Dalmage, *Tripping On the Color Line: Black-White Multiracial Families in a Racially Divided World* (New Brunswick: Rutgers University Press, 2000); Kim Williams, *Boxed In: The U.S. Multiracial Movement* (Cornell University: unpublished dissertation, 2001).

9. Some discrepancy exists about the exact origination date of this organization. The 1987 mission statement flyer of I-Pride states the date as February 1979. The Association of MultiEthnic Americans (AMEA) homepage states the date

as 1978. In either case, as AMEA notes, it is the oldest multiracial organization in the country.

10. Based on personal interview conducted by Heather Dalmage on July 19, 1996.

11. See AMEA Home Page at http://www.ameasite.org/.

12. See Kimberly McClain DaCosta, "All in the Family: The Familial Roots of Racial Divisions," in this volume for an elaboration of the historical and political interaction between definitions of community, kinship, and race. See also, Naomi Zack, *Race and Mixed Race* (Philadelphia: Temple University Press, 1994).

13. Omi and Winant, *Racial Formation in the U.S.: 1960–1990* (New York: Routledge, 1994).

14. For a broader discussion see Omi and Winant, *Racial Formation*.

15. Kim Williams, *Boxed In: The U.S. Multiracial Movement* (Cornell University, unpublished dissertation, 2001).

16. See Dalmage, *Tripping on the Color Line*.

17. Thanks to Kim Williams for drawing my attention to this meeting/award ceremony.

18. Williams, *Boxed In*.

19. Michael Omi and Howard Winant raised the issue of multiracialism for discussion within a broader racial theoretical framework in *Racial Formation in the U.S.* Other explorations followed, see for instance, Angela Davis, "Discussion," in *Black Popular Culture*, ed. Gina Dent (Seattle: Bay Press, 1992); Rhonda M. Williams, "Living at the Crossroads: Explorations in Race, Nationality, Sexuality, and Gender," in *The House that Race Built*, ed. Wahneema Lubiano (New York: Vintage, 1998); Michael Eric Dyson, "Essentialism and the Complexities of Racial Identity," in *Multiculturalism: A Critical Reader*, ed. David Theo Goldberg (Cambridge: Blackwell, 1994).

20. See for instance, Maureen Reddy *Crossing the Color Line: Race, Parenting, and Culture* (New Brunswick: Rutgers University Press, 1994); Lise Funderburg, *Black, White, Other: Biracial Americans Talk About Race* (New York: Morrow House, 1994); Jane Lazarre, *Beyond the Whiteness of Whiteness: Memoir of a White Mother of Black Sons* (Durham: Duke University Press, 1996); Claudine Chiawei O'Hearn, *Half + Half: Writers on Growing Up Biracial + Bicultural* (New York: Pantheon, 1998); James McBride, *The Color of Water: A Black Man's Tribute to His White Mother* (New York: Riverhead Books, 1996).

21. Williams, *Boxed In*.

22. Omi and Winant, *Racial Formation*, 88.

23. See for instance Maria P. P. Root's broadly cited, "Bill of Rights for Multiracial People," which first appeared in *The Multiracial Experience*, 7.

24. Omi and Winant, *Racial Formation*.

25. Howard Winant, "The Theoretical Status of the Concept of Race," in *Theories of Race and Racism: A Reader*, ed. Les Back and John Solomos (New York: Routledge, 2000), 181.

26. W. E. B. DuBois. "Conservation of Races," in *Theories of Race and Racism*, 80.

27. See for instance, Randall Kennedy, "Orphans of Separatism: The Painful Politics of Transracial Adoption," *American Prospect* 17 (Spring 1994): 38–45; and

Peter Hayes, "Transracial Adoption Politics and Ideology," *Child Welfare League of America* 72, 3 (1994): 304–308.

28. Quoted in Gary Peller, "Race-Consciousness," in *Critical Race Theory*, eds. Kimberle Crenshaw, Neil Gotanda, Gary Peller, and Kendall Thomas (New York: New Press, 1995), 128.

29. Levonne Gaddy, an open letter released to "AMEA Affiliate members and newsletters," March 11, 2000.

]

PART I

CONTEXT OF THE MULTIRACIAL MOVEMENT

The history of framing race through family and family through race has created a lightening rod to multiracial families. In this section the authors address the historical and contemporary battles around the construction of race and family in the United States. Ultimately, the authors point to the places from which multiracial family members struggle to name their own identities and in the process have created a movement that is reshaping racial meanings and practices in society.

Race exists in the practices of society and the way in which people think about those practices.[1] The current trend in racial thinking and practice in mainstream America is toward color blindness, a denial that race matters. But it is precisely because race matters that multiracial families and people have become the battleground for those wanting to uphold white supremacy, those wanting to deny that race matters, and those hoping to undermine racism. Multiracial families are living on racial borders; the very borders that have been created, imagined, and codified to make the complexities of human difference appear simple, discrete, and immutable. The fact that these families exist calls into question the construction of racial categories in the United States.

Omi and Winant have suggested that "social movements create collective identity by offering their adherents a different view of themselves and their world; different, that is, from the world view and self-concepts offered by the established social order."[2] The context of the Multiracial Movement can be discovered in the struggle by multiracial family members to step

17

outside of the ideologies and practices that maintain single-race white families as the ideal, the stick-with-your-own racial community members as authentic, and census categories as common sense. Kimberly McClain DaCosta, Abby L. Ferber, and Charles A. Gallagher each address the way racial categories and hierarchies have been defined and maintained through interlocking discourses of race, family, and community. The construction of family reflects gender, race, and sexual politics—politics called into question (and at times reinforced) through the civil rights movement. Kim M. Williams argues that the civil rights movement created a space for individual-based politics from which the Multiracial Movement has developed.

In this first section we are uncovering the context of the Multiracial Movement through an exploration of the established social order and the shifting world views of multiracial family members. Thus, DaCosta, Ferber, Gallagher, Williams analyze the ideologies, politics, and practices from which the Multiracial Movement developed.

NOTES

1. Omi and Winant, *Racial Formation*.
2. Omi and Winant, *Racial Formation*, 99.

ONE

ALL IN THE FAMILY:
THE FAMILIAL ROOTS OF RACIAL DIVISION

KIMBERLY McCLAIN DaCOSTA

[Incest] even combines in some countries with its direct opposite, inter-racial sexual relations, an extreme form of exogamy, as the two most powerful inducements to horror and collective vengeance.

—Claude Levi-Strauss, *The Elementary Structure of Kinship*

To pass out of a race always requires one to pass out of a family.

—Shelby Steele and Thomas Lennon, "Jefferson's Blood"

DEBATES ABOUT MULTIRACIAL POLITICS have tended to focus on the most obviously "racial" nature of the issues at stake (Will a multiracial category alter race-based social policies? Will such a category reify a biological notion of race? Do multiracials seek to escape a stigmatized status?). Yet even a brief glance at the forms of collective organization, goals, and activities of persons of mixed descent make it clear that the Multiracial Movement is as much a politicization of kinship as it is one of racial identity—one in which multiracial families[1] are emerging *as* families. Most of the more than sixty local community groups formed in the last twenty years were formed by interracial couples and multiracial people to meet others like them and share experiences. Through the formation of groups and the attempt to name their experience ("multiracial"), interracial families try to make visible and normalize that which is conventionally invisible and pathologized (given that the family is usually thought of as a monoracial institution and interracial sex is taboo). The attempt to create a new multiracial label is partly an attempt to make visible *relationships* that are often not assumed by others— that between parents and children who appear racially different.[2]

While the familial roots of multiracial politics have been largely ignored, this case offers a chance to see quite clearly the very real connections between concepts and histories of race and family in the United States. In this chapter I demonstrate the importance of the family as both a structure and strategy in the creation and maintenance of racial division in the United States. Through the family, individual and group aspirations for economic and social advancement or maintenance (or the frustration of such ends) are realized. The family is fundamentally connected to the system of stratification since nearly all families ascribe their economic and social status to their children. Much of U.S. social policy has been designed to distribute resources *through* families, and the unequal treatment of families according to race has resulted in large and persistent inequalities between blacks and whites. This relationship between family and race is the implicit basis of social stratification research, but it has been explicitly studied only recently, and most vividly in studies examining the gap in wealth between blacks and whites.[3] My analysis begins with what the social stratification literature takes largely for granted—namely, why distributing resources through the family so effectively creates and reproduces racial inequality. That it does so suggests that the legitimate and socially recognized family was itself constituted with race in mind.

In this chapter I show that American notions of race and family are mutually constituted and that understanding this relationship makes clear why multiracial activism necessarily concerns the family. The notion of a "multiracial family" has, until very recently, been an oxymoron in American cultural consciousness. As such, the emergence of multiracial families *as* families represents a significant cultural shift in American conceptions of family and race. Paradoxically, the invisibility (and rarity) of multiracial families, which essentially reflects a breaking of family bonds across racial categories, owes its genesis to the very tight *relatedness* between American notions of race and family. This tight relationship is born of two processes— what I call "the racialization of the family" (how racial premises came to be buried in our understanding of family, in which genetic/phenotypic sharing is coded to signify cultural sharing, intimacy, and caring) and "the familization of race" (how it came to be that members of the same racial group feel a kin-like connection and how that familial understanding is used politically). These two processes form the context in which "multiracial" becomes a distinctive social identity in the United States, and are the subtext of multiracial politics. I show how the concept of family became racialized, and in turn, how notions of race are constructed through kinship practices by examining the logic underlying American racial classifications and antimiscegenation laws.[4] Finally, I explore what has changed since 1967 and how these processes relate to the current emergence of multiracial politics in general, and multiracial families in particular.

In using the term *multiracial families* I run the risk of flattening the differences in experience and social location of such families.[5] My goal is not to describe "the" multiracial family as if there is or could be a single multiracial family experience. Multiracial families are not defined by a specific cultural tradition, ancestry, or experience of migration, and are diverse by class, sexuality, religion, and family form.[6] Rather than look at multiracial families as an interesting variation on a uniform version of the American family, I am interested in the family as a contested concept—one that is at stake in social struggles over legitimate definitions of the social world. It is for this reason I do not focus on describing comparisons between various ethnoracial combinations in multiracial families (i.e., black/white versus Asian/white). This chapter focuses instead on how the family became racialized and race familized in an effort to discuss the emergence of multiracial families as part of "broader transformations in kinship, ideology, and social relations."[7] Similar to the argument that lesbian and gay families represent not merely an alternative to, but a transformation in the heterosexist basis of legitimized family forms, I am interested in showing that the symbolic and political emergence of multiracial families represent the beginnings of a transformation in the *racial* basis of American notions of kinship.

RACIALIZING FAMILY

After having an abortion upon receiving a prenatal diagnosis of Down's syndrome and feeling "inconsolable," Emily, a white woman, describes how she came to terms with her decision:

> We were watching the parade on Main Street . . . and a family with a kid with Down's Syndrome was standing in front of me. Right there at the parade, honest to God, like a sign direct to me. And the thing was, I really looked at the kid, how she dripped her ice cream all over, how she couldn't be made to do what the other kids wanted, I looked at her and thought, "She doesn't belong in that family." She didn't look like them, she looked like someone else. Like a lot of someone elses, not quite from the same race, if you know what I mean. And it made me feel, well, that I'd done the right thing, that the one I aborted wasn't quite from my family, either.

Rayna Rapp interprets this quote from her study of the social and cultural meaning of amniocentesis as an example of the ascription of "alien kinship" to children with genetic abnormalities.[8] Yet it also illustrates perfectly what I call a racialized conception of family. Notice how Emily associates appearance and family. Appearance as racially "other" disqualifies the (potential) child from membership in the family, as it serves to justify her decision to terminate her connection to the "alien" fetus.

Emily's response is but one example, albeit stark, of the ways in which an assessment of racial difference plays into the interpretation of familial relatedness and responsibility. These racialized assumptions of kinship, however, can be found in other, more common experiences faced by people in multiracial families. Lena, a black/white woman whom I interviewed as a part of a larger study on multiracial collective organization,[9] recalls what is was like when her large family was out in public.

> We came to expect that complete strangers would approach us, bending down for a closer look and smiling enthusiastically as they commented on how "beautiful" we all were. It almost felt as if they were trying to figure out which parts of us were white, which black, and which too blended to really tell the difference. To the liberal-types we were their equivalent of poster children for racial harmony. But other times I sensed that some people thought we were freaky.

When people stare at multiracial families in public, when they are "horrified" at the prospect of having a racially different son-in-law and grand-children, and when they "match" families in public according to how they look, they are attempting to reconcile the intimacy displayed between differently "raced" people acting like family with their own racialized conceptions of what families are supposed to look like. While this can be interpreted as relatively benign ("racial harmony") or hostile ("freaky"), Lena's story underscores that in either case, the multiracial family is positioned as an object to be gazed *at*. Most Americans think of multiracial families as different because of the racialized notions of kinship they carry around in their heads, and which their objective reality bears out.[10] In the United States, family members are presumed to "look alike," and looking alike is often interpreted to mean that one has the same phenotypic markers (hair texture, skin color, eye shape, etc.). Phenotypic sharing signifies cultural sharing, intimacy, and caring. As a result, people have difficulty conceptualizing intimacy between people who look different, or who are perceived to look different by virtue of differences in the most obvious racial markers such as eye shape and skin color.

This often unspoken, unconscious racialized concept of family defines the parameters of the normal family. Most people do not often think explicitly that their ideas of family are racialized. But when confronted with the interracial family and the feelings of strangeness they arouse, the "normal" family against which they are implicitly being measured, is made *explicit*. It is when Emily sees the girl with Down's syndrome in a *familial* setting that an imputed "racial" difference is highlighted, and the "abnormality" of that family is heightened. Moreover, this attribution of racial difference can be called upon to explain (as Emily does), because it is immediately culturally intelligible, why it is that we do not form intimate caring relationships across racial boundaries.

MULTIRACIAL FAMILIES AND THE COMMON SENSE

That the notion of "multiracial families" makes sense in the United States is generally not in dispute. That is, when someone describes a family as "multiracial" or "interracial," others are likely to assume that family is comprised of persons of "different races." They are unlikely to be completely at a loss for what it means, as they might be if someone described a family as "papgurdle" (a term I, not surprisingly, made up). In other words, they have a common frame of reference to discern, even if they have never heard the term, what "multiracial family" might mean. "Everyone knows," for instance, that Tiger Woods is from an "interracial family" *because* he has a "black" father (although this turns out to be a simplification of his ancestry) and a Thai (read Asian) mother. Similarly, if asked to classify the families in the following examples along a multi/monoracial dimension, where at least one member is of Ancestry A and Ancestry B, most Americans would assign such descriptions similarly.

Ancestry A	Ancestry B	Racial Classification
African American	Swedish	multiracial (black)
English	Irish	monoracial (white)
Chinese	Japanese	monoracial (Asian)

That such classifications make sense to most Americans stems from the fact that when it comes to race, Americans have been socialized in a similar manner. For those who have been socialized differently, such classifications will not make sense. In other societies, and at other historical periods in the United States, such classifications would differ. In seventeenth-century China, for example, the fundamental social distinction was drawn between the Chinese and Barbarians. The more remote a group was said to be from the Chinese center, the more barbaric that group was thought to be physically and culturally.[11] In the early-twentieth-century United States, an English-Irish pairing would have been considered a mixed union. While only the

African American/Swedish family in our example is designated multiracial in the early twenty-first century, the others, despite varied ancestry, are given a racial designator that is considered "mono"racial—unmixed and unified under the racial designator.

Paradoxically, as much as the idea of "multiracial families" makes cognitive sense, the stories of Emily and Lena above demonstrate that in cultural terms it does not. People are unaccustomed to seeing and knowing what to do with family relations that cross racialized boundaries. To understand why "multiracial families" both do and do not "make sense" in the United States, it is helpful to first recognize that the category "multiracial family" is a recent creation. For most of U.S. history, multiracial families did not exist as such and were actively prevented from forming. Despite the fact that since 1967 formal institutionalized sanctions against interracial marriage and recognition of offspring have been declared unconstitutional, the stigma attached to interracial couples and multiracial families has not completely dissipated.[12] Considerations of race still structure marriage and relationship patterns, as evidenced by the relative rarity, despite recent increases, of interracial unions.

Accounting for why multiracial families do and do not make sense is a more difficult question. To do so requires that we look at the principles underlying the classifications of race, but also of family, and then multiracial families. Such classifications are rooted in objective social structures, as well as in the subjectivity of people's minds. These categories we use to see the world help to make the reality that they describe. Taken together, they make the world appear self-evident, real, and natural.[13]

RACIAL CLASSIFICATION, ANTIMISCEGENATION, AND NOTIONS OF KINSHIP

Underlying both Emily's and Lena's stories is a taken-for-granted sense of what a "normal" family is that relies upon the common sense of how differently raced people are supposed to interact. To understand, then, how the family became racialized (or why Emily's explanation "makes sense"), we need to look at the relationship between American notions of kinship and race. This relationship is evident in American racial classifications and antimiscegenation statutes, which form the ground upon which the notion of "multiracial families" is a distinct social position.

Dominant American notions of kinship define and differentiate kin by relations of marriage (a legal relationship) and "blood" (a biogenetic relationship).[14] Obviously, whom we consider kin often contradicts such rules. That is because kinship systems are cultural systems—not a simple list of biological relatives—but "a system of categories and statuses which often contradict actual genetic relationships."[15] Kinship systems are social systems that contain within them rules for which and in what manner kin relationships are granted, legitimized, and recognized.[16]

Just as kinship systems do not merely apply labels to relationships (mother, son, aunt) given in nature, the American system of racial classification has never been about a simple labeling of an objective fact (race). On the contrary, racial classifications, like kinship systems, reflect an "imposition of social ends upon a part of the natural world. [They are] therefore 'production' in the most general sense of the term: a molding, a transformation of objects (in this case people) to and by a subjective purpose."[17] These social categories are the means through which social relationships and people get classified, and which prescribe and prohibit certain relations between bodies defined in particular ways. These classifications are backed by law, science, custom, and force, and are often given religious significance.

The relationship between American racial categories and notions of family, however, is far deeper than this. It is impossible to understand "American kinship" without considering race. American racial categories are based on a conception of kinship just as notions of family are based on conceptions of race.[18] In the United States, the dominant principle for allocation of individuals into racial categories is descent. In other words, one's racial classification is determined by how one's ancestors were racially defined.[19] Yet how one's ancestors were racially defined was never a simple reading of biological "fact," as evidenced by the "one-drop rule." The "one-drop rule"— the practice of identifying those with any known African ancestry as black[20]— illustrates that some descent categories mattered more in the determination of racial classification. In the United States, a person with any African ancestry is socially, if not always legally, classified as "black." A black person is someone with a black ancestor, who is someone with a black ancestor, and so on. It is because of this "one-drop rule" that persons with *no* visible physical characteristics associated with African heritage can be black in the United States.[21]

Hypodescent is often analyzed as a mechanism through which whites maintained control over resources in lieu of slavery.[22] What is often forgotten are the ways in which the logic of hypodescent is aimed at preventing the formation of *family* ties across racial boundaries. For according to the one-drop rule[23], it is impossible for a black woman to give birth to a white child, yet a white woman *can* bear a black child.[24]

ANTIMISCEGENATION LAWS

The relationship between kinship and race is perhaps made most explicit in antimiscegenation laws. In the service of maintaining white domination, and justified by eugenicist thinking on the importance of preserving white racial "purity" through the control of sexual practice,[25] antimiscegenation laws prevented marriage and the formation of family relations (both material and emotional) between differently racialized people. Much as lesbian and gay relationships are culturally positioned outside law and nature today (although this is being challenged), antimiscegenation laws did the same for persons of mixed descent and interracial couples. Because intermarriage was illegal, such couples and their offspring were denied a legal basis of kinship. The justification of such laws stigmatized multiracial offspring as "degenerates," asserting the unnatural basis of interracial procreation and sexual relations.[26] Multiracial children were denied the status of "legitimacy." In fact, antimiscegenation laws made legitimacy an *impossibility* if one was born to differently classified parents. Seen in this light, multiracial persons were, perhaps more than any other social group, the quintessential "bastards."

The interpretation of kinship embedded within the logic of antimiscegenation is not merely symbolic, but also had material consequences. Marriage is, after all, far more than the sentimentalized consecration of love that modern actors imagine it to be. It is also a legal mechanism that regulates the transmission of property. Louisiana courts, for example, created explicit restrictions to assure that property was not transferred from whites to their colored offspring. Since without paternal acknowledgment a child could not inherit from his father, the courts restricted the right of a multiracial person to prove paternity if the suspected father was white. Even white men who sought to voluntarily acknowledge their colored children were at times prevented from doing so, even when they had no other legitimate children. Such laws remained on the books well into the 1960s.[27] Moreover, laws restricting the rights of Negroes and mulattos to testify in court made it virtually impossible to make white men accountable to their mixed offspring or to punish them for violating antimiscegenation laws.[28] But even if one were found to have committed the offense of intermarriage, one's children would not necessarily be provided for since, at least in theory, if a marriage could be declared null and void the parties involved would not be subject to either the benefits or obligations of marriage.

My comments on the extent of economic transfers between white and nonwhite kin must be tentative since to date there has been little systematic research in this vein. Work by legal scholars who study antimiscegenation laws have reached very general, and sometimes contradictory, conclusions. Eva Saks has reported that despite precedent for designating some "illegitimate" offspring as "children" for inheritance purposes, Southern state courts often denied offspring because they were "mulatto."[29] Randall Kennedy, however, argues that "[v]irtually all of the states that were fiercely opposed to interracial marriage granted limited recognition for purposes of property inheritance and related matters."[30] It is not clear, however, if most or even many of these cases granted such recognition so that interracial or nonwhite kin could inherit from white relatives. The case Kennedy cites (*Miller v. Lucks*) resulted in an ironic circumstance in which the state of Mississippi *did* recognize an intermarriage between a black woman and a white man that had taken place out of state, but with the result that the *white* relatives of the husband inherited property once belonging to the black wife and that would have been given to her (black) relatives. Moreover, of the miscegenation cases that Kennedy cites where "judges injected on an ad hoc basis bits of decency into a massively indecent regime of racial hierarchy"—by which he means they did not allow the parties to escape providing for kin—all concern parties whose phenotype and ancestry are very ambiguous. Such cases do not disrupt the basic underlying principle that founds obligation and recognition of relatedness on the degree to which racial difference is or can be denied.

Yet even a cursory reading of American history tells us that such economic and symbolic capital transfers between white and nonwhite kin did occur. Historically black colleges offer a particularly visible example of such transfers.[31] Wilberforce University in Ohio is a case in point. Originally a hotel for slave masters, their concubines, and their children, it was bought by a group of white planters and converted into a school for the children from their interracial unions.

The social and legal "discouragement" of interracial sex and marriage was also a prohibition against the development of emotional ties across racial lines. Yet just because interracial emotional ties were discouraged does not mean they did not develop. Recent memoirs and historical accounts of interracial families make clear that such ties did exist,[32] even in an atmosphere of social stigma and physical threat.[33] Even so, very low numbers of intermarriages today testify that whom Americans love, care for, and feel responsible to is hardly natural and spontaneous but has very much been shaped by racial division. A statistical manipulation illustrates the point. If marriages were randomly distributed with regard to race, we should expect that 45 percent of marriages would be between partners of different racial classifications (based on 1996 Current Population Survey data).[34] Yet 1990 census figures show that only about 3 percent of U.S. marriages were between differently classified individuals. This is not particularly surprising given that we know marriage patterns are shaped by spatial and social distance between individuals—distance that is exacerbated through a variety of mechanisms of racial domination. But even in places (such as college campuses) where the social distance between individuals by race (in terms of income, occupation, and education) is muted and where many theories of intermarriage locate the rise in intermarriage rates for some groups, the rates of cross-category unions are relatively low and skewed toward some groups and not others (Asian/white versus black/white).

How then should we evaluate the impact of antimiscegenation laws if, as the above discussion shows, the laws themselves (and/or their spirit) were sometimes subverted? My argument does not depend on there being *no* emotional or materially based kin connections across racial lines, or on the extent to which people were punished for violating antimiscegenation laws. What is important here is the symbolic importance of antimiscegenation laws. As much work in the sociology of law demonstrates, laws often achieve more of their impact by providing simplifying schemas, evocative symbols, and constitutive scripts than by meting out concrete rewards and punishments. This point helps to explain why even in states that never had antimiscegenation statutes the taboo against intermarriage and interracial sex has been culturally potent.

What does matter here is that antimiscegenation laws restricted the major privileges that family membership tends to provide, and which in dominant discourse are definitional of family—access to a family name, household, and the accumulation and transmission of cultural, economic and symbolic capital from one generation to the next—along racial lines.[35]

Antimiscegenation laws represent the refusal to grant social and legal status to interracial unions, and to deny the relationship between parents and offspring. In structuring the tracing of descent, the determination of acceptable marriage partners, inheritance, the power to name as kin (or not) and to legitimize or abolish particular sexual relations and any resultant offspring according to the dictates of white supremacy, the "multiracial family" was effectively made an oxymoron. In so doing, the normative family was constructed as monoracial. But more than that, in legally prohibiting interracial families, monoraciality was made a *necessary condition* of family.

FAMILIZING RACE

There is another way that understanding the relationship between notions of family and race helps us better understand the current activism over multiraciality. As has been described in the literature on multiraciality, multiracials often express feeling (or being made to feel) "inauthentic" around "monoracial" people. Questions about multiracials' cultural authenticity are never far removed from suspicions about their ethnic loyalties. Many multiracials cite this sense of being perpetually "suspect" as a major reason why they have joined collectively with other multiracials.[36]

Questions of ethnic loyalty and authenticity owe much to dominant conceptions of family—much as the family is "racialized," our notions of race are "familized." People experience racial membership as a kin-like connection. This entails an expectation that those within a given category should behave in familistic ways toward each other. For example, family members do not air each other's "dirty laundry"—they are expected to remain loyal to the group and present to outsiders a particular impression. In the highly charged arena of U.S. identity politics, racial membership exacts a similar kind of loyalty, particularly among groups of color. In this context, people who identify themselves as "multiracial," or who are involved in cross-category relationships are often seen as being disloyal to the group, and are accused of trying to escape membership in a stigmatized category.

Many scholars have discussed how a key dimension of how people think about race and ethnicity is a belief in real or assumed bonds of kinship between members of the group.[37] Stephen Cornell puts it succinctly when he writes, "Ethnicity is kinship writ large."[38] Just as "races" are popularly understood as subcategories of the human family, members within a "race" are presumed to be more closely related to *each other* than they are to those outside their subcategory. This "relatedness" is understood in genetic, historical, and cultural terms. And genetic sharing is also understood as warranting other forms of political, economic, and cultural sharing. A well-known representation of a familized notion of race can be found in African American usage of kin terms ("sister" and "brother") to refer to other African Americans outside one's immediate family; much the same can be found in nationalistic discourse.

One might argue that the use of kin terms to describe ethnic affiliations is mere metaphor—that people use such kin terms to signal or create a feeling of closeness to others.[39] Carol Delaney states that "because family and kinship relationships are felt to be natural, the imagery of the family used in other contexts helps to naturalize them."[40] No doubt this is true, and an important part of understanding the relatedness between conceptions of race and family. But more than that, I argue that we need to account for why ethnic and racial affiliations feel natural in the first place. U.S. conceptions of race were constructed in familial ways *not* through mere metaphor, but through concrete social practices and legal codes. Again, clues to how race becomes "familized" can be found in the logic of antimiscegenation and hypodescent. Not only did antimiscegenation laws and the one-drop rule racialize kinship, but also they serve as the basis through which racial groups (1) were produced and (2) came to be culturally understood in familial ways.

Mary Waters found that her respondents used the symbol of the ethnic group to link themselves and their families to a wider collectivity, precisely because there was "little conceptual terminology that allows [Americans] to link their nuclear families to institutions beyond them."[41] The social psychological and behavioral traits they labeled as specifically "ethnic" about them, however, were the same characteristics that others thought were unique to their own ethnic group, and which Waters suspects owed more to their similar middle-class status than their ethnic affiliation. Just as the language of ethnicity is used to link individuals and families to a broader collectivity, family is understood to be the vehicle through which one acquires ethnoracial authenticity.

CREATING RACE

The one-drop rule, in creating black/white bodies as black bodies, was essential for hardening boundaries between racial categories.[42] Before the *Plessy* decision (1896), racial categories and the rights and privileges they afforded their bearers, allowed for some recognition of mixed categories.[43] With the codification of the one-drop rule that the *Plessy* decision set in motion, recognition of mixed categories waned and the lot of mixed descent persons was cast with that of Negroes. Legal definitions of American racial classifications claimed to be able to determine ancestry with precision (one fourth Indian, five-thirty-seconds Negro, etc.). They reified "blood" as an objective fact, and contributed to the commonsense understanding of "races" as fundamentally different and unrelated.

To the extent that the one-drop rule has been important in shaping kinship practices, it follows that "races" are produced through kinship practices as well. Many scholars have shown how local kin terminologies, marriage patterns, and inheritance practices are shaped by, and in turn, shape wider social relations. Weber pointed out that " 'endogamy' of a group is probably everywhere a secondary product" of the monopolistic closure of political, status, economic, and religious groups.[44] E. P. Thompson and his colleagues showed how inheritance practices relate to class formation.[45] Ellen Ross and Rayna Rapp have argued that "inheritance laws legislated by a central state implicate family formation and sexual patterns." Gayle Rubin argued that kinship practices create gender.[46] In the same vein, kinship practices help create and maintain races.

Robert Merton noted fifty years ago, more directly than most commentators, the role endogamy plays in creating and maintaining group boundaries. He wrote:

> Endogamy is a device that serves to maintain social prerogatives and immunities within a social group. It helps prevent the diffusion of power, authority and preferred status to persons who are not affiliated with a dominant group. It serves further to accentuate and symbolize the "reality" of the group by setting it off against other discriminable social units. Endogamy serves as an isolation and exclusion device, with the function of increasing group solidarity and supporting the

social structure by helping to fix social distances between groups. All this is not meant to imply that endogamy was deliberately instituted for these purposes; this is a description in functional, not necessarily purposive, terms.[47]

As Merton describes, antimiscegenation laws (like racial classifications) worked to draw rigid boundaries around social groups, again by controlling kinship. Antimiscegenation laws did their race-making work in partnership with laws against incest. Incest laws delineate permissible marriage partners, and mandate that marriage alliances be struck outside one's immediate family. Antimiscegenation laws also delineated permissible marriage partners, yet bound that pool of partners within racial groups. It is interesting to note that in Louisiana, while the legal definition of what constitutes incest has fluctuated over the years (for example, sometimes allowing first-cousin marriage, other times prohibiting it), "the ban on interracial marriages has, by contrast, always been *absolutely* null and void (except when temporarily repealed under Reconstruction)."[48] According to Dominguez, the location of the law in the same code article that deals with "the least acceptable" incestuous relations is telling of the "intended strength of the legal prohibition against miscegenation." I agree, yet I think there is more to it. These laws are associated because prohibitions against interracial and intergenerational sex play supporting roles in maintaining the racial order. Antimiscegenation laws not only prohibited cross-racial unions. They also marked the limit of the incest boundary: that is, antimiscegenation laws presume that one should have sex and marry persons outside one's immediate family, but not *so* far outside one's "family" as to cross racial lines. It is interesting to note that throughout most of U.S. history, the right to marry has been relatively unrestricted, subject to only three kinds of limitations—those based on heterosexuality, race, and consanguinity.[49] Those restrictions, however, are particularly important for my argument here. They underscore the connectedness between kinship practices, represented by incest and antimiscegenation laws, in shaping racial formation. Antimiscegenation laws act like a companion bookend to incest laws, shaping marriage patterns in accordance with racial domination and shaping the familized way in which race is understood.[50]

Thus, Levi-Strauss's contention, quoted at the beginning of this chapter, begins to make sense. Given the importance of the control of sexuality and the family for maintaining group prerogatives, it is no accident that the occurrence or even mere suggestion of interracial sex was a principle incitement to lynching and vigilante raids—the most obviously violent forms of racial domination—because sexual intimacy, love, and property (each constituent elements of the family) raise the specter of blacks' humanity and equality with whites.[51] As applied to the U.S. example, however, Merton understates the purposive dimension of the use of endogamy in maintaining racial division and, indeed, domination.[52]

RACE AS KINSHIP WRIT LARGE

As discussed in the "racializing family" section, antimiscegenation laws prevented not only the transfer of property, but also obligation (in the form of emotional ties and caring), and the recognition of relatedness between differently classified people. While obscuring kin connections across racial boundaries, antimiscegenation *emphasizes* a sense of relatedness among members of the *same* category. Moreover, while the original purpose of restrictive policies on interracial sex and marriage was to maintain white control over material resources and not to prevent race mixture per se, in the twentieth century eugenic arguments were increasingly used to justify antimiscegenation laws. Eugenicists played on the fear that interracial sexual unions would make dangerous, degenerate, sterile offspring. Such fears played on and elaborated the idea that racial difference represented a kind of species difference, where people of different races were distinctly *un*related.[53]

Americans understand race in familized ways in part because they learn "race" (their own racial position and the meaning of racial difference) in the context of family. This is because racial membership tends to follow family membership (due to the cultural dominance of the idea that both race and family membership have a biological basis) and because one's everyday life is heavily mediated by the social position of one's family, which itself tends to be already separated from members of other racial categories (indicated in part by high degrees of spatial and social segregation by race in the United States, see Massey and Denton).[54] In and through kinship practices we come to know, accept, and think of ourselves in racial terms.[55]

While the origins of familized understandings of race and racialized understandings of family extend to defunct policies developed decades and even centuries ago, the cultural impact of those policies remains, evident in practices such as disowning. Although there is no systematic data on the extent of disownings due to outmarriage currently or in the past, recent biographical work suggests such disownings did occur in the not-too-distant past.[56] When family members disown their kin, they condemn them for loving and/ or marrying a person of another racial category, and impose as penalty the severing of material and emotional ties with that person, and often with their children as well. At the same time, the "transgressor" is often accused of being a "race traitor"—disqualified from full membership in a particular racial group. Under the logic of disowning, "mixed" relations and their parents are exiled outside the family, because they have gone outside "the race." In other words, relatedness to a person of another racial group disqualifies one from membership in the family because it disqualifies one from full membership within the "race." Disowning underscores the extent to which people construct racial identity through notions of family, and family identity through notions of race.

MULTIRACIAL KINSHIP POST-1967

The "racialization of the family" and the "familization of race" form the social and cultural subtext of the current activism of multiracials. Racial classifications and antimiscegenation laws are but two mechanisms among a host of other forms of racial domination[57] that facilitated the creation of sharp divisions (symbolically, politically, culturally, and socially) between social groups, defined them as racially different, and in so doing shaped the cultural common sense in which racial difference and the division of families along racial lines appears to be natural. The objective effects of these laws and policies on families today and in the past have been quite real. During slavery and since, restrictions on marriage, the transfer of property, and public acknowledgment of interracial kin were mapped onto physical space (determining where biologically related but socially unrecognized kin could live, work, and be buried) and shaped our very conceptions of whom one could and should care about along those racial divisions. This history lives on, evidenced by very low U.S. intermarriage rates (roughly 3 percent in 1990).[58] Moreover, this objective reality forms the basis of our subjective understandings of what a family is. Families are presumed to be monoracial, "races" are presumed to be significantly different, and what is more, that construction of family and race appear to us as self-evident and natural.

Despite appearances to the contrary, the construction of families as monoracial and the unrelatedness of "races" is the outcome of a historical, not natural process, and as such, is subject to change. The dismantling of antimiscegenation statutes in 1967, for example, represents an important turning point in the racialization of kinship and the familization of race. In the last thirty years, we have witnessed what has been called a "biracial baby boom" in which the number of children born to interracial unions has more than quadrupled.[59] The number of intermarriages has increased tenfold,[60] while the demographic profile of multiracial families has changed. Most intermarriages are Asian/white, not black/white, while gender patterns of black/white unions (mostly black men/white women) are the reverse of the dominant pattern when antimiscegenation laws were first enacted. If a general blocking of the development of familial and emotional ties across racial lines characterizes the period before 1967, the period since has witnessed a gradual opening in the frequency and social acceptance of such ties. The younger cohort of mixed descent persons grew up with close personal ties not only to both parents, but also to extended kin. Intermarriage statistics suggest that most Asians and Latinos now have white relatives while about one-sixth of whites have a nonwhite relative.[61] Moreover, such statistics most likely underestimate interracial kin ties since they do not count unmarried heterosexual couples and lesbians and gays for whom legal marriage is disallowed.

Trends in intermarriage and the everyday circumstances of mixed descent persons' lives are important for understanding the advent of multiracial politics and why "family issues" are central in multiracial organizations. They suggest why multiracial activists think of state racial categories—created to serve political and administrative ends—as representative of themselves, their parents, and their relationships. While the multiracial family is a cultural oxymoron, it is no longer a rarity. The formation of collective organizations for multiracial families and their assertions that they are indeed families challenges a fundamental feature of American racial domination, yet its implications are not entirely clear. Intermarriage patterns and the political and cultural response to them and to mixed racial identity have always been linked to the broader system of racial domination that demarcates white from black (and less rigidly, white from other ethnoracial groups), and the fates of those of African descent (whether one is putatively "mixed" or not) have always been linked.[62] While the possibility exists that the greater visibility of multiracial families will lead to more acceptability of all kinds of relations across racial boundaries—from intimate and familial ones to spatial and social ones—this cannot and should not be taken as evidence that the problem that defined America in the twentieth century—the color line—has not followed us into the twenty-first.

NOTES

Claude Levi-Strauss, The Elementary Structures of Kinship (Boston: Beacon Press, 1969 [1949]),10.

Thomas Lennon, "Jefferson's Blood," Frontline, Airdate May 2, 2000.

1. I use the term *multiracial* in the context of this movement to refer not only to people of multiple racialized ancestry, but to the so-called "monoracial" people involved in these multiracial groups (typically intermarried individuals and parents of mixed-descent children).

2. Multiracial activists have framed their push for state classification as a family issue. Representatives from the Association of Multiethnic Americans testified to the House Subcommittee on Census, Statistics and Postal Personnel in 1993 that "[w]hen government compels a multiracial/multiethnic family to signify a factually false identity for their child, it invades a fundamental right of privacy. Every multiracial family is entitled to safeguard its integrity against unwarranted intrusions by the government. No child should be forced to favor one parent over the other by any governmental agency."

3. See Dalton Conley, *Being Black, Living Red: Race, Wealth, and Social Policy in America* (Berkeley: University of California Press, 1999); Melvin L. Oliver and Thomas M. Shapiro, *Black Wealth/White Wealth: A New Perspective on Racial Inequality* (New York: Routledge, 1995). The black/white wealth gap serves as striking evidence for the importance of the family in transmitting economic, social and symbolic capital across generations, and the devastation that results when a group is systematically prevented from doing so. Conley finds that racial inequality in the post-1960s generation is better explained by differences in access to property (and that of one's parents) than by differences in occupation, income, and education. Differential levels of wealth between blacks and whites are linked to a variety of policies targeted at families, such as redlining and access to home mortgages, that over time have "sedimented" racial inequality. Conley writes, "Race, family, and life chances seem to be inextricably linked in a vicious circle of inequality over the life course" (1999), 12.

4. Technically, I am *not* describing a process, since to do so would require a sustained historical analysis of the social, economic, and political conditions that resulted in this race/family nexus. Neither am I making a causal argument (i.e., that racial classification and antimiscegenation laws *caused* the mutual construction of race and family), which is frustratingly vague as to who did what, when, and why and which leaves unanswered why a taboo against cross-racial unions exists even in those states that did not have antimiscegenation laws. My goal is much more modest. I use racial classification and antimiscegenation laws as social and legal practices that illustrate a deeply ingrained aspect of American culture wherein race and family are intricately intertwined.

5. See Barrie Thorne and Marilyn Yalon, eds. *Rethinking the Family: Some Feminist Questions* (Boston, Northeasern University Press, 1992).

6. According to the U.S. Census, in 1990 about one-third of interracial marriages were Asian/white, followed closely by 25 percent Other/white, and 22 percent American Indian/white. Only 14 percent of interracial marriages in the United States in 1990 were black/white, and even fewer are between two nonwhite partners (Sanjek 1994).

7. Kath Weston, *We Choose: Lesbians, Gays, Kinship* (New York: Columbia University Press, 1991), 7. Some of these sociohistorical developments include attempts to build "multiracial community" through the creation of organizations, collective efforts to obtain federal classification for multiracials, the biracial baby boom, and changes in the context in which multiracial kin interact and in which multiracials assert identity.

8. Rayna Rapp, "Heredity, or: Revising the Facts of Life," in *Naturalizing Power: Essays in Feminist Cultural Analysis*, eds. Sylvia Yanagisako and Carol Delaney (New York: Routledge, 1995), 81.

9. This study (DaCosta 2000) is an ethnographic and interview-based study on the social, political, and cultural factors that have led to the emergence of the Multiracial Movement. Interviewees were drawn from a pool of individuals involved in organizations for persons of mixed descent and their families.

10. The vast majority of American marriages are formed between people of the same racial category.

11. Frank Dikotter, *The Discourse of Race in Modern China* (Stanford: Stanford University Press, 1992).

12. According to Schuman et al., in 1972 fewer than 30 percent of whites approved of racial intermarriage. By 1996, that percentage has grown to approximately 70 percent. For blacks, approval of intermarriage has hovered around 80 percent since 1972, showing slight increases since 1994. Yet there is a marked difference between attitude and behavior when it comes to intermarriage, as evidenced by very low intermarriage rates.

13. This chapter draws on Bourdieu's analysis of family (1996). It takes the ethnomethodological challenge seriously, aware of the power of language (instituted by statistical agencies and law) to construct a legitimate definition of the "normal" family (with words such as house, home, household) and critical of the tendency in dominant discourse about family to talk about the family as if it were capable of action as an entity. This discourse presupposes that the family exists as a separate social universe that is both self-contained and natural. Breaking with ethnomethodologists, Bourdieu emphasizes that although family is only a word, it is also "a collective principle of construction of social reality"; "the family as an objective social category (a structuring structure) is the basis of the family as a subjective social category (a structured structure)" ("Family.." 1996, 21) and both are the basis of how the family seems to be self-evident, natural. Moreover, Bourdieu emphasizes that families are continually made and remade. The idea of family endures, shaping (objective and subjective) social reality, not only because institutions recognize such a category, but also because in everyday life people do. The family is reproduced through such everyday actions as gift exchanges, service, assistance, visits, attention, and kindnesses, as well as through special occasions. Taken together, institutional and individual actions comprise what Bourdieu calls a "labour of institutionalization" that is both ritual and technical and aimed at producing "obliged affections and "affective obligations."

14. David M. Schneider, *American Kinship: A Cultural Account* (Englewoods Cliffs, NJ: Prentice-Hall, 1968).

15. Gayle Rubin, "The Traffic in Women: Notes on the Political Economy of Sex," in *Toward an Anthropology of Women* ed. Reyna Reiter (New York: Monthly Review Press, 1985), 169.

16. Pierre Bourdieu, "The Family as a Realized Category," in *Theory, Culture and Society* 13, no. 3 1996: 19–26; Schneider, *American Kinship.*

17. Rubin, "The Traffic in Women," p. 176.

18. In the assignment of an individual's race, the family is a key principle of construction. American racial classifications are determined by descent (ancestors), a key criterion for classifying families. Yet this racial classificatory schema for individuals works somewhat differently when applied to families. While a family with a black partner and a white partner has long been understood as an interracial family, the offspring of that union have more often been understood to be black socially. Even now, the assigning of children to the black category seems more common than the assignment of "black family" to the group as a whole. Classification of mixed individuals and their families, however, is similar with respect to whiteness—that is, the "mixed" family and individual would almost never be described as white.

19. Charles Wagley, "On the Concept of Social Race in the Americas," in *Contemporary Cultures and Societies in Latin America*, ed. Dwight B. Heath and Richard N. Adams (New York: Random House, 1965) 531–45.

20. While persons of other ethnoracial combinations have been affected by the logic of the one-drop rule (since they could not officially claim multiple ancestry), these individuals were, in some cases, depending on physical appearance, able to claim the status as whites. This system of racial classification was created with the express purpose of maintaining white supremacy by disenfranchising Southern *blacks*. See Davis 1991.

21. The one-drop rule was not a uniformly applied legal rule in all cases (e.g., in some states, the offspring of octoroons and white were white, and could sue for libel if called a "Negro." See Costello 1992).

22. The one-drop rule replaced the antebellum system of classification in which multiracial individuals were classified in ways that reflected that multiplicity. The slave system provided the institutional apparatus to keep the "races" socially separate—not only blacks from whites, but *multiracial* people from whites—in an effort to maintain white control over resources (Davis 1991). As such, the recognition of mixedness was not threatening to whites. The abolition of slavery dismantled that apparatus but in its place came legal standards such as the one-drop rule that served the same purpose (Degler 1971; Wacquant 1997). The one-drop rule effectively blocked multiracial access to the white category while also taking away a multiracial or "mulatto" category. This "tightening" of racial boundaries afforded the implementation of policies designed to maintain white control over the South. By the 1920s the category *mulatto* was removed from the U.S. Census, and the state no longer recorded multiple racial ancestry (Marx 1998; Davis 1991). Not until 1997 did the census bureau agree to allow individuals to choose more than one racial category on federal forms.

23. The one-drop rule was developed with specific reference to blacks, and has not been applied to other groups with any consistency. Multiracials of non-African ancestry have been accepted as whites. Davis (1991) argues, "[R]acially mixed persons in the United States, except for those with black ancestry, generally have been treated as assimilating Americans after the first generation of miscegenation." Multiracials of one-fourth or less Asian or Mexican (Indian) ancestry are "most likely to be accepted the same way an assimilating immigrant from Europe is. . . . They do not have to hide their racial minority background if it is one-fourth or less, so there is no need to pass as white" (118).

24. The state's understanding of race gradually became accepted in everyday life as well. While for a time the mulatto elite resisted its classification with blacks, with a growing awareness that partial European ancestry would no longer afford them any legal benefits, and that whites would treat mulattoes as black, they began to accept and even embrace their categorization with "un-mixed" blacks. This alliance consolidated around the era of the Harlem Renaissance, with the formation of a "New Negro" ideal that downplayed distinctions of color and class among blacks (Drake and Cayton 1993 [1945]; Frazier 1957; Williamson 1980). Much of the impetus behind broader acceptance of this new understanding of "Brown America"

came from the Harlem Renaissance artistic movement. A significant portion of these artists was of multiple ancestry.

25. Siobhan Somerville, *Queering the Color Line: Race and the Invention of Homosexuality in American Culture* (Durham: Duke University Press, 2000); Dorothy Roberts, *Killing the Black Body: Race, Reproduction, and the Meaning of Liberty* (New York: Pantheon Books, 1997). By 1940, thirty states had anti-miscegenation laws (Roberts 1997), 71.

26. John D'Emilio and Estelle Freedman, *Intimate Matters: A History of Sexuality in America* 2nd ed. (Chicago: University of Chicago Press, 1997); Cynthia Nakashima, "An Invisible Monster: The Creation and Denial of Mixed Race People in America," in *Racially Mixed People in America,* ed. Maria P. P. Root (Newberry Park, CA: Sage, 1992), 162–78.

27. Virginia Dominguez, *White by Definition: Social Classification in Creole Louisiana* (New Brunswick, NJ: Rutgers University Press, 1986), 63.

28. George Fredrickson, *White Supremacy: A Comparative Study in American and South African History* (New York: Oxford Press, 1981), 106.

29. Eva Saks, "Representing Miscegenation Law," in *Interracialism: Black-White Intermarriage in American History, Literature, and Law* ed. Werner Sollors (New York: Oxford University Press, 2000 [1988]), 67.

30. Randall Kennedy, "The Enforcement of Anti-Miscegenation Law," in *Interracialism: Black-White Intermarriage in American History, Literature, and Law* ed. Werner Sollors (New York: Oxford University Press, 2000), 156.

31. W. E. B. DuBois commented on some of the beneficiaries of their white fathers' aid (his classmates at Fisk) in his second autobiography, of which David Levering Lewis writes, "Willie was bedazzled by the likes of Ransom C. Edmondson and his younger brother, elegant sons of a white planter; by the unnamed relative of a future U.S. president, chauffeured to campus daily" (Lewis 1993, 61). "Lots and lots of mulattoes of that sort," DuBois writes, "some of whom were financed by their fathers, and some of them were financed by the fact that as mulattoes they got the better jobs" (DuBois 1962 quoted in Lewis 1993).

32. Gregory Howard Williams, *Life on the Color Line: The True Story of a White Boy Who Discovered He Was Black* (New York: Penguin Books, 1996); Shirley Taylor Haizlip, *The Sweeter the Juice: A Family Memoir in Black and White* (New York: Simon and Schuster, 1998); Carl Degler, *Neither Black Nor White: Slavery and Race Relations in Brazil and the States* (Madison: University of Wisconsin Press, 1970); Dominguez, *White By Defintion.*

33. See Martha Hodes, *White Women and Black Men: Illicit Sex in the Nineteenth Century South* (New Haven: Yale University Press, 1997).

34. I thank Bradley Herring for generating the statistics supporting this claim.

35. See Bourdieu (1996) for more discussion of the privileges of family membership and their importance in maintaining the social order.

36. Kimberly McClain DaCosta, *Remaking the Color Line: Social Bases and Implications of the Multiracial Movement* (University of California, Berkeley: unpublished dissertation, 2000).

37. Brackette Williams, "Classification Systems Revisited: Kinship, Caste, Race, and Nationality as the Flow of Blood and the Spread of Rights," in *Naturalizing*

Power: Essays in Feminist Cultural Analysis ed. Sylvia Yanagisako and Carol Delaney (New York: Routledge, 1995).

38. Stephen Cornell, "The Variable Ties that Bind: Content and Circumstances in Ethnic Processes" in *Ethnic and Racial Studies* 19 no. 2 (April 1996), 268.

39. Anthony Appiah, *In My Father's House: Africa in the Philosophy of Culture* (London: Methuen, 1992).

40. Carol Delaney, "Father State, Motherland, and the Birth of Modern Turkey," in *Naturalizing Power: Essays in Feminist Cultural Analysis* (New York: Routledge, 1995), 177.

41. Mary Waters, *Ethnic Options: Choosing Ethnic Identities in America* (Berkeley: University of California Press, 1990), 134.

42. F. James Davis, *Who is Black: One Nation's Rule* (University Park: Pennsylvannia State Press, 1991); Degler, *Neither Black Nor White*.

43. Hodes, *White Women and Black Men*.

44. Max Weber, "Ethnic Groups," in *Economy and Society* (Berkeley: University of California Press, 1978 [1918–1920]), 386.

45. Jack Goody, Joan Thirsk, and E. P. Thompson, *Family and Inheritance: Rural Society in Western Europe, 1200–1800* (New York: Cambridge University Press, 1976.

46. Rubin, "The Traffic of Women."

47. Robert Merton, "Intermarriage and the Social Structure," in *Interracialism: Black-White Intermarriage in American History, Literature, and Law* (New York: Oxford University Press, 2000), 483.

48. Dominguez, *White By Definition*, 61.

49. Kristin Luker, *Abortion and the Politics of Motherhood* (Berkeley: University of California Press, 1984); Werner Sollors, *Neither Black Nor White Yet Both: Thematic Exploration in Interracial Literature* (New York: Oxford University Press, 1997).

50. Others have explicitly equated "amalgamation" with incest. In his 1854 treatise on sociology, Henry Hughes wrote: "Hybridism is heinous. Impurity of races is against the law of nature. Mulattoes are monsters. The law of nature is the law of God. The same law, which forbids consanguineous amalgamation, forbids ethnical amalgamation. Both are incestuous. Amalgamation is incest."

51. The recent cross burning at the home of an intermarried couple in California testifies to the power intermarriage still has to incite threats and intimidation.

52. The control of sexuality is an integral part of systems of domination in other societies as well, particularly those who have a descent-based understanding of how relevant social group membership is acquired, such as Japan, South Africa, and Germany. Descent-based systems lend themselves to concerns over "purity," which entails a concern with sexuality, oriented toward maintaining the putative purity of the dominant group. In South Africa, for example, the 1949 Prohibition of Mixed Marriages Act and the 1950 Immorality Amendment Act, which prohibited interracial sex, only applied to unions between whites and nonwhites (Dikotter 1992). See Burckhardt (1983) for an elaboration of the unequal treatment afforded the "konketsuji" or mixed blood children in Japan, and Burleigh and Wippermann (1991) for information on Germany's Law for the Protection of German Blood and Honor that prohibited cross-category sexuality and marriage.

53. Sommerville, *Queering the Color Line*; Stephen Jay Gould, *The Mismeasure of Man* (New York: W.W. Norton, 1981).

54. Douglas Massey and Nancy Denton, *American Apartheid* (Cambridge: Harvard University Press, 1996).

55. My point is quite similar to that made by Gayle Rubin in "The Traffic in Women" (1975), in which she argued that the creation of gender was required for patriarchal kinship systems to function. Patriarchal kinship systems rest on marriage, she argued, an alliance that exchanged women so as to amass power for men. In order for women to participate in such a system they had to be gendered, transformed from females to women, while males were made into men, each "incomplete opposites" of the other. Similarly, these men and women are also "raced" in a way that constructs sexuality in accordance with the structure of racial domination.

56. Williams, *Life on the Color Line*; James McBride, *The Color of Water: A Black Man's Tribute to his White Mother* (New York: Riverhead Books, 1997).

57. Other mechanisms include discrimination, segregation, ghettoization, and racial violence. See Wacquant, "For an Analytic of Racial Domination."

58. Intermarriages represent 3 percent of an estimated 51.5 million marriages in 1990. U.S. Bureau of the Census, 1990 Census of Population and Housing, Public Use Microdata Samples.

59. Maria P. P. Root, ed. *The Multiracial Experience: Racial Borders as the New Frontier* (Thousand Oaks, CA: Sage, 1996).

60. According to the U.S. Census, from 1960 to 1990, the number of interracial married couples increased from roughly 157,000 to almost 1.5 million. The number of multiracial births rose from 460,000 in 1970 to 1.9 million in 1990. It must be pointed out that these numbers are always subject to question, since it is only now that we can count such statistics, given that such categories did not exist and/or have changed over time.

61. Roger Sanjek, "Intermarriage and the Future of Races in the United States," in *Race* ed. Steven Gregory and Roger Sanjek (New Brunswick: Rutgers University Press, 1994). Potential kinship links such as these are far fewer between blacks and whites, or between blacks and Hispanics or Asians. These kinship ties bear upon future developments in racial coalitions. Sanjek (1994) estimates that of those whites that marry interracially, the vast majority marry Hispanics or Asians (about 77 percent), and only about 23 percent marry blacks. Some argue that we may be seeing a "race-to-ethnicity" conversion for Hispanics and Asians similar to that of the Irish and Jews in early twentieth century, but not for African Americans. With each generation in the United States and as income and education levels rise, Hispanics and Asians are more likely to marry whites. While Asian and Hispanic outmarriage rates have risen sharply, black/white intermarriage rates have remained flat.

62. "Miscegenation" has played various roles in the different institutional arrangements oriented toward controlling African Americans. In the period of slavery, the threat of insurrection and abolition led to growing hostility toward miscegenation and the development of one-drop ideology to bolster slavery. In the Jim Crow South from the end of slavery to 1965 black emancipation and political rights threatened to erode the color line and whites' access to cheap labor. The development of Black Codes, political disenfranchisement, and systematic exclusion from all major institu-

tions, however, bolstered the color line. The creation of antimiscegenation statutes during this period was one part of the strategy of limiting black/white social contact that might imply equality between racial groups. The establishment of the northern ghetto from around 1915 to 1968 served both to exclude blacks from the rest of society and to protect them from that society. At the same time, urbanization "melted" mulattoes into an overarching African American identity in part because it was impossible for them to go elsewhere. As Drake and Cayton (1947) document, the ghetto was a source of protection for intermarried couples and their offspring as well. By the end of the 1960s, the communal ghetto began to break down in part because opportunities for African Americans became available in predominantly white institutions, of which the more educated and economically secure were most able to take advantage. As retrenchment of welfare state policies has taken hold since the 1970s, a growing class split has developed among African Americans, one that is important for the development of multiracial politics. The demographic roots of the Multiracial Movement emerge largely from the middle-class side of the split among the African American population, where many activists grew up in middle-class circumstances, were raised in white or somewhat integrated neighborhoods, and have uncharacteristically high levels of education, as did their parents (DaCosta 2000). For a broader analysis of the development of the "four peculiar institutions" that have structured African Americans' lives, see Wacquant 2001, "Deadly Symbiosis: When Ghetto and Prison Meet and Mesh."

TWO

DEFENDING THE CREATION OF WHITENESS:
WHITE SUPREMACY AND THE THREAT
OF INTERRACIAL SEXUALITY

ABBY L. FERBER

> There is a double standard for hatred, as there is for so much else. . . . We are not allowed to hate. They are. . . . Every oppressed people worth its salt hates its oppressors. We should feel no more guilty about hating our enemies than a rodent should feel about hating a snake. . . . Enmity is a key component of the art of individual and group survival. The man who hates to hate is only half a man and a poor defender of his family and race. . . . Without love there is no creation. *Without hate the creation cannot be defended.* Hate is just as much a unifier as love.[1] (Italics added)

FOR THE WRITERS and readers of *Instauration*, an overtly racist and anti-Semitic white supremacist journal, hatred is an integral part of life. It is every man's duty to defend his own kind against his enemies: in this case, Jews, African Americans, and all nonwhites. And as this passage suggests, hatred is essential to protecting the race. In sharp contrast to the increasingly subtle deployment of racist codifications that pervade mainstream discourse, white supremacist hatred is blatant.

Throughout white supremacist discourse, whites are depicted as the victims of racial oppression. Another article asks,

> How much damage does minority racism do as it requires the Majority to keep its mouselike feet on the treadmill; fork over a disproportionate share of the taxes; or battle in the overseas wars? . . . daily, at all hours, the minority racist makes his appearance, alternately complaining, accusing, plotting, sleuthing, whining, gloating, demanding, inserting and twisting his ideological dagger, as he attacks the majority in a thousand different ways.[2]

Inverting the reality of racial oppression, thousands of articles in dozens of different white supremacist publications paint an overwhelming picture of the white race under attack.

Since race is believed to be something that shapes the lives of people of color, whites often fail to recognize the ways in which their own lives are shaped by race. Recent scholarship argues that we need to extend our analyses to explore white identity and privilege.[3] As Toni Morrison maintains, we need to examine "the impact of racism on those who perpetuate it."[4] Not only do traditional conceptions of race exclude the experiences of whites, they also prevent us from understanding racial privilege, relieving whites of responsibility for racism. "Racism, from this perspective, disadvantages others, but is not shown to advantage whites."[5] Oppression and privilege, however, are tied together. And as recent studies demonstrate, white identity developed historically as a consolidation of privilege.[6]

When we focus only on the victims of racism, privilege remains invisible. We often fail to explore the way race shapes the lives of white people, treating whites as if they were raceless and, therefore, the norm. Embarking on a new course, Toni Morrison asserts that white American identity is constructed through its relationship with and representation of an African other, created in opposition to this Africanist presence. Recently, sociologists and other scholars have begun to take a similar approach, systematically exploring the construction of white racial identity.[7]

Surprisingly, even much research on the white supremacist movement has failed to explore whiteness itself, and the central threat posed by multiracial identity. However, I do not think we can understand the white supremacist movement and its adherents without exploring the ways in which they construct both white and multiracial identities. I argue that the white supremacist movement is primarily a project to reconstruct whiteness and maintain white privilege and power. In white supremacist discourse, whiteness is elaborated and defended because it is perceived to be threatened, and it is this threat that interests me. In studying white supremacist literature, what surprised me most was the way in which this threat was articulated, almost exclusively, as the threat of interracial sexuality. It is an understatement to claim that white supremacy is obsessed with interracial sexuality and multiracial people. For white supremacists, multiracial people serve as a powerful symbol of the dangers of transgressing racial boundaries. Poststructuralist theory has revealed the centrality of borders to the construction of coherent identities. Far more than a lurid preoccupation, the obsession with interracial sexuality is part of the process of boundary maintenance essential to the construction of both race and gender identity.

The construction of racial difference is central to racism.[8] The study of the white supremacist movement then, is not only the study of racist ideology, but of the construction of races themselves. Rather than reading white supremacist discourse as one that is *descriptive* of race, I am reading it as one that actively constructs race. Representations of the white supremacist movement traditionally define it as one that attempts to champion white interests while espousing hatred toward blacks and Jews, taking the given reality of race for granted. Instead, I read this movement as actively producing the differences that it seeks to exploit. Deconstructing our taken-for-granted text/reality distinction shows the reality of race to be one that is constantly being written and read.

In *Reading Rodney King/Reading Urban Uprising*, Kimberle Crenshaw and Gary Peller assert that to explore race in America, it is imperative to "examine critically how ideological narratives work as a form of social power."[9] Extending this approach to the study of race, they suggest that "the realm of interpretation, ideology, and narrative is a critical site in the production of American racial domination. . . . At stake . . . is a contest over which, and whose, narrative structure will prevail in the interpretation of events in the social world."[10] Rather than seeing ideological narratives as mystifications of the truth, this approach emphasizes that all seeing takes place within a narrative field. The power of ideology comes from its power to define what it does and does not make sense to say, the power to define knowledge and reality.

In white supremacist publications, fears of multiracial identity emerge in relation to the construction of race and gender. Interracial sexuality emerges as the central issue in white supremacist discourse. While considered extremist in their beliefs, the white supremacist construction of identity is based on modern Enlightenment conceptions of identity that have been taken for granted by mainstream discourse. White supremacist beliefs are rooted historically in mainstream American beliefs about the significance of race and the necessity of racial segregation. While white supremacists are usually labeled extremist for their support of violence, most hate crimes are not performed by members of white supremacist groups.

White supremacist antagonism toward interracial sexuality is also not as extreme as we might expect, especially when viewed within the context of American history. Prior to the 1967 U.S. Supreme Court ruling in *Loving v. Virginia*, seventeen states had laws against interracial marriage. At one point, forty of the fifty states banned interracial marriage.[11] It is imperative, then, that we situate white supremacist constructions of race and interracial sexuality within a broader the historical context.

HISTORICAL CONTEXT

Carolus Linnaeus, a prominent naturalist in the eighteenth century, developed the first authoritative racial division of humans in his *Natural System*, published in 1735.[12] Considered the founder of scientific taxonomy, he attempted to classify all living things, plant and animal, positioning humans within the matrix of the natural world. As Cornel West demonstrates, from the very beginning, racial classification involved hierarchy and the linkage of physical features with character and cultural traits.[13] For example, in the descriptions of his racial classifications, Linnaeus defines Europeans as "gentle, acute, inventive . . . governed by customs," while Africans are "crafty, indolent, negligent . . . governed by caprice."[14]

The construction of racial classifications has been an inherently ideological and political project. This explains why scientific theories of race failed to gain widespread acceptance and importance until 1865, with the emancipation and rise of blacks as a strong political force.[15] Because race is not grounded in genetics or nature, the project of defining races always involves drawing and maintaining boundaries between those races. From the moment the concept of race was invented, interracial sexuality became a concern. Robert J. C. Young observes that "the idea of race here shows itself to be profoundly dialectical: it only works when defined against potential intermixture."[16] While whiteness has been defined in opposition to blackness, multiracial identity poses the greater threat to the construction of these essential racial classifications; multiracial peoples reveal that the borders between races are permeable and penetrable. Further, the existence of multiracial peoples throws into question the "purity" of white identity, making it difficult to distinguish who is and is not white.

Conceptions of race were carved out of the fear of interracial sexuality, and ideas about miscegenation from this time period are practically indistinguishable from the beliefs of contemporary white supremacists. Louis Agassiz argued for rigid segregation and warned against the dangers of miscegenation:

> Conceive for a moment the difference it would make in future ages,
> for the prospect of republican institutions and our civilization gen-

erally, if instead of the manly population descended from cognate nations the United States should hereafter be inhabited by the effeminate progeny of mixed races. . . . I shudder from the consequences. . . . How shall we eradicate the stigma of a lower race when its blood has once been allowed to flow freely into that of our children.[17]

The issue of miscegenation, and questions of how to define and identify mulattoes, played a central role in scientific theories of race. Any discussion of the existence of races had to address the question of the mixing of races, and any attempt to define the distinctive characteristics of races also had to address the characteristics of the mulatto, the product of racial mixture. Robert J. C. Young argues that "from the 1840s . . . discussions of the question of hybridity became a standard discursive feature of any book on natural history or race, and one of the most persuasive means through which any writer on racial theory established himself as being, in Foucault's phrase, 'in the true.' "[18]

Count Joseph Arthur de Gobineau, in his 1854 *Essay on the Inequality of Human Races*, asserted that race mixing would inevitably lead to the "deterioration of humanity."[19] Zoologist and paleontologist Edward D. Cope, editor of the *American Naturalist*, wrote in 1890 that "the greatest danger which flows from the presence of the Negro in this country, is the certainty of the contamination of the race."[20] Race was assumed to be an inherited essence, shaping biological, physical, and cultural characteristics.

Throughout the second half of the nineteenth century, discussion of race and racial purity grew increasingly popular in both academic and mainstream circles as Americans developed distinctive beliefs and theories about race for the first time. As scientific beliefs about race were increasingly accepted by the general public, support for the one-drop rule became increasingly universal. Popular opinion grew to support the belief that no matter how white one appeared, if one had a single drop of black blood, no matter how distant, one was black.[21]

Throughout the history of racial classification in the West, miscegenation and interracial sexuality have occupied a place of central importance. The science of racial differences has always displayed a preoccupation with the risks of interracial sexuality. Popular and legal discourses on race have been preoccupied with maintaining racial boundaries, frequently with great violence. This chapter suggests that racial classification, the maintenance of racial boundaries, and racism are inexorably linked. The construction of biological races and the belief in maintaining the hierarchy and separation of races has led to widespread fears of integration and interracial sexuality. Throughout U.S. history, the fear of black political and economic equality has been rearticulated as the fear of interracial sexuality and guarded with force.

Additionally, gender has been central to this fear, as the protection of white womanhood and the threat of interracial sexuality have become synonymous. While interracial sexuality has been condemned historically, it has only been the relationship between white women and black men that has been the focus of attention; the exploitative relations between white men and black women have largely been ignored by the white community. The construction of whiteness as racially pure, and the enforcement of the one-drop rule, provided white males with the freedom to engage in interracial sexual relations, often through the rape of black women, while at the same time defending white womanhood against the fictional black male rapist. The myth of black sexuality as animal-like and out of control has served to justify the myth of the black male rapist and the institution of lynching. Additionally, for the white community, this myth has erased from view white males' sexual abuse of black women, who were defined as sexual creatures and therefore incapable of being raped. Defining black women as promiscuous and oversexed, combined with the belief that all women were the property of white men, meant that the only form of rape that was actually considered such was the rape of white women by black men. In this case, rape is seen as a violation of white male property rights. The intersections of race and gender are revealed in the entrenched paradox that while interracial sexuality has been condemned, it is only the relations between white women and black men that have been considered a threat to the white community.

Racial classification is essential to the preservation of white, and especially male, power and privilege. As this chapter highlights, racism is often a method of maintaining racial classification, and racial classification serves to support racism. As West argues, the

> basis for the idea of white supremacy is to be found in the classificatory categories and the descriptive, representational, order-imposing aims of natural history . . . the genealogy of racism in the modern West is inseparable from the appearance of the classificatory category of race.[22]

The history of racial classification, and beliefs about race and interracial sexuality, can be characterized as inherently white supremacist. White supremacy has been the law and prevailing world view throughout U.S. history, and the ideology of what is today labeled the white supremacist movement is firmly rooted in this tradition. Accounts that label the contemporary white supremacist movement as fringe and extremist often have the consequence of rendering this history invisible. Understanding this history, however, is essential to understanding and combating both contemporary white supremacist and mainstream racism. Further, this history provides the context for understanding the rise of the contemporary Multiracial Movement. Accounts that fail to address the important link between the U.S. history of white supremacist thought and contemporary racial identity movements, including the white supremacist movement and the Multiracial Movement, will fail to comprehend the strength and appeal of these contemporary movements, while minimizing the centrality of racism to American history and identity. After all, while a great deal has changed over the past three decades, the one-drop rule is still generally accepted, and interracial unions remain controversial.

Today, interracial marriages constitute only about 2 percent of all marriages,[23] suggesting that strong cultural taboos against intermarriage still exist. The vast majority of these marriages, however, occur between white and nonblack others. In fact, marriages between whites and nonblack others are three times more likely than marriages between whites and blacks, and respondents to a Knight-Ridder poll were most approving of marriages between "other combinations of races, and were least critical of Asian and Hispanic unions."[24] Clearly, black/white relations remain the most problematic.

Each year, dozens of television talk shows focus on the "problems" of interracial dating, interracial marriage, mixed-race adoptions, etc. Numerous movies have focused on this "problem," ranging from *Imitation of Life* and *Guess Who's Coming To Dinner* to the more recent *Jungle Fever*, *Mississippi Masala*, *Made in America*, and *Secrets and Lies*. These texts both illustrate and recreate the Western preoccupation with interracial sexuality, and my analysis will explore just why interracial sexuality plays such an integral role in white supremacist discourse and, especially, in the construction of racialized, gendered identities. Interracial sexuality is not simply one among many issues that preoccupy white supremacists; it is my contention that the issue of interracial sexuality is key to comprehending the white supremacist worldview.

CONSTRUCTING RACE AND GENDER IN WHITE SUPREMACIST DISCOURSE

Historically, interracial unions were problematic because they threatened the construction of a pure white identity. Maintaining the borders between the races is essential to their construction. I argue that the construction of racial classifications and the regulation of interracial sexuality are inextricably linked; one cannot be understood without the other. Recognizing and analyzing the construction of race aids us in comprehending just why interracial relations are seen as so threatening.

While white supremacist discourse adamantly supports the notion that race is a biological and/or god-given essence, my review of the discourse reveals the social construction of that essence. Exploring this discourse reveals the construction of both race and gender as inner essences, immutable and natural.

Throughout white supremacist discourse, whiteness is defined in terms of visible, physical differences in appearance. According to one article, true whites are Nordics, "the thin, fair and symmetric race originating in Northern Europe."[25] In another article, Nordics are described as the only cleanly chiseled faces around. And there are other ways they stand out. The world's finest hair and finest skin texture are in Scandinavia. Some of the world's tallest statures, largest body size and most massive heads are also found in Northern European regions.[26] A great deal of effort is put into physically distinguishing races from one another. Both the book and film entitled *Blood in the Face* take their name from some white supremacists' supposition that Jews cannot blush and only true whites show "blood in the face."[27] Rather than revealing race as a biological essence, this discourse reveals the continued effort required to construct racial differences, demonstrating Judith Butler's assertion that identities are constructed through reiterative and citational practices.[28] The construction of identity is not a singular act or gesture, but rather a process, or performance, as Butler calls it, which must be continually repeated. The elaboration of racial and sexual difference must "*repeat itself* in order to establish the illusion of its own uniformity and identity."[29]

These identities are always at risk and never secure. The endless repetition through which they are constructed suggests that they require this repetition for their existence and even though racial identity is posited as a biological or god-given fact of nature, the definition of whiteness is in constant flux. There is disagreement among groups and individuals over the characteristics that define whiteness and who is, or is not, white. In some of the discourse, Aryans are defined as strictly Northern Europeans, and there is debate over exactly where to draw the line in Europe. As one white supremacist claims in the film *Blood in the Face*, "We're more Nazi than the Nazis were!"

White supremacists construct Jews as a separate, nonwhite race. Jews are said to be identifiable by physical markers such as "long kinky curls and typical hooked nose, thick fleshy lips, slant eyes and other typical Jew features."[30]

Because the visible characteristics constructed as markers of race are not always evident, discerning the race of individuals is of the utmost importance to white supremacists. Articles such as "Racial Tagging" in *Instauration* reveal surprises in the racial identity of public figures. As this article explains,

Racial identification is a tricky game. As we keep our eyes open, we stumble across the most surprising information. Recently we have been looking into the Portuguese origins of public figures considered to have been solidly Northern European in racial makeup.[31]

Racial identity is constructed as an essence within each person that merely needs to be discovered. Like the approach of much traditional sociological analysis of intermarriage, individuals are assumed to possess, a priori, an essential racial identity, which they bring to the marriage. This discovery, or reporting, of race, however, is actually part of the process of production of the racialized subject. In Butler's terms, these comprise the reiterative and citational practices which construct race.

While a great amount of effort and written space is devoted to delineating physical racial differences, these physical differences are always interpreted as signifying deeper, underlying differences. Intelligence, morality, character, and culture are all posited as racially determined. As an *NSV Report* article proclaims, "[R]acists believe that values and ideals are a manifestation of race and are thus biologically inherited."[32] Mirroring the work of earlier generations of scientists and anthropologists, physical and cultural characteristics are linked, both assumed to be determined by race and therefore unchanging. Politics, music, art, and science are all shaped by race in this discourse. *The Thunderbolt* proclaims that

> [T]he White Race has created and developed most of the world's present and past civilizations . . . responsible for almost all of the scientific, engineering and productive know-how that has raised the world's standard of living . . . the only race which has been able to maintain a free democratic government. Liberty, justice and freedom only exist in White nations . . . culture, art, humanities. . . . The charity and goodness of the White Race have time and again saved the non-White peoples of the world from famine and plague. The White Race in the past has established moral codes, rules and laws, and educational systems for the advancement of society that have been unsurpassed by any other race in the world.[33]

Like conceptions of race developed in the eighteenth and nineteenth centuries, civilization is a marker for whiteness. Additionally, this racial essence is represented as immutable. An *NSV Report* article about Jews claims,

> We fight for things that they cannot understand because of their nature; and because of their nature, they can never understand because they are aliens. Even if they changed their religion, they will not be a part of our Folk. They can never be a part of our Folk

for they are aliens. They might as well be from another planet because they are not of our world.[34]

Not surprisingly, the characteristics that identify whites are always found to be superior to the characteristics of nonwhites. Differences in intelligence or brain size, as well as the accomplishments of "Western civilization," are frequently referenced to construct the superiority of whites, and the beauty of white women is invoked to signal the superiority of white aesthetics. A *Thunderbolt* article proclaims, "The negro in our midst is an inferior being."[35] On the other hand, the superiority of whites is constructed through frequent reiterations, as in this *New Order* article:

> America and all civilized society are the exclusive products of White man's mind and muscle. . . . [T]he White race is the Master Race of the earth . . . the Master Builders, the Master Minds, and the Master Warriors of civilization. Without the White race, the world would still be a Stone Age swamp.[36]

Throughout white supremacist discourse, race and gender are constructed as differences, and difference is equated with inequality. The difference/equality dichotomy recasts equality as necessarily requiring sameness, while difference necessarily requires and justifies hierarchy.

Like racial difference, gender difference is imagined as not merely differences in physical characteristics, but differences in character and personality as well. For example, a *White Power* article explains that

> [o]ur ancestors wisely realized that women were different from men not just biologically, but psychologically and emotionally as well. They recognized that the sexes had distinct but complementary roles to play in society . . . ordained by natural law.[37]

And like racial difference, sexual difference, is believed to be a fact of nature and immutable.

Both race and gender are constructed as genetic and/or god-given essences, and they are often interdependent. Gender and racial differences are linked throughout this discourse: the former are considered essential features distinguishing races from one another. A number of articles point out that "sexual dimorphism [the difference between the sexes] is greatest in the Caucasoids."[38] Drawing upon the assumptions of early evolutionary theorists, differentiation is seen as the key to advancement. The more pronounced degree of differentiation between white men and women is offered as one factor separating whites from other races and signaling their supposed supe-riority. At the same time, males are posited as more differentiated than females, establishing white males as superior to white women and nonwhite men and women. As one author explains, "[S]exual dimorphism is greatest in the Caucasoids. We know further that women are less varied (smaller standard deviations) on most physical components, such as height, weight, and intelligence (relative brain size)."[39] This convenient matrix of differen-tiation perches white males firmly at the top.

While white supremacists cite the degree of gender difference between white men and women as one factor separating whites from other races and establishing white superiority, they also emphasize the differences between white and nonwhite females as a feature distinguishing the white race and signaling its superiority. The belief that white women represent the ideal of female beauty is widespread and considered commonsense knowledge in this discourse. An *Instauration* article credits "25,000 years of tough natural selec-tion on the edge of glaciers" with producing "these beauteous products of a very special kind of evolution . . . these magnificent-looking women."[40]

Even more significant, gender is central to white supremacist discourse because the fate of the race hinges upon white women's sexual and reproduc-tive acts. Images of white women define them as breeders of the race, and the property of white men, who owe them protection.

PATROLLING THE BORDERS

White supremacist discourse is obsessed with interracial sexuality. This point cannot be overemphasized. Newsletters devote huge amounts of space to the issue. Perusing a few publications yields a plethora of titles decrying the phenomenon: "More Mixed Breeds Born,"[41] "God Commanded Racial Seg-regation; Holy Bible Condemns Mixed Marriage," "Brainwashed Into Inter-racial Marriage," "Mixed Babies are Colored,"[42] "Mixed Marriage Mongrelizing Russia,"[43] and "Interracial Marriages On Increase."[44]

Mixed-race people are seen as inferior, and almost inhuman. One ar-ticle argues, they are "negroidal mongrels who on their own could not build a pyramid or modern city."[45] Elsewhere, we are told that "a mulatto or mongrel race is a shiftless, lazy, mindless, leaderless and slave-like race which must have a racial superior 'boss-man' to tell them what to do."[46]

Interracial sexuality threatens not only racial identity but gender iden-tity as well. Because white female beauty is constructed as a sign of racial difference and white superiority, interracial sexuality is represented as a threat to that defining feature of whiteness. One publication provides a fictional account of a white survival demonstration, where protestors chant,

"Sweden is going Brown." "No more Ingrid Bergman." "America is going brown." "No more Cheryl Tiegs." "France is going brown." "No more Catherine Deneuve," . . . "What is the solution?" "White separatism!"[47]

Interracial sexuality is constructed as eliminating difference, making everyone the same inhuman brown, and because white female beauty is defined as a distinguishing feature of whiteness, interracial sexuality is depicted as a threat to that beauty as well as white aesthetic standards.

To white supremacists, mixed-race people are far more dangerous than other nonwhites. Because interracial sexuality threatens the borders of white identity, mixed-race people become the living embodiment of that threat. White supremacist publications are filled with images of "mongrels" who are to be feared and despised because they straddle and destabilize those racial boundaries essential to securing white identity and power.

It is through the construction and maintenance of racial boundaries, and the demarcation of "whiteness" as a racially pure identity, that the white subject is constructed. While those who are discovered to be of mixed black/white ancestry have been traditionally defined as black in the United States, they nevertheless represent a potential threat to the construction of racial identity based on the illusion of white racial purity. More importantly, mixed-race people signal the instability and permeability of racial boundaries; the regulation of interracial sexuality is required in order to secure the borders.

For white supremacists, mixed-race people also make racial separation and segregation more difficult. Race is constructed through the reiteration of physical differences that are visible and knowable, and the existence of mixed-race individuals is represented as a threat to this surety. In a *National Vanguard* article entitled "Beware The Almost Whites!" readers are warned that interracial sexuality produces

a continuous range of mongrels between the two racial extremes. Near the White end of the spectrum there will be some who . . . will be almost indistinguishable from the true Aryans. Drawing the line between what is Aryan and what is not becomes more and more difficult.[48]

Mixed-race people then make it more and more difficult to construct whiteness. An article in *The New Order* further explains, "The 'murder by miscegenation' device works all too well when . . . 'almost Whites' . . . can gain acceptance when a nigger cannot."[49] The existence of "almost whites" poses a threat to the constructed surety of racial identity and symbolizes the insecurity and permeability of racial boundaries, threatening the possibility of racially pure reproduction. It is for this reason that white supremacists see race mixing as the ultimate tool being used against them. They fear genocide of the white race, and argue that their ultimate enemy, the Jews, are trying to race mix whites out of existence. One publication argues, "[W]e could never again rebreed the White Race out of interracial mongrels."[50]

In William Pierce's popular white supremacist novel, *The Turner Diaries*, which was reputedly used as a blueprint for the Oklahoma City bombing, readers are warned, "The enemy we are fighting fully intends to destroy the racial basis of our existence. No excuse for our failure will have any meaning, for there will be only a swarming horde of indifferent, mulatto zombies to hear it. There will be no White men to remember us."

CONCLUSION

This chapter has argued that (1) race is a social construct; (2) race and gender are intertwined; (3) the regulation of interracial sexuality is key to the construction of race; (4) white supremacist discourse is primarily concerned with constructing and defending white racial identity and privilege; and (5) interracial sexuality and multiracial people are perceived to pose the greatest threat to white power.

Too often, fears of interracial unions are dismissed as merely individual prejudice, as simply a result of some people's dislike of Others. In a similar fashion, white supremacists are often assumed to simply be prejudiced individuals who hate all nonwhites. While not entirely wrong, these explanations are entirely too simple. First, all nonwhites do not pose the same threat to white power. Clearly, the existence of multiracial peoples are perceived as most threatening, as we have seen. Further, these assumptions fail to consider race as a social construct, and instead take racial identities and categories for granted. In order to understand fears of interracial unions and multiracial people, as well as contemporary racial identity movements, we must explore the historical construction of race and whiteness. Both the regulation of interracial sexuality, and the white supremacist movement, are about the construction of whiteness and white power. They are not only about hatred of others, but about the construction of the white self and the preservation of white privilege. Whiteness here is constructed as privilege; it is central to the definition of what it means to be white. Any threat to white privilege is therefore perceived as a threat to whiteness itself. Interracial sexuality and multiracial people threaten the entire house of cards. I began this chapter with the words of a white supremacist author who argued that "without hate the creation cannot be defended." While he probably imagined a very different creation, his words ironically ring true: white supremacist hatred defends the human/social creation of race.

This historical context also provides an important backdrop for evaluating the potentially subversive power of the Multiracial Movement. An analysis of the construction of race and white supremacy reveals that the Multiracial Movement's revolutionary potential lies in its threat to racial essentialism. Attempts to reify multiracial identity as simply another racial identity classification will neutralize that threat and instead contribute to maintaining the hierarchical classificatory system. However, a Multiracial Movement which relentlessly disrupts and destabilizes racial classifications, revealing their constructed nature, can instead contribute to the broader movement against white power.

NOTES

1. *Instauration* (January 1977):10–11.

2. *Instauration* (August 1976):5.

3. Ruth Frankenberg, *White Women, Race Matters: The Social Construction of Whiteness* (Minneapolis: University of Minnesota Press, 1993); Toni Morrison, *Playing in the Dark: Whiteness and the Literary Imagination* (New York: Vintage, 1992).

4. Morrison, *Playing in the Dark*, 11.

5. Betsy Lucal, "Oppression and Privilege: Toward a Relational Conceptualization of Race," *Teaching Sociology* 24 (July): 246.

6. Noel Ignatiev and John Garvey, *Race Traitor* (New York: Routledge, 1996); George Lipsitz, "The Possessive Investment in Whiteness: Racialized Social Democracy and the "White" Problem in American Studies," *American Quarterly* 47, no. 3 (September):369–87; David R. Roediger, *The Wages of Whiteness: Race and the Making of the American Working Class* (New York: Verso, 1991); Alexander Saxton, *The Rise and Fall of the White Republic* (New York: Routledge, 1987).

7. Frankenberg, *White Women, Race Matters*; Suzanne Harper, *The Brotherhood: Race and Gender Ideologies in the White Supremacist Movement*, Ph.D. Dissertation (University of Texas, Austin, 1993).

8. David Theo Goldberg, *Racist Culture: Philosophy and the Politics of Meaning* (Oxford: Blackwell, 1993); Cornel West, *Prophecy Deliverance! An Afro-American Revolutionary Christianity* (Philadelphia: Westminster Press, 1982).

9. Kimberle Crenshaw and Gary Peller, "Reel Time/Real Justice," in *Reading Rodney King, Reading Urban Uprising*, ed. Robert Gooding-Williams (New York: Routledge, 1993), 62.

10. Crenshaw and Peller, "Reel Time/Real Justice," 57.

11. Robert J. C. Young, *Colonial Desire: Hybridity in Theory, Culture and Race* (New York: Routledge, 1995), 148.

12. West, *Prophecy Deliverance!* 56.

13. West, *Prophecy Deliverance!*

14. West, *Prophecy Deliverance!* 56.

15. Michael Banton and Jonathan Harwood, *The Race Concept* (New York: Praeger, 1975), 28.

16. Young, *Colonial Desire*, 19.

17. Stephen Jay Gould, *The Mismeasure of Man* (New York: Norton, 1981), 49.

18. Young, *Colonial Desire*, 11.

19. Banton and Harwood, *The Race Concept*, 28.

20. Edward D. Cope, quoted in John G. Mencke, *Mulattoes and Race Mixture: American Attitudes and Images, 1865–1918* (Ann Arbor: University Microfilms Research Press, 1979), 57.

21. Mencke, *Mulattoes and Race Mixture*, 37.

22. West, *Prophecy Deliverance!* 55.

23. F. James Davis, *Who Is Black? One Nation's Definition* (University Park: Pennsylvania State University Press, 1991).

24. Elsa C. Arnett and Tony Pugh, "Mixed-Race Unions Up," *Denver Post*, Dec. 6, 1997.

25. *Instauration* (February 1980):13.

26. *Instauration* (January, 1980):15.

27. James Ridgeway, *Blood In The Face* (New York: Thunder's Mouth Press, 1990).

28. Judith Butler, *Bodies That Matter: On The Discursive Limits of Sex* (New York: Routledge, 1993), 2.

29. Judith Butler, "Imitation and Gender Insubordination," in *Inside/Out: Lesbian Theories, Gay Theories*, ed. Diana Fuss (London: Routledge, 1991), 24.

30. *The Thunderbolt* (no. 301):6.

31. *Instauration* (October 1976):10.

32. *NSV Report* (October/December 1991):3.

33. *The Thunderbolt* (May 30, 1975):8.

34. *NSV Report* (October/December 1987):1.

35. *The Thunderbolt* (May 1982):3.

36. *The New Order* (March 1979):8.

37. *White Power* (105):4.

38. *Instauration* (March 1981):7; *Instauration* (January 1980):14–15.

39. *Instauration* (March 1981):7.

40. *Instauration* (May 1981):36.

41. *The Thunderbolt* (January 1979):8.

42. *The Thunderbolt* (May 1981):7.

43. *The Thunderbolt* (July 1981):12.

44. *The Thunderbolt* (August 1981):4.

45. *The Thunderbolt* (August 1979):9.

46. *The Thunderbolt* (no. 297):3.

47. *Instauration* (June 1980):18.

48. *National Vanguard* (August 1979):5.

49. *The New Order* (March 1979):2.

50. *The Thunderbolt* (January 1979):12.

THREE

RACIAL REDISTRICTING: EXPANDING THE BOUNDARIES OF WHITENESS

Charles A. Gallagher

My family would object to a biracial relationship if the person I was seeing were African American. I'm dating someone from El Salvador now and they are okay with the relationship.

—nineteen-year-old white female college student

My dad would be more upset if the guy was black than if he was Asian. I think this is because of the slavery situation in America, the hatred towards black and vice versa.

—eighteen-year-old white female college student

We are most likely to see something more complicated: a white-Asian-Hispanic melting pot—a hard to differentiate group of beige Americans—offset by a minority consisting of blacks who have been left out of the melting pot once again.

—Political Analyst Michael Lind on the future of interracial relationships

THE MULTIRACIAL MOVEMENT has raised public awareness that millions of individuals with mixed-race backgrounds do not fit into the racial categories established by the government. What this movement has ignored however, are the ways in which existing racial categories expand to incorporate groups once considered outside of a particular racial category. The social and physical markers that define whiteness are constantly in a state of flux, shifting in response to sociohistoric conditions. Groups once on the margins of whiteness, such as Italians and the Irish, are now part of the dominant group. National survey data and my interviews with whites suggest a process similar to the incorporation of Southern and Eastern Europeans into the "white" race is taking place among certain parts of the Asian and Latino populations in the United States. I argue that the racial category "white" is expanding to include those ethnic and racial groups who are recognized as being socially, culturally, and physically similar to the dominant group.

How borders of whiteness have evolved over time provides theoretical insight into how racial categories are redefined and how this process affects the relative mobility of racial and ethnic groups.[1] Not long ago Italian and Irish immigrants and their children had a racial status that placed them outside the bounds of whiteness.[2] Both of these groups now fit unambiguously under the umbrella of whiteness. Like the process of racialization[3] that transformed Italians and Irish into whites, some light-skinned, middle-class Latinos and multiracial Asians are being incorporated into the dominant group as they define themselves, their interests, and are viewed by others as being like whites. As white respondents in my study made clear, Asians, and to a lesser extent Latinos were viewed as having the cultural characteristics (a strong work ethic, commitment to family, focus on schooling) that whites believe (or imagine) themselves as possessing. In what was an extension of the model minority myth, many whites in this study saw Asians as potential partners in the demonization of African Americans, further legitimating the existing racial hierarchy.

I argue that we are currently experiencing a "racial redistricting" where the borders of whiteness are expanding to include those groups who until quite recently would have been outside the boundaries of the dominant group. Within the context of contemporary race relations those groups who do not "conform" to cultural and physical expectations of white middle-class norms, namely blacks and dark-skinned Latinos who are poor, will be stigmatized and cut off from the resources whites have been able to monopolize; good public schools, social networks, safe neighborhoods and access to primary sector jobs. These expanding borders serve to maintain white or nonblack privilege by casting blacks in negative, stereotypical terms. As whites and other nonblack groups inhabit a common racial ground the stigma once associated with interracial relationships between these groups is diminishing. These trends in racial attitudes and how these perceptions may influence mate selection have important implications for multiracial individuals and how racial categories will be defined in the near future.

The initial focus of the twenty individual interviews and eight focus groups (a total of seventy-five randomly picked white college student at a large northeastern urban university) was to examine the political and cultural meaning they attached to being white. What emerged in the interviews was a narrative about their whiteness that was intricately tied to how similar or dissimilar respondents saw other racial groups, why discussions of race relations tended to focus only on blacks and whites, and why Asians, and not blacks, could be absorbed or folded into the dominant group. These interviews revealed that many whites saw Asians and blacks in starkly different terms. At another large urban university in the southeast I administered an open-ended survey to a large undergraduate sociology class asking white respondents if they or any family members would have any reservations about them dating or marrying across the color line. The questionnaire was designed to examine to what extent, if any, white respondents' views about interracial relationships varied by race of the potential partner. Fifty-nine white students of traditional college age participated in the open-ended survey. The trends in these two samples point to how racial attitudes, social distance, and the perception of assimilation may shape dating preferences and how the cultural and phenotypical expectations that define racial categories change.

MULTI OR MONO RACIAL: NATIONAL TRENDS

Over the next twenty years we are likely to witness the children of Asian/white and Latino/white unions identifying themselves as many of their parents have already; as whites with multiple heritages where expressions of ancestry are "options" that do not limit or circumscribe life chances. According to the 1990 census native-born Asian wives were almost equally likely (45 percent) to have a white or Asian husband. Almost one third (31.4 percent) of native-born Latinas had white husbands while 54 percent of married American Indian women had white husbands. Only 2.2 percent of black wives had white husbands. The percentage of husbands who had white wives was also quite high; 36 percent of native born Asian, 32 percent of Latino, and 53 percent of American Indian men married white women. Only 5.6 percent of black husbands, however, had white wives.[4]

Self-identifying as white rather than a combination of races is the choice made by a sizable number of multiracial offspring. In fact, a 2000 study by the National Health Interview Surveys allowed respondents to select more than one race but were then asked in a follow-up interview to choose their "main race." More than 46 percent of those who marked white and Asian as their racial identity chose white as their "main race," 81 percent of those who marked white and American Indian marked white as their "main race," whereas only 25 percent of those who marked black and white marked chose white as their "main race." In the 2000 census almost half (48 percent) of the nation's Latino population defined themselves as white.[6]

What is perhaps more important for understanding how the contours of racial categories expand and contract is an examination of the racial definition parents in interracial marriages give to their children. A significant proportion of interracial couples where one partner is white and the other is Asian or Latino choose to define their offspring as white.[7] In families where the father was white and the mother was Asian Indian 93 percent defined their children as white. Where the father was white 51 percent of Native American, 67 percent of Japanese and 61 percent of Chinese mixed-race families defined their children as white. Only 22 percent white father and black mother unions defined their children as white. Among white mothers who married nonwhite husbands Waters found "50 percent of the offspring of white mothers and Native American fathers are reported to be white, 43 percent of Japanese/white children are reported as white, 35 percent of Chinese/white children are reported as white, and 58 percent of Korean/white children are reported *by* their parents to be white" while only 22 percent of black/white children were defined as white.[8] Given these trends, it is possible that the progeny of some of these relationships will have the option to self-identify as white and live their lives in white social networks, occupy white neighborhoods, and marry white partners. It is possible then that the white race can "grow" without an influx of "white" immigrants.

ASIAN ASSIMILATION VERSUS BLACK SEPARATISM

One theme that emerged in my interviews was that whites viewed Asians as model minorities driven to assimilate and move up the socioeconomic ladder while blacks were viewed as refusing to adopt the styles, mannerisms, and habits that would aid in their upward mobility. The sense that Asians were working to be part of system while blacks were not was evident in the following focus group discussion:

Interviewer: Why is our conversation mostly about blacks.

Theresa: Because [Asians] are so quiet.

Martha: That's exactly what I was going to say. They don't make a big deal like the blacks do. They don't jump up and down and scream and yell. They just do their thing.

Theresa: [Asians] don't want to be bothered. They want to get through so that they can have a chance to get into the system, figure it out, work up to what they want and they don't need anyone to bother them. They'll be fine. They can depend on themselves. They know that. I think they figure that if they try and depend on other people or try to make a voice about it they'll just get pushed down.

Interviewer: So why don't they make demands on the system?

Kathleen: I don't think they particularly lose out like the blacks did. And now the American Indians are starting to get more vocal because they've just been pushed down so much. I don't know that [Asians] ever have. I know that during World War II when they were put in the camps and stuff, whatever, but I don't see discrimination against them.

Theresa's comments point to the stages of assimilation some whites believe groups need or should pass through in order to gain upward mobility. The expectation is that groups will learn to work within the ethnic and racial hierarchy, not challenge it. The reference that blacks "jump up and down and scream and yell" suggests that organized resistance and opposition by African Americans to racial inequality is not a legitimate way to bring about social change or create economic opportunity for blacks. If Asians are no longer discriminated against, as Kathleen argues, the reason must be that they have properly integrated themselves in dominant group. What was implied in many of these exchanges was that whites perceived blacks as not trying hard enough to mirror the beliefs and behaviors of the dominant group while Asians did. Culturally, then, whites view Asians (and Latinos) as fellow immigrants who also worked their way up the racial and ethnic hierarchy; these groups are, as implied by my respondents, kindred spirits.

In sharp contrast to the idea that Asians have been accepted because of individual self-reliance, blacks' wearing clothing that expressed black unity, black nationalism, or critiques of institutional racism (e.g., wearing Malcolm X shirts or caps) was perceived as intimidating to whites and the antithesis of the assimilation narrative whites see blacks rejecting. The view that Asians wished to be mainstream culturally where blacks did not was evident in this exchange:

Mitch: They just go about and do what they have to do and blend in with the background. They're not so much asserting themselves.

They kind of work around you to get done what they have to get done, more than trying to break through a whole blockade of stuff.

Interviewer [addressing Frances]: Were you going to say something about intimidation?

Frances: I mean, [Asians] don't intimidate us. They don't walk around with Oriental hats or clothes. They don't make a big issue of it. They keep their culture to themselves. If you want to join their culture they don't have a problem with that. If you want to marry an Oriental, granted, that can be a problem. A lot of times that can really be a problem. But, the only problem we would run into would be the parents of the kids our age, because most of them have come from their country but the second generation, *they're American and they know American ways.* There's no pressure.

Mitch: I think there's a lot in the press about discrimination and its time is coming. I mean it's true, though. But, I mean, it's all over the place, stuff about discrimination. It's just becoming like really, really popular for black students to be black and proud and racist. But with Asians it's not that way. I mean there is a magazine *Ebony* for strictly black people—I've never really read it. I mean there is no magazine for just Asian people. There's nothing saying, like, Asian power. But it's [a black focus] all over the place.

That which makes race a salient form of social identity, such as wearing a Malcolm X cap or "black theme" shirts that call for pan-African unity, was viewed by some whites as a form of racial intimidation. The perception that blacks self-segregate and promote separatism by reading a black magazine such as *Ebony* while Asians do not, reflects the belief that Asians and whites have rejected race politics and share a common vision of what it means to being an American. It is important to note that dozens of magazines exist that are directed primarily at Asian and Asian Americans on a wide range of social, cultural, and business topics.

Having a strong work ethic, taking responsibility for your own mobility and embracing assimilation was a point Sharie made to contrast why she believes Koreans have been more successful than blacks:

Interviewer: Why do you think the Koreans have succeeded where the blacks haven't?

Sharie: Because they don't blame anybody. They try. They work, work, work and they succeed. And if they don't succeed they take it and they accept it and they don't blame anybody for it. They just take it and they don't cause any problems. And we don't blame them for anything. They don't do anything to us wrong. They're nice to us. You know what I mean? There shouldn't be a struggle. The black people have every opportunity. We try to give them every opportunity. Look at the schools—if you are a black person you can practically go to school free here, practically. And, uh, and I'm glad to see that there's so many black people going to college and that they're all trying to succeed but they can't blame us all the time.

Interviewer: Whom do they blame?

Sharie: The white society, that we're not giving them enough op-portunity. I don't know. I think that's why the Koreans . . .

Interviewer: What do you think that does, the blaming, in terms of what whites think about blacks?

Sharie: That they're losers. That they're putting the blame on some-body who's not—it's an excuse for them—it's your fault; it's the white society's fault. I think it just makes them think less of them. It makes them think that they don't have a work ethic. I mean when we came to this country no one had anything—I mean, they had less than the blacks when they came over to this country, way less. And look at where this country has come. They can work just as hard and succeed way above their expectations if they just stopped and looked at themselves.

This depiction of Asians collectively starting out with "way less" than African Americans yet achieving the American Dream because they are the model minority serves a number of functions; it minimizes social distance between whites and Asians while crafting a narrative where each group can point to the other's immigration experiences and shared upward mobility. What is also shared however, as evidenced in surveys of perceived social distance racial attitudes, is the tendency for both whites and Asians to stereotype blacks.[9]

ASIAN PASSIVITY, BLACK INTIMIDATION: REFLECTIONS OF SOCIAL DISTANCE

The theme of black racial intimidation and Asian passivity emerged in this focus group exchange:

James: It's because—I think they're quiet and they're smaller in stature than black people and they seem less threatening. I mean, that's not all of them. You know, I have a couple Asian friends, and they can be loud sometimes, but, I think, as a group they're all right.

Rita: They don't walk around with Mao Tse-tung hats on or shirts that say Asian Power. They're not being threatening. They're acting, they're making themselves useful, not making themselves useful, that's really awful to say, but they're working within the framework that they're given and they're making the best of their opportunities.

James: Maybe it's because of their culture.

Interviewer: So does that mean that since they're not asking for anything so they're not a threat? Is that what goes on?

Jeff: They're not demanding anything—a lot of the time in dealing with the black cause it won't work—please, "can we have equal rights," demanding . . .

Interviewer: So, why is that so different?

Jeff: Because demanding takes on an aggressive stature whereas asking doesn't.

And if I personally see someone being aggressive to me my first impulse is to be aggressive back and, again, that's another vicious circle.

As Rita sees it, Asians work "within the framework" where blacks presumably do not, and unlike blacks, Asians do not use past racial injustices to explain current racial inequities. Rita's reference that Asians do not use racial identity politics (no Mao Tse-tung hats) to advance group interests taps a strong sentiment among whites that the assertion of group rights (demanding "equal rights") to ameliorate racial inequality is a rejection of the ideals that made America great: rugged individualism, embracing an achievement ideology, and believing the socioeconomic playing field is level for all. In the last exchange Jeff explains that race relations between black and whites are tense because blacks are "aggressive" where Asians are not.

The amount of perceived social distance between whites, blacks, and Asians was evident in this exchange concerning which groups whites view as a threat:

Mike: Asians are different about being Asians and blacks are different about being black.

Joshua: You don't usually see Asian Power T-shirts.

Mike: And they're just not militant—that's not the word I'm looking for but it seems like the Asians are like, scholars.

Christel: They seem more complacent.

Lori: Yeah. They laugh at us. You know, they can say, make fun of me now, but . . .

Mike: They're so academic. I don't really think they're worried about finding a place and getting up in the university.

Lori: They're not as concerned with social issues. It doesn't seem like it, anyway.

Interviewer: Are they less threatening as a group?

Mike: They're not threatening, I don't think, to anybody.

Rejecting identity politics, blending in, not being threatening or militant; all these characteristics serve to make blacks cultural outsiders and by contrast, make Asians insiders. In addition to James's earlier comment about Asians being less threatening because they are smaller in stature, a few other respondents identified appearance as central to race relations.

One of the few nontraditional-aged students in the interviews, Pauline, a thirty-eight-year-old student, links color and culture in her explanation of group dynamics.

Interviewer: And why don't we talk about white and Asian?

Pauline: Like I said, I think it's because they're a little more accepted than the blacks.

Interviewer: Why are they more accepted?

Pauline: I think because their skin color is not as dark.

Interviewer: Do you think it's just that, just the skin color?

Pauline: Uh, maybe their culture is more accepted.

Interviewer: In what way?

Pauline: Well, you hear about how, like the Asians, a lot of them have families that believe in respect, respect for the family, so maybe their ideas in those ways are more accepted than the ways that blacks have lived.

Rob uses what he perceives as the physical similarities between whites and Asians also as the reason there seems to be less hostility between whites and Asians than whites and blacks.

Interviewer: It seems that I don't really hear students, that is, white students talk about Asian students that much. They don't seem to be an issue about anything. What's your take on that? I mean, why do you think that is?

Rob: I don't know. That is an interesting perspective. I don't know. I don't know. Maybe it gets down to something as simple as, you know, the contrast of skin color. Maybe it's just that blunt. I don't know.

Interviewer: What do you mean by that, though?

Rob: I mean that if you had a mass of people, just a crowd of people standing right there you could obviously pick out black Americans much easier than you might an Asian. You know what I mean? Because there is an obvious difference. Maybe it's something like that. I don't know. I really don't know.

These exchanges suggest that whites view Asians as having made every effort to assimilate by embracing a work ethnic, striving for the American Dream, and doing so in a color-blind fashion.

Many whites in this study saw Asians as possessing similar attitudes, beliefs, ambitions and even viewed Asians as being physically similar to whites, while blacks were seen as aggressive, threatening, and demanding.

Herbert Blumer succinctly described how racial identities are constructed and understood by observing: "To characterize another racial group is, by opposition, to define one's own group."[10] However, groups are not only defined through an oppositional relationship; solidarity between groups can emerge when social distance between two groups is less than the social distance of a different, and often more stigmatized group. My respondents' comments suggest that a racial repositioning is taking place where whites imagine Asians as occupying a place within the existing racial hierarchy that minimizes the social distance between whites and Asians, while blacks are placed farther on the social margins.[11]

SHADES OF ROMANCE: COLOR, PREFERENCE, AND STIGMA

The focus group interviews above suggest that many whites view Asians as being culturally more similar to them than blacks, a finding that mirrored my survey on interracial relationships. My open-ended questionnaire asked respondents if any family members would "object to you bringing home a romantic partner that was from a different race." An overwhelming major- ity (86 percent) of the fifty-nine white respondents in my survey said that at least one family member would object to dating outside the white race but most wrote that being involved with Asians and Latinos would be viewed as less of a problem for family members. This finding is consistent with national survey data on intermarriage rates. A Knight Ridder poll in 1997 found that although whites were generally accepting of interracial marriage, 30 percent of respondents opposed black and white unions but were less critical of interracial marriages involving Latinos and Asians.[12] Mary Waters reports that "one in five whites still believes interracial mar- riage should be outlawed, and a majority of whites, 66 percent, said they would oppose a close relatives marrying a black."[13] In their analysis of 1990 General Social Survey data, Herring and Missah found that whites, Jews, Asians, and Hispanics had the greatest opposition to one of their own marrying someone who was black.[14] While there was variation in the levels of opposition to interracial marriages for all groups, marrying someone who was white generated the least amount of disapproval. Using data from a 1992 study of Los Angeles County, Bobo and Smith found an "unambigu- ously greater average level of hostility to contact with blacks among non- blacks than occurs in reference to any other group."[15] Their survey found that whites, Asians, and Hispanics were more likely to oppose residential integration and interracial marriage with blacks and viewed blacks as being more dependent on welfare, harder to get along with, and less intelligent than other racial and ethnic groups. These attitudes serve as an important backdrop in understanding which racial groups whites might consider as romantic partners and how the resulting multiracial families would be positioned in the U.S. racial hierarchy.

MY FATHER WOULD DISOWN ME....

The responses below typify the anger that crossing the color line was imagined to trigger with family members, especially when it was a white female being involved with a black male:

> If I were to bring home a black man or a man of any other racial group home with me, my father would disown me! My father would kick me out of the house and would financially disown me, and never talk to me again. He was raised in a very old fashion traditional blacks are slaves, lower on the social scale and not anywhere close to being on the same level as the rest of the world. I have never been involved with a black man, but I did go to my senior prom with a black friend. It started a big fight between everyone in my family. (eighteen-year-old white female)

> If I were to bring someone home from a different racial background as my boyfriend, my family would be very confused. The person that would be most upset would be my dad. He would completely object to me having a black male date his daughter. My dad grew up in Atlanta, and now works in Atlanta. He is surrounded by the black race all day. He has set in his mind there are blacks and there are niggers. He says the black men and women that speak where people can understand them, and that have respect for people and their things are respectable black people. He will then explain that the niggers in the world that are lazy, disrespectful, stealing, cheating, Ebonics speaking blacks who will never earn respect by him. Don't get me wrong. My dad has black friends too. (nineteen-year-old white female)

> My father would object, my mom and dad will both be upset. They said that it looks bad when a white girl is dating a black guy because it looks like she cannot do any better than a black guy. (eighteen-year-old white female)

> We moved, as part of the white flight, to a whiter area. A part of why we moved was so that I would date a white girl, in my opinion. (nineteen-year-old white male)

What stands out in these survey responses was that blacks, but not Asian, American Indian, or Latino were the reference group these white respondents used to explain how family members might react to an interracial relationship. Perhaps that as the quintessential racial "other" in the United States "black" was automatically inserted as what was understood as a worst-case scenario for their families. Only a minority of white respondents (14 percent) wrote that their family would be indifferent or supportive of an interracial relationship, a finding that calls into question recent national surveys that suggest America has come to accept interracial relationships.

ASIAN OR LATINO—BUT NO BLACKS

A number of respondents made it clear that crossing the color line would *only* be a problem if their partner were black.

> My dad and brother. I think men are intimidated by other men that are different from them. I do think that there is a big difference from Asian or Latin to black. My dad would be more upset if the guy was black than if he was Asian. I think this is because of the slavery situation in America, the hatred towards black and vice versa. (eighteen-year-old white female)

> My ultra-liberal parents wouldn't care. I assume the only race that would shock them (assuming I was still living in the south) is black. Considering the drastic habitual differences and tastes on a general level they would question our compatibility. As for Asians, Latino, Middle Eastern, etc. I've had a diverse group of friends so neither of us would feel awkward. My family would object to a biracial relationship if the person I was seeing was African American. I'm dating someone from El Salvador now and they are okay with the relationship. (nineteen-year-old white female)

> Most of my family is pretty open-minded. To be honest, my step-father wouldn't care unless my partner were African American (black). (twenty-year-old white male)

> My dad would object to the relationship the most. He is very traditional. Especially towards a relationship between myself and a guy of African American decent. I have had a relationship with a Filipino-American and he addressed little objection however it was clear that he wasn't thrilled about it. (nineteen-year-old white female)

These last open-ended survey responses and the responses in the epigraph underscore trends in the national survey data discussed at the beginning of this chapter; whites are more willing to cross the color line when their potential mate is not black.

GROWING THE WHITE RACE: THEORETICAL PREDICTIONS

The Multiracial Movement seeks to highlight how the existing racial categories used by government and state agencies deny multiracial people the right to self-definition. Moreover rejecting the monoracial categories imposed on multiracial people is taken as an act of revolution and ultimately such insurgency can bring about positive social change by acknowledging how the idea of race as a socially constructed category reflects power, politics, and the maintenance of white privilege.[16] In a society fixated on creating an infinite amount of consumer choices and willing to impose free market principles on almost every social interaction, the beliefs that undergird the Multiracial Movement would appear to fit easily into post–civil rights race politics. This however, has not happened as evidenced by the relatively small number of multiracial people who could have defined themselves as multiracial in the 2000 census but did not. What appears to be taking place is a reconfiguring of existing racial categories. Richard Alba advises that "rather than speak of the decreasing White population," our collective notion of majority group might undergo a profound redefinition as "some Asians and Hispanics join what has been viewed as 'White' European population."[17] Herbert Gans makes a similar yet more problematic prediction about the future of racial categories:

> [T]oday's multiracial hierarchy could be replaced by what I think of as a dual or bimodal one consisting of "nonblack" and "black" population categories, with a third "residual," category for the groups that do not, or do not yet, fit into the basic dualism. More important, this hierarchy may be based not just on color or other visible bodily features, but also on the distinction between undeserving and deserving, or stigmatized and respectable, races. The hierarchy is new only insofar as the old white-nonwhite dichotomy may be replaced by a nonblack one, but it is hardly new for blacks, who are likely to remain at the bottom once again.[18]

Gans's collapsing of our current racial hierarchy into a dichotomous one where a sizable part of the population is placed in an intergenerational racial holding pattern is consistent with cultural critic Michael Lind's comment in the epigraph which suggests that racial borders may be fluid but the end result will be a further cementing of blacks to the bottom of the racial and economic hierarchy.

Sociologist Mary Waters writes that "[i]n general in the United States, those who are nonwhite racially have not been granted this opportunity by society but have been identified racially *by* others even if they wanted to disregard their racial or ethnic identity" (emphasis hers).[19] What is of particular importance in Waters's analysis is that the inability to select from the full range of the racial or ethnic options is imposed by "others," a point that underscores the racism on which the one-drop rule was founded. But just as the dominant group can impose measures that exclude individuals from their ranks so too can it create discourse, privilege traits, and stereotypes that assume group behavior. It is not that nonblacks aspire to be white but "in the racial context of the United States, in which Blacks are the defining other, the space exists for significant segments of groups today defined as non-White to become White."[20] What is suggested here is that educated, assimilated Asians and Latinos will be accepted into the dominant group. Those Asians and light-skinned Latinos who are well educated, economically secure, and/or with a white partner, may be able to take advantage of and exploit the perks, privileges, and prerogatives of being a member of the dominant group.

Access to amenities such as suburban housing and good schools are linked to race. Reynolds Farley notes that when Asians and Latinos move to metropolitan areas "they find themselves less residentially segregated than blacks."[21] More than one-half of all Asians (50.6 percent) in 1998 lived in suburban areas. Douglas Massey found that "the largest and most segregated Asian communities in the United States are much less isolated than the most integrated Black communities." In addition, he found that class did not lessen the extent to which black communities were racially segregated. "The most affluent blacks," Massey explains, "appear to be more segregated than the poorest Hispanics and Asians; and in contrast to the case of Blacks, Hispanic and Asian segregation levels fall steadily as income rises, reaching low or moderate levels of $50,000 or more."[22] Adelman and associates found that "even when group differences in socio-demographic are controlled, blacks were located in neighborhoods with higher levels of poverty and female headship and fewer college-educated residents than were their non-Hispanic white counterparts."[23] It is likely Asian/white and Latino/white families are part of these suburbanization trends.

But these assertions concerning residential segregation, social isolation, and which racial minorities are denied access to the resource rich middle-class white suburbs also miss what is slowly taking place: white suburbs are absorbing, even welcoming certain multiracial families because they are viewed as being culturally similar to the dominant group. Sociologist Orlando Patterson chides African Americans for not creating the rich and dense web of social networks that result from interethnic and interracial marriages. He argues that "[a]ll other American ethnic groups, including the more recently arrived Asians are intermarrying at record rates. . . . [W]hen one marries into another ethnic group one greatly expands one's social networks."[24] He advises, "[A]fter four centuries of imposed social—although not sexual reproductive—endogamy, Afro-Americans could do with a good deal of exogamy."[25] But Patterson's inability to understand why interracial marriage rates look as they do is analogous to the Multiracial Movement's blind spot on how a sizable part of the multiracial population define themselves or go on to define their children as white rather than multiracial. Patterson suggests that each racial group has a cultural dowry they bring to their marriages. The problem is that in a society structured around white racial dominance Asians and Latinos are defined as having those traits while blacks do not. We are now (or perhaps again) at a unique juncture in the history of racial and ethnic identity construction where racial categories may be mutating. Expanding the boundaries of whiteness to include those groups who subscribe to the existing racial status quo is one way racial dominance is "reorganized." White privilege is not being challenged by the incorporation of new groups into the category "white." It is revitalized as potential challengers to the existing hierarchy are co-opted and rewarded with the perks of membership in the dominant group. What is typically required, however, is that the racist beliefs and practices of the dominant group are internalized by those who join the ranks of the dominant group. In the end the Multiracial Movement may not be able to count on assimilated, economically successful light-skinned Latinos or Asians or their even lighter-skinned multiracial children, because like the Italians and Irish before them, racial redistricting will have allowed them to glide easily into the category "white."

NOTES

Michael Lind, "The Beige and the Black," *New York Times Magazine*, September 6, 1998, 39.

1. See Roediger and Ignatiev. See also Ruth Frankenberg, *White Women, Race Matters: The Social Construction of Whiteness* (Minneapolis: University of Minnesota Press, 1993); Birgit Brander, ed., *The Making and Unmaking of Whiteness* (Durham: Duke University Press, 2001); Ashley W. Doane Jr., "Dominant Group Identity in the United States: The Role of "Hidden" Ethnicity in Intergroup Relations," *The Sociological Quarterly*, 38, no. 3; Charles A. Gallagher, "White Reconstruction in the University," *Socialist Review* 24 (1995); Amanda Lewis, "Whiteness Studies: Past Research and Future," *African American Research Perspectives*, 8, no. 1 (2002).

2. See David Roediger, *Towards an Abolition of Whiteness: Essays on Race, Politics, and the Working Class* (New York: Verso, 1994); David Roediger, *The Wages of Whiteness: Race and the Making of the American Working Class* (New York: Verso, 1991); Noel Ignatiev, *How the Irish Became White* (New York: Routledge,1995); Karen Brodkin Sacks, "How Did Jews Become White Folks?" in *Race*, ed. Steven Gregory and Roger Sanjek (New Brunswick: Rutgers University Press, 1994); Charles A. Gallagher, "White Racial Formation: Into the Twenty-First Century," in *Critical White Studies: Looking Behind the Mirror*, ed. Richard Delgado and Jean Stefancic (Philadelphia: Temple University Press, 1997).

3. Omi and Winant define this process as a "socio-historical process by which racial categories are created, inhabited, transformed and destroyed." Michael Omi and Howard Winant, *Racial Formation in the United States: From the 1960s to the 1990s* (New York: Routledge, 1994), 55.

4. Reynolds Farley, "Racial Issues: Recent Trends in Residential Patterns and Intermarriage," in *Diversity and Its Discontents: Cultural Conflict and Common Ground in Contemporary American Society*, ed. Neil Smelser and Jeffrey Alexander (Princeton: Princeton University Press, 1999), 114–15.

5. Annie E. Casey Foundation, "Using New Racial Categories in the 2000 Census," www.aecf.org/kidscount/categories/bridging.htm.

6. U.S. Census.

7. Mary Waters, "Multiple Ethnic Identity Choices," in *Beyond Pluralism: The Conception of Groups and Group Identities in America*, ed. Wendy F. Katlin, Ned Landsman, and Andrea Tyree (Chicago: University of Chicago Press, 1998).

8. Waters, 41.

9. Cedric Herring and Charles Amissah, "Advance and Retreat: Racially Based Attitudes and Public Policy," in *Racial Attitudes in the 1990s: Continuity and Change*, ed. Steven A. Tuch and Jack Martin (Westport: Praeger, 1997), 139.

10. Herbert Blumer, "Race Prejudice as a Sense of Group Position," in *Rethinking the Color Line: Readings in Race and Ethnicity*, ed. Charles A. Gallagher (Mountain View, CA: Mayfield Press, 1999).

11. Michael Omi argues that we should not think about increased rates of intermarriage between white men and Asian women as an "indicator of assimilation" because such a description negates "differences in group power." It may be, as Omi suggests, that the assimilation framework masks patriarchy, sexist stereotypes of Asian women, and group-based inequalities in the name of minimizing social distance but it does not alter the fact that these marriages and the children of these unions challenge and blur existing racial categories. The ability to have both racial and ethnic options in how these individuals construct their identity suggests that under certain conditions the one-drop rule will cease to accurately describe the experiences of certain mixed race individuals. See Michael Omi, "The Changing Meaning of Race," in *America Becoming: Racial Trends and Their Consequences*, ed. Neil Smelser, William J. Wilson, and Faith Mitchell (Washington, DC: National Academy Press, 2001), 258.

12. Anne-Marie Connor, "Interracial Unions Have a Ripple Effect on Families, Society," *Los Angeles Times*, www.ebony1ivory/datingstories.html.

13. Waters, 43.

14. Cedric Herring and Charles Amissah, "Advance and Retreat: Racially Based Attitudes and Public Policy," in *Racial Attitudes in the 1990s: Continuity and Change*, ed. Steven A. Tuch and Jack Martin (Westport: Praeger, 1997),139.

15. Lawrence Bobo and Ryan Smith, "From Jim Crow Racism to Laissez-Faire Racism: The Transformation of Racial Attitudes," in *Beyond Pluralism: The Conception of Groups and Group Identities in America*, ed. Wendy Katlin, Ned Landsman, and Andrea Tyree (Chicago: University of Illinois Press), 202.

16. Root, 7.

17. Omi, 258.

18. Herbert Gans, "The Possibility of a New Racial Hierarchy in the Twenty-First Century United States," in *The Cultural Territories of Race*, ed. Michele Lamont (Chicago: University of Chicago Press, 1999), 371.

19. Waters, 29.

20. Jonathan W. Warren and France Winddance Twine, "White Americans, the New Minority?: Non-Blacks and the Ever-Expanding Boundaries of Whiteness," *Journal of Black Studies*, 28, no. 2 (Nov. 1997).

21. Farley, 102.

22. Douglas Massey, "Residential Segregation and Neighborhood Conditions," in *America Becoming: Racial Trends and Their Consequences*, ed. Neil Smelser, William J. Wilson, and Faith Mitchell (Washington, DC: National Academy Press, 2001), 411.

23. Robert Adelman, Hui-shien Tsao, Stewart Tolnay, and Kyle Crowder, "Neighborhood Disadvantage Among Racial and Ethnic Groups: Residential Location in 1970 and 1980," *The Sociological Quarterly*, 42, no. 4.

24. Orlando Patterson, *The Ordeal of Integration: Progress and Resentments in America's Racial Crisis* (Washington, DC: Civitas, 1997), 195.

25. Patterson, 197.

FOUR

LINKING THE CIVIL RIGHTS
AND MULTIRACIAL MOVEMENTS

KIM M. WILLIAMS

IN THIS CHAPTER I make four primary claims, the most fundamental of which is that the Multiracial Movement could not have happened, nor could it have taken the forms it has, had it not been for both successes and failures of the civil rights movement. At first glance, the trajectory of largely acrimonious relations between the multiracialists and civil rights advocates throughout the 1990s might seem to suggest little overlap between these two movements. Yet, I will demonstrate that the Multiracial Movement is a spin-off movement of the civil rights movement. More strongly stated, the outcomes of the civil rights movement are imprinted on the Multiracial Movement: they explain important aspects of the timing, characteristics, and even the goals of the latter. To advance these arguments, I draw upon a number of social movement concepts to demonstrate the ways in which the civil rights successes helped to set in place a working definition of race that is currently under considerable strain.

Although conceding that there are no pure races in a biological sense, the civil rights establishment, most prominently the NAACP, the Urban League, and the National Council of La Raza registered steadfast opposition to Multiracial Movement demands for mixed-race recognition in the 2000 census. The crux of their objection centered around the belief that the addition of a multiracial category on the census would dilute the traditional minority count; giving substantial numbers of people who are now counted as black or Hispanic the opportunity to choose "multiracial." A new multi-racial category would not only undercut the aims of the Voting Rights Act, they argued, it would also jeopardize various state and federal programs aimed at minorities, such as minority business development programs and some affirmative action plans. In short, civil rights groups have perceived the contemporary assertion of multiracial identity as a threat because it disrupts a logic of race in which such organizations have become increasingly invested over time. Racial statistics began to hold new political potential for disadvantaged minority groups in the 1960s and 1970s, which explains why civil rights organizations have been so adamant in their defense of the status quo regarding the collection of racial statistics since then. Throughout history, racial designations have been employed by the United States as tools of dominance, serving to separate and penalize those not defined as white.[1] However, a crucially important shift began to emerge around 1970, when minorities, through the political leadership of civil rights organizations, were able to use racial counts to their material advantage. In the 1960s, the "very classifications that had previously been employed [to deny] civil rights now became useful in enforcing and monitoring these same civil rights."[2] As a result of a number of civil rights successes (i.e., the outcomes of the civil rights movement), racial statistics became valuable to U.S. minority groups in new ways.

In this chapter I will address three interrelated points: (1) how the legal, political and cultural outcomes of the U.S. civil rights movement prompted the establishment of a "working definition" of race in the United States over the past thirty to forty years; (2) how and why this working definition is changing; and, (3) the political positioning of Multiracial Movement activists. First, I examine the working definition of race established through the major civil rights legislation of the 1960s.

RACIAL UNDERSTANDINGS AND CIVIL RIGHTS LEGISLATION: CREATING A WORKING DEFINITION OF RACE

The Voting Rights and Civil Rights Acts, as well as the programs associated with the Great Society spurred the reallocation of millions of dollars and a significant redistribution of political power. First, I will review the ways in which racial data took on new importance as a result of these policy outcomes. Next, I will turn to the problematic definition of race upon which these outcomes were conceptually based.

The Civil Rights and Voting Rights Acts of 1964 and 1965 dismantled the most egregious of discriminatory mechanisms: black disenfranchisement in the South and various types of public and private discrimination throughout the United States. The new laws required the collection of racial and ethnic data in order to monitor legislative compliance and the delivery of new social services and programs. For example, to implement and regulate the Civil Rights Act, racial data became important in order to identify the numbers of minorities employed in firms and the racial composition of schools. Similarly, for the purposes of redistricting and the creation of "majority-minority" electoral districts, enforcement of the Voting Rights Act required population tabulations by race at the level of city blocks.

The War on Poverty and the Great Society programs initiated by the Johnson administration in the late 1960s and early 1970s can be viewed in the same vein. Specifically intended to address problems faced by groups and to improve living conditions in cities, several of the social welfare programs of the Great Society distributed funds by means of statistically driven grant-in-aid formulas. By 1978, more than one hundred such programs had been developed, using some measure of population to allocate funds for programs from preschool education to urban mass transportation.[3]

With funding and redistricting driven by federal census counts, it should be no surprise that "across the country communities and minorities began to examine closely their population numbers. Each one had the same goal: to maximize its own numbers."[4] As a result, the operating procedures used to collect these data took on greater significance. Perhaps most politically consequential for census taking in the post–civil rights era was Statistical Directive No. 15, issued by the Office of Management and Budget (OMB) in 1977. This directive (known as Directive 15) served as the authoritative word on federal racial statistics[5] for more than twenty years. Directive 15 mandated the use of four standard racial categories (in addition to one ethnic category, Hispanic) to be used in the official collection and reporting of racial data in the United States:

- *White*: A person having origins in any of the original peoples of Europe, North Africa, or the Middle East.

- *American Indian or Alaskan Native*: A person having origins in any of the original peoples of North America, and who maintains cultural identification through tribal affiliations or community recognition.

- *Asian or Pacific Islander*: A person having origins in any of the original peoples of the Far East, Southeast Asia, the Indian subcontinent, or the Pacific Islands. This area includes, for example, China, India, Japan, Korea, the Philippine Islands, and Samoa.

- *Black*: A person having origins in any of the black racial groups of Africa.

- *Hispanic*: A person of Mexican, Puerto Rican, Cuban, Central or South American, or other Spanish culture or origin, regardless of race.[6]

Instituted for the purposes of civil rights enforcement, Directive 15 specifically cautioned that the mandated categories "should not be interpreted as being scientific or anthropological in nature," rather, they were developed to meet expressed congressional and executive needs for "compatible, non-duplicated, exchangeable" racial and ethnic data.[7] Gone was any reference to a purportedly scientific basis of race; these categories were intended as political instruments.

Accordingly, they were treated as such by elected officials, the Census Bureau, and various lobbying groups endeavoring to protect, change, and/or add categories. For instance, Mexican American groups successfully lobbied to add the "Hispanic Origins Question" to the 1980 census, and several Asian categories were included in the 1980 and 1990 enumerations in response to pressure exerted by Asian American organizations. At the other end of the spectrum, the Arab American Institute has worked, so far in vain, to reassign persons of Middle Eastern origin from "white" to a new "Middle Eastern" category. Meanwhile and from a different angle, other groups (the Celtic Coalition, the Society for German American Studies) have also been trying to disaggregate the white category.[8] A wide array of lobbying groups and other interested parties questioned the conceptual foundations behind the basic categories reported in Directive 15, and in response, the OMB began a comprehensive review of the directive in 1993. This review culminated in a number of changes that were implemented in the 2000 census.[9]

However, for twenty years (1977–1997), and thus, until recently, the directive mandated the use of official racial categories by the federal government, even as the definitions used in the directive became increasingly anachronistic. For instance, reflective of Census Bureau data from the 1960s to the early 1970s, the 1977 directive used terms such as "majority race" and "principal minority race" to refer to whites and blacks respectively. (Census Bureau data from that period indicated that blacks constituted 96 percent of the minority population; in 2000 the bureau reported that blacks constituted about 50 percent of the minority population.)[10]

In summary, these sorts of demographic changes have created problems not only for Directive 15, but also for the dated view of race relations set forth in the Civil Rights and Voting Rights Acts.[11] The policy outcomes associated with the civil rights movement of the 1960s rightly focused on racism, discrimination, and equality. Yet, the question of what race is, and the possibility of ongoing and considerable changes in racial demographics, remained largely outside of the scope of consideration in the civil rights decade. Since the mid-1960s, racial statistics have provided a powerful means for civil rights organizations to make claims on the state and its services. However, such statistics are themselves characterized by both inconsistencies and anachronistic assumptions. In short, while the civil rights successes certainly created opportunities, this new fusion of statistics and politics would also usher in an attendant set of problems.

UNDOING THE "WORKING DEFINITION"

The racial assumptions upon which the civil rights movement was predicated are showing perceptible signs of strain. In fact, it is arguable that the developments discussed below "combine to render the concept of race less powerful than it has ever been at any time in American history."[12] This is not at all to suggest that racism does not still pervade American institutions, or that race does not continue to have a strong grip on the American psyche. Rather, my claim is that a number of contemporary dynamics are seriously disrupting the logic of race as it was legally and socially understood and instituted, only thirty to forty years ago. Three factors have upended the dominant concept of race in recent years: (1) rapidly changing demographics, especially new immigration trends and an exponential increase in interracial marriages and births; (2) a weakening sense of black unity; and (3) the publicizing of these developments.

DEMOGRAPHICS, IMMIGRATION, AND INTERRACIAL MARRIAGES AND BIRTHS

The contemporary racial landscape of the United States looks radically different than it did forty years ago. The civil rights movement occurred at a time when blacks were by far the largest minority group in the country, and whites were by far the majority. Depending on how one counts, data from the 2000 census indicate that Latinos are now the majority-minority in the United States.[13] Moreover, in the nation's most populous state, California, whites are now in the minority. If current demographic trends persist, within the next sixty years, as everyone is currently categorized, whites will no longer make up a majority of the U.S. population.[14] While almost all of the discussion of race in the civil rights decade focused upon the nation's discrimination against blacks, racial debates in the post–civil rights era are more multidimensional. Demographic shifts are blurring existing racial landmarks; immigration and intermarriage trends represent two of the most notable causes in this regard.

Over the past thirty years, an increasing number of immigrants have come to the United States from areas other than Europe, largely due to a 1965 change in immigration laws. In scope, this influx of immigrants is comparable to the massive migration stream from Europe in the early part of the twentieth century; however, contemporary immigrants to the United States are coming from primarily Latin America, the Caribbean, and Asia. In 1970, 4.8 percent of the total U.S. population was foreign-born; by 1994, the percentage had nearly doubled, to 8.7 percent.[15] By 2000, 10.4 percent of the U.S. population was foreign-born, and 76.5 percent of the foreign-born population came to the United States from Latin America, the Caribbean, or Asia.[16]

These figures raise a host of issues, but most relevant for our purposes is that increasing numbers of Americans do not perceive race in the terms dictated by the U.S. Census Bureau. The most obvious evidence along these lines comes from the Census Bureau itself. Unable to find a box that applied to themselves, more than seven million people marked "Other" on the 1980 census race question, and close to ten million did so in 1990. In 2000, more than fifteen million Americans selected "Some Other Race."[17] Many of these people clearly do not understand the Census Bureau's mandates. Furthermore, considering the way in which a segment of the "Other" responses were handled by the Census Bureau in 1990, it is comparably evident that the Census Bureau has found it difficult to categorize them:

> For the 1990 census, people who wrote that they were "multiracial" or "bi-racial" were left in the "Other" race classification. Respondents who wrote "black-white" were counted as blacks; those who wrote "white-black" were counted as whites. Finally, imputation processes . . . are used to assign a standard race to more complicated cases. This usually involves checking the racial responses of other people in the same household or similar households in the neighborhood.[18]

Immigration has amplified an already growing awareness that racial categorizations, and coexisting understandings about race, are not immutable, universal facts. Moreover, millions of immigrants who have come to this country have had no prior experience with formal racial categorization (about half of the countries in the world do not collect racial data in their censuses).[19]

Intensifying the effects of changing immigration patterns, there has also been a meteoric rise in the number of interracial marriages in the United States over the past thirty years. Such marriages grew from about 150,000 interracially married couples in 1960 (when antimiscegenation laws were still in effect in sixteen U.S. states) to more than one million in 1998. In 2000, interracial marriages numbered 1.46 million.[20] A word of caution: a logic whereby we can identify a subset of marriages as "interracial" implies that all other marriages are between two people of the same (pure) race. This type of reasoning poses an unresolved dilemma for Multiracial Movement advocates, to which I will return at the end of the chapter. But nevertheless, popular ideas of race are certainly challenged when we hear that between one-quarter and one-third of all marriages involving Japanese Americans are now out-group marriages, that more indigenous people marry outside the indigenous population than marry within it, and that marriages between blacks and whites have increased sevenfold since 1960 (from 51,000 in 1960 to 363,000 in 2000).[21] Like it or not, a society long hostile to acknowledging racial mixture will have to come to terms with a growing population of multiracial families and individuals.

Perhaps such acknowledgment is taking place more rapidly than one might otherwise suspect. Recent scholarly work demonstrates that even though interracial marriage rates are still relatively low, kinship ties multiply their effect dramatically.[22] Defining kin as those related by blood or marriage, a recent study conducted at Princeton University found that interracial kin relations are so plentiful that "one in seven whites, one in three blacks, four in five Asians, and more than nineteen in twenty Native Americans are closely related to someone of a different racial group."[23] Although those related by blood or marriage do not inevitably form close emotional bonds, kinship ties increase the possibility of such attachments among individuals who might otherwise have little to do with one another. In this way, inter-marriage patterns can potentially be viewed as an engine of social change.[24]

WEAKENING BLACK UNITY

Numerous studies have documented the fact that racial identity and solidarity were powerfully cohesive forces in creating the culture of protest upon which the civil rights struggles were launched and sustained. While black unity and assumptions of black homogeneity underpinned the civil rights movement, this can be at least in part attributed to the brutality of white racism. In 1965, Jim Crow laws were just being lifted and interracial marriage was still illegal in sixteen states. Institutional racism certainly helped to ensconce race as an objective fact, but it also had the "unintended consequence of defining, legitimating and provoking group identity and mobilization."[25] Yet, in part as a result of the successes of the civil rights movement, black solidarity has gradually weakened. In short, the civil rights movement helped to create the legal and social space for new possibilities and differentiations within "the black community" that were not previously possible or imagined.

For example, the civil rights movement is rightly attributed as the catalyst for the dramatic expansion of the black middle class over the past thirty to forty years. While this is certainly a positive development, numerous studies have also documented that the civil rights movement marked the beginning of a profound (and still growing) class cleavage between middle-class and poor blacks.[26] In a similar vein, the civil rights movement also helped to create the social space for other disenfranchised groups within the black community to assert themselves politically. Thus, while the civil rights movement has often been seen as a model for other socially and politically excluded populations, such as women and gays, it also served as a powerful example for women and gays *within* the black community. These groups began to recast the ideological and organizational lessons learned from the civil rights struggles toward other ends, namely, in order to critique sexism and homophobia in black communities. In this way, although the civil rights movement was itself a largely Southern, church-based movement that did not exemplify much in the way of a progressive attitude toward the rights of black women or black gays, its example gave rise to broader assertions of difference within black communities.[27]

The outcomes of the civil rights movement altered more than public policy; the movement also marked a profound cultural shift in how racial identity has since been expressed and understood, both within black communities and beyond. I am asserting that the civil rights movement marked the beginning of the end for uncomplicated notions of race in this country. That is *not* to say that the meaning of blackness was not questioned or disputed before, or even during the civil rights era,[28] but such debates were fewer, more contained, and generally less conceivable for both the general American public and for American elites (e.g., politicians, educators, artists) than they are now. In other words, in the civil rights era both analysts and activists could refer to blackness and evoke the same idea. When the civil rights era ended, so did this common understanding. Black unity can no longer be taken for granted as a given, and ironically, this can be partially attributed to outcomes of the civil rights movement.

PUBLICIZING THESE DEVELOPMENTS

If racial lines, as we have generally tended to conceive of them in this country over the past forty years, are rapidly eroding, this is largely due to the fact that discussions in this regard have extended well beyond the walls of academia. The concept of race is now considered, debated, and increasingly refuted in an unprecedented array of popularized arenas such as television talk shows and weekly news magazines. From the ivory tower to Oprah and on to the golf course, the mid-1960s concept of race has begun to unravel at the seams.

FROM CIVIL RIGHTS TO THE MULTIRACIAL MOVEMENT:
CYCLES OF PROTEST

In spite of all the evidence presented above, the undoing of a working definition of race does not a social movement make. Clearly, the structural

circumstances outlined above greatly facilitate the possibility for a movement to challenge entrenched ideas about race. But racial understandings are
always problematic and debatable, and it is only in recent years that they
have become widely problematized and debated in the United States. Thus,
a number of questions remain. Obviously, important queries about the timing, characteristics, and even the goals of the Multiracial Movement can be
examined by considering the ways in which, ironically, it is part of a larger
cycle of protest initiated by the civil rights movement.

"Cycles of protest" refers to the idea that different social movements are
in fact connected. The concept helps us address questions of how one movement might be said to create the political and/or social space in which a later
one can emerge, the similarity in tactics and/or appeals through which movement leaders foster an insurgent consciousness, and the ways in which different
movements can be said to respond to each other ideologically. Along these
lines, the civil rights movement is referred to as an "initiator" movement in
the social movement literature. Initiator movements "signal or otherwise set in
motion an identifiable protest cycle;"[29] "spin-off" movements model themselves, to varying degrees, after the initiator movement.

In this section, I argue that the Multiracial Movement is a spin-off
movement of the civil rights movement. More strongly stated, the Multiracial Movement could not have happened, nor would it have taken the forms
it has, had it not been for both the successes and failures of the civil rights
movement. At first glance, this is perhaps counterintuitive. The friction and
hostility that have persisted over the past ten years between civil rights and
multiracial groups might compel an observer to conclude that these two
movements must necessarily have sharply divergent profiles. However, the
Multiracial Movement has not reinvented the wheel of protest. Rather, it
has creatively adapted, reinterpreted, and built upon tactics, ideologies, and
legal outcomes established through the civil rights struggles. A closer look at
the timing, characteristics, and goals of the Multiracial Movement should
drive this point home.

Timing of the Multiracial Movement in Relation to Civil Rights

Broad structural processes such as immigration and the increase in multiracial births and marriages have been so habitually pointed to by the authors
currently writing on multiracial issues that an analyst could comfortably
conclude that these developments inevitably led to the rise of the movement. I want to dispel this notion by providing an alternative and more
analytical account. In order to explain the rise of multiracial activism in the
1970s, as well as many of its successful campaigns in the 1990s, one must
look at specific ways in which, from the 1960s onward, the political climate

became less hostile, and eventually, even favorable to the politicized concept of multiracial identity. To this end, we need to make a distinction between broad structural processes and specific "dimensions of the political environment that provide incentives for people to undertake collective action by affecting their expectations for success or failure."[30] Such changes in the political environment create "political opportunities," a concept that is especially helpful in answering the "why now?" question regarding the timing of a social movement. For our purposes, political opportunities can be understood as changes in the legal or institutional structure that grant more formal political access to challenging groups.[31]

In terms of timing, it is no surprise that the first contemporary multiracial organizations began to form in the 1970s. Legal/institutional changes brought about by the civil rights struggles were crucial for the development of multiracial activism: until antisegregation laws were implemented, and until antimiscegenation laws were fully repealed in the United States, the possibility for a Multiracial Movement to materialize and prosper was remote. The legal system went from being overtly hostile toward interracial contact and unions in the early 1960s, to one in which such contact was at least not regarded as criminal activity by the end of that decade. In other words, the civil rights movement helped to remove fundamental barriers, which in turn produced the legal and political space for multiracial organizations to form across the country in the 1970s and 1980s. Carlos Fernandez, the first president of the Association of Multi-Ethnic Americans (AMEA), now the largest multiracial umbrella group in the United States, seems to concur, as he has identified the people who have created and joined these organizations over the past twenty years to be the "generation literally born from the successes of the civil rights movement."[32]

CHARACTERISTICS OF THE MULTIRACIAL MOVEMENT IN RELATION TO CIVIL RIGHTS

Any number of factors involved in the rise of a movement and the chances of its success are obviously beyond the direct control of the activists involved. Movements can ride the wave of political opportunities, and they can benefit from broader structural circumstances such as demographic shifts, but they cannot be said to ordain the terms of such things. Thus, I am addressing the aspects of a movement that are more purposely coordinated by the activists involved. The influence and example of the civil rights movement is also apparent when looking at key characteristics of the Multiracial Movement that its leaders have had some control over, including ideological framing and the tactics utilized to draw attention to the cause.

Ideological Framing: Given the rigid definition of race that has been characteristic of American institutions and social attitudes, the Multiracial Movement has certainly brought challenging ideas about race to the fore. Through
key documents and statements made by leading multiracial activists involved
in the movement over time, we can see that this has largely been achieved
through the adept and creative recasting of appeals made popular by the civil
rights struggles. This is most obvious in the fact that multiracial activists
routinely insisted upon framing the official recognition of multiracialism as
a civil right. By arguing that the recognition of multiracial people was the
"next logical step in civil rights,"[33] multiracial activists drew shrewdly on the
symbolism of the civil rights movement, yet in the process, cast themselves
as more progressive than the so-called progressives (i.e., the civil rights lobby).

I have conducted interviews with every major leader of the Multiracial
Movement, and in the course of the interviews, each of the national leaders
alluded to the fact that they see the Multiracial Movement (and/or their
personal involvement in it) *related to, but somehow a step beyond* the civil
rights movement. Ramona Douglass, recent past president of AMEA, said
that she has "been a part of the civil rights movement since the early 1970s
and marched in the South with the Ku Klux Klan dancing in my face . . . we
[multiracial activists] are changing race as we know it."[34] Susan Graham,
president of Project RACE, said "our objective is civil rights and equality for
all."[35] My point is that the Multiracial Movement has not so much created
an ideological schema itself as it has creatively and effectively adapted an
ideological framework that was readily available from the example of the
civil rights movement.

Take, for example, the Voting Rights Act. The definition of race or
color was left implicit in the law; in practice, it meant "black" and "white"
or "white" and "nonwhite." To this, Carlos Fernandez, AMEA's first president, claimed that "it is the biological aspect of race and racial mixture that
is essential to racist thinking . . . this attitude finds expression in the failure
of our society and its institutions to officially acknowledge racial mixture,
potentially the basis for a unifying national identity and a crucial step for
breaking down traditional lines of social separation."[36]

Tactics: Another aspect of the movement's characteristics concerns its tactics; again, this is an element of movement activity that is more purposely
directed than the sort of structural processes previously discussed. Over the
past ten years, a number of the forty active multiracial organizations across
the country[37] have joined forces at various times and in diverse venues to
stage "solidarity" marches, write and deliver position papers, organize forums,
events, and symbolic commemorations, and plan street boycotts. While the

multiracial leadership has at times been sharply divided over some of these maneuvers,[38] the movement has nevertheless used a repertoire of actions that clearly found inspiration in the civil rights struggles. The most conspicuous connection in this regard can be seen in the fact that a number of multiracial groups have come together in recent years to stage two "Multiracial Solidarity Marches," one held in Washington, D.C., in 1996, the other in Los Angeles in 1997. The 1996 march was even called a "March on Washington," an apt appropriation of terminology that is widely associated with civil rights efforts.

GOALS OF THE MULTIRACIAL MOVEMENT IN RELATION TO CIVIL RIGHTS

Multiracial activists have utilized and reframed the tactical and ideological tools of the civil rights movement, and they have also greatly benefited from and capitalized on the legal precedents established in the context of that earlier set of struggles. I would further argue that the very goals of the Multiracial Movement flow from the outcomes of the civil rights movement. An examination of the mission statements of the three national multiracial organizations demonstrates this point.

In AMEA's mission statement, the objectives are normative and philosophical; its position is that multiracial people should have a right to claim or incorporate their entire heritage, and embrace their total identity. AMEA says its "primary goal is education: to promote a positive awareness of interracial and multiethnic identity, for ourselves and for society as a whole."[39] For Project RACE, the "major, overall objective is to mandate a multiracial category on all forms requiring racial data,"[40] so that multiracial children do not have to suffer the adverse consequences of being regarded as "Other." A Place For Us (APFU), primarily a religious organization, views the "support and encourage[ment] of interaction between anyone involved with interracial relationships"[41] to be their purpose. APFU has engaged in extensive political activity to realize this aim: its founders, Ruth and Steve White, delivered speeches at both Multiracial Solidarity Marches (APFU sponsored the Los Angeles March). Moreover, APFU was heavily involved in the (failed) effort to add a multiracial category to California state forms in 1996–1997.

Perhaps the most extensively reproduced statement exemplifying the movement's broad goals can be found in Maria Root's "Bill of Rights for Racially Mixed People," which has become something of a charter statement within the activist multiracial community. Some of the rights that Root identifies include: "the right not to keep the races separate within me; the right to not be responsible for people's discomfort with my physical ambiguity; the right to not be forced to justify my ethnic legitimacy; the right to change my identity over my lifetime—and more than once."[42]

The underlying theme in these mission statements and the Bill of Rights is inextricably intertwined with claims that gained newfound vigor in this country through the civil rights struggles: the importance of self-naming and the ostensible connection between recognition, identity, and the state. In fact, the Multiracial Movement's philosophical grounding is remarkably consonant with Charles Taylor's understanding of the politics of recognition. The themes of rights, recognition, and identity tie the mission statements together conceptually:

> The thesis is that our identity is partly shaped by recognition or its absence, often by the misrecognition of others, and so a person or group of people can suffer real damage, real distortion, if the people or society around them mirror back to them a confining or demeaning or contemptible picture of themselves. Nonrecognition or misrecognition can inflict harm; can be a form of oppression, imprisoning someone in a false, distorted, and reduced mode of being.[43]

The politicization of these normative and philosophical objectives denotes another conceptual link between the outcomes of the civil rights movement and the goals of the Multiracial Movement. It is one thing to assert that a group deserves acknowledgment and recognition; it is yet another matter altogether to look to the state for that endorsement. In considering the trajectory of the Multiracial Movement, we can see that even from very early on (i.e., efforts to get the Berkeley, California, school district to add a multiracial category in the late 1970s), a primary goal has been recognition in one form or another from the local, state, or federal government.

In thinking about how, in general, claims for the recognition of a group's existence and its identity became viewed as a matter for the state to address, we must again look to the cycle of protest set in motion by the civil rights movement. If "the appearance of a highly visible initiator movement significantly changes the dynamics of emergence for all groups who mobilize as part of the broader protest cycle,"[44] then we can certainly see how the civil rights movement facilitated the entry of not only blacks, but later of Latinos, Asian Americans, American Indians, and women into the political process. Their entry not only transformed the dynamics of racial politics, but also acted as a catalyst in the transformation of identity, difference, language, and "the personal" into political issues. In other words, the very definition of what is legitimately regarded as "political" can be said to have shifted as a result of this cycle of protest. (The OMB's 1977 decision to recognize the importance of self-naming on the census can be identified as one of the state's tangible responses to these kinds of claims.) It is in this context that we should place the stated goals of the Multiracial Movement, which had the benefit of witnessing these prior struggles and of learning from their example. All of this is not to suggest that the Multiracial Movement has nothing new to tell us, however, it does indicate that the movement could not have happened had it not been for both the premises on which the civil rights project relied, and for a number of key legal, political, and social outcomes of that movement.

HOW HAVE MULTIRACIAL MOVEMENT ACTIVISTS POSITIONED THEMSELVES POLITICALLY?

While the working definition of race of the civil rights era may be coming undone at the seams, in and of itself, this does not answer a number of urgent questions about the usefulness of the multiracial challenge to this emergent situation. In other words, we must also ask: Is the Multiracial Movement actually challenging race as we know it, as its leaders passionately aver? Are Multiracial Movement activists well positioned to, and seriously concerned about waging an assault against institutional and other forms of racism, or is this movement simply another interest group marketing a fashionable iden-tity at the expense of established minority populations?

My final assertion in this chapter is that evidence on this important matter of "political location"[45] is mixed. In interviews I conducted from 1996 to 1999 with all of the organizational leaders of multiracial groups across the country ($n = 40$, response rate: 75 percent), in addition to four case studies of groups in the Bay Area, Washington, D.C., Atlanta, and Chicago (see note 37), a serendipitous string of interesting facts converged: (1) Ironically, and in spite of the fact that multiracial leaders *say* that multiracial identity is constitutive of "people across all racial mixes,"[46] there are not very many multiracial adults involved in the Multiracial Movement. This is largely an effort of monoracially identified parents *on behalf of their children*; (2) al-though there are by far more documented Asian/white marriages in the United States than black/white marriages, multiracial social movement orga-nizations are *almost exclusively comprised of black-white couples*; (3) in accord with Census Bureau data suggesting that the vast majority of black-white interracial marriages in the United States are between black men and white women,[47] multiracial social movement organizations mirror this gender/race dynamic; (4) in accord with most organizations of this sort (i.e., local groups concentrated on family issues), there is a gender gap whereby women tend to become the leaders of these groups more often than men do: and finally, (5) across the board, most local-level organizational leaders are middle class and live in suburbs. And so, we end up with the compelling fact that most multiracial organizations are in fact run by white, middle-class women living in suburbs.

The basic socioeconomic indicators of my respondents, generally speaking, show that people involved in these groups look a lot like mainstream middle-class Americans, if somewhat more affluent. 47.5 percent of all respondents[48] reported that their family income is above $60,000 per year; 20 percent said it is between $45–60,000. Only 10 percent of all respondents reported annual family incomes below $30,000. In terms of educational attainment, 50 percent of all respondents reported having earned at least a college degree; within that group, an additional 30 percent have earned master's degrees. Only 6.3 percent of all respondents reported that their formal education ended with a high school degree only.

In terms of individual measures of political attitudes, most respondents identified as either strong (26.3 percent) or moderate (41.3 percent) Democrats and declared themselves either strongly (32.5 percent) or moderately (37.5 percent) in favor of affirmative action. However, in part because only 30 percent of organizational leaders reported that combating racism in their local communities was a priority in their groups, it is difficult to link these broad measures of liberalism on the part of multiracial activists to any evidence of support for a wider progressive platform and/or to sustained consideration of racial or class issues within or beyond local multiracial social movement organizations. Furthermore, 53.6 percent of all respondents said that the Multiracial Movement should welcome the support of Republicans, while 40 percent said that the multiracial community should be wary of support from Republicans.

Looking at the issue of political attitudes in another way, when asked, "What do you think of the idea that multiracial people can or should be able to act as a bridge between 'the races'?" respondents were lukewarm as to the viability of such a prospect: 40 percent of all respondents said it was a good idea, but almost as many registered aversion to the concept (22 percent said that multiracial people should not be held responsible for diminishing racial tension on a broad scale; 17 percent said it was a good idea, but it would place a big and unwarranted burden on multiracial individuals). These data seem to fly in the face of the national leaders' claims as to the ostensible sociopolitical aspirations of the Multiracial Movement to act as a bridge across the racial divide and to diminish racial tension. Moreover, although many local leaders lament the lack of diversity in their organizations, these groups remain disproportionately white and female. Looking at data from all respondents, when asked an open-ended question as to how they identify racially, 56.3 percent said "white," 22.5 percent said "black," and 17.5 percent said "multiracial." The remaining 3.7 percent include those identifying as Asian American, Latino, Native American, or of the "Human" race.

A second important question that these data on racial identification in multiracial organizations raise is: Why, for the most part, do we overwhelmingly see black/white identified couples involved in the *Multiracial* Movement? On this issue, almost all respondents (90 percent) said that they felt less stigma attached to all other combinations, for instance, Asian/white; Latino/white; or Native American/white. While this plausibly explains the predominance of black-white couples in multiracial organizations, it concurrently implies a sharp divergence in the lived experiences of interracial couples on the basis of how they are perceived/feel they are perceived (racially) by the outside world. This may help to explain why multiracial organizations do not look all that multiracial; perhaps those who feel most stigmatized are also the ones most likely to join multiracial groups. What this means is that it is probably unlikely that people "across all racial mixes" would identify with the Multiracial Movement in similar proportions, or with similar effect. Thus, although the multiracial population is growing, this demographic shift does not seem likely to translate into a mass-based *Multiracial* Movement in that it is not resonating with people across the range of different racial combinations.

Finally, and logically pursuant to the issues already discussed, is the matter of what respondents viewed as the appropriate political articulation of multiracial identity. Interestingly, and in spite of national leaders' proclamations to the contrary, support for the multiracial category initiative was subdued even within multiracial organizations. My data show that only 40 percent of the organizational leaders, and 47.5 percent of all respondents, approved of the effort to get a multiracial category added to the census. Meanwhile, 36.7 percent of leaders, and 23.8 percent of all respondents preferred to check all that apply, while 13.3 percent of leaders and 22.5 percent of all respondents favored "abolishing racial categorization altogether."[49]

Summing up, a rather unexpected picture emerges when we explore the sociopolitical positioning of local level multiracial organizations. Overwhelmingly, adult participants do not identify as multiracial themselves, and they have not been able to attract a particularly diverse membership base (either "racially" or on measures of socioeconomic status). They are also divided as to what a political articulation of "multiracialness" should entail and whom they should welcome and/or eschew as allies. Furthermore, they are hazy on the matter of whether or not multiracial people can or should be at the forefront of efforts to lessen racial tension. Although they exhibit predominantly liberal attitudes as measured by party affiliation and stance toward affirmative action, by and large these traits have not been connected to any broader social justice platform within local level multiracial organizations.

SUMMARY

This chapter has aimed to make three closely related main points, and it is suggestive of a fourth. First, racial categorization is not only imposed from "above" (i.e., by the state); it is also appropriated from below. Categorizing by race can result in consequences that the state did not bargain for, particularly when those who are subordinated are able to adopt the terms of their definition as the basis for mobilization.[50] This is how we can make sense of the apparent irony that racial categories in this country were originally used to keep track of and augment the number of slaves, yet current-day civil rights groups are ardently defending the practice and logic of racial categorization. In the hands of the socially or politically disenfranchised, numbers can provide a powerful means for race-ethnic groups to make themselves visible, articulate their differences, and make claims on the state and its services. As a result of the civil rights successes, racial counts provided new political potential for disenfranchised groups, which their leaders earnestly seized.

The second point asserted in this chapter is that while the civil rights movement left us with a working definition of race, inscribed both in law and in cultural practice, various trends over the past thirty to forty years have combined to radically undermine this set of understandings about "what race is." These trends, which include rapidly changing demographics, rising immigration rates, increasing interracial marriages and births, and widening divisions within "traditionally defined" minority groups, make it difficult to refer to race in the sense in which it was understood only a generation ago. Indicative of this, the U.S. Census Bureau, the source of the most authoritative data available about the U.S. population, itself admits that it has become increasingly ineffectual in terms of its ability to reflect the racial complexity of the United States.

My third contention is that broad scale structural changes do not in and of themselves adequately explain much about the timing and other dynamics related to the Multiracial Movement. To this end, I have introduced and applied key social movement concepts in order to grant us more analytic leverage on questions regarding aspects of the Multiracial Movement that its leaders have purposely generated (such as tactics, ideological framing, and goals), as well as aspects that are beyond their direct control (such as the repeal of antimiscegenation laws). In both cases, evidence is marshaled to demonstrate that the Multiracial Movement is in fact a part of a larger cycle of protest, initiated by the civil rights movement. Finally, and at the least, my work studying multiracial organizations suggests that the multiracialists' claim to change "race as we know it" is something to be proven, not assumed.

NOTES

1. See for example, Sharon Lee, "Racial Classifications in the U.S. Census: 1890–1990," *Ethnic and Racial Studies* 16 (1993): 238–42.

2. Carlos Fernandez, "Government Classification of Multiracial/Multiethnic People," in *The Multiracial Experience: Racial Borders as the New Frontier*, ed. Maria P. P. Root (Thousand Oaks, CA: Sage, 1996), 24.

3. Harvey Choldin, *Looking for the Last Percent: The Controversy over Census Undercounts* (New Brunswick: Rutgers University Press, 1994), 27.

4. Ibid., 41.

5. Although Reynolds Farley aptly notes that the directive "had a much greater impact since employers, schools and firms linked in any fashion to federal spending had powerful incentives to gather data consistent with the government's requirement." Reynolds Farley, "Identifying with Multiple Races: A Social Movement that Succeeded but Failed?" Population Studies Center at the Institute for Social Research, University of Michigan. Research Report No. 01-491. December 2001.

6. Office of Management and Budget, *U.S. Directive No. 15*, 1977.

7. Ibid. Note: Prior to the directive, federal agencies used their own categorization policies, leading to recognition by several agencies of the need for a uniform set of race and ethnicity categories.

8. See for example, Yen Espiritu, *Asian American Pan-Ethnicity: Bridging Institutions and Identities* (Philadelphia: Temple University Press, 1992), especially pp. 82–133.

9. In an unprecedented move, for the 2000 census, the OMB decided to allow respondents to "mark all that apply" on the race question.

10. Because the 2000 census allowed respondents to mark more than one race, the size of racial groups is reported from minimum to maximum counts. Thus, depending on how one counts, blacks constituted either 49.5 percent or 50.7 percent of the minority population in 2000.

11. References to race relations in the Voting Rights Act are unmistakably bipolar in their orientation: the act treats race as if it is an exclusively black and white issue. However, a number of recent court cases have challenged the Voting Rights Act in this assumption (*Johnson v. DeGrandy*, 1994; *Vera v. Bush*, 1996) raising the issue of how to construct districts where no one racial group comprises a majority of the voting age population. See for example, Lawrence Morehouse, "Redistricting in the Multiracial Twenty-First Century," in *Race and Representation*, ed. Georgia A. Persons (New Brunswick: Transaction Publishers, 1997), 116.

12. Richard J. Payne, *Getting Beyond Race: The Changing American Culture* (Boulder: Westview, 1998), 169.

13. The Latino population share for 2000 constituted 12.5 percent of the total U.S. population. At the "maximum" range, the black population share for 2000 is 12.9 percent, but at the "minimum" range—blacks who marked only black and no other races—the black population share was only 12.3 percent. Thus, depending on the definition used, either blacks or Latinos can be considered the largest minority group.

14. U.S. Bureau of the Census, "Projections of the Population of the United States by Age, Sex, Race, and Hispanic Origin: 1995 to 2050," *Current Population Reports*, P-25, No. 1130 (February 1996).

15. U.S. Bureau of the Census, "The Foreign-Born Population: 1994," *Current Population Reports*, P-20-486 (August 1995), 1.

16. U.S. Bureau of the Census, "Profile of the Foreign-Born Population in the United States: 2000," *Current Population Reports*, P23-206 (December 2001).

17. Elizabeth Grieco and Rachel Cassidy, "Overview of Race and Hispanic Origin: Census 2000 Brief," U.S. Department of Commerce (March 2001), 3.

18. Lee, "Racial Classifications in the U.S. Census: 1890–1990," 83.

19. Barry Edmonston and Charles Schultze, eds., *Modernizing the U.S. Census* (Washington, DC: National Academy Press, 1995), 154, footnote 1.

20. U.S. Bureau of the Census, "America's Families and Living Arrangements: March 2000," and earlier reports. *Current Population Reports*, P-20-537 (March, 2000).

21. U.S. Bureau of the Census, "Interracial Married Couples: 1960 to Present," *Current Population Reports*, P-20-537 (29 June 2001).

22. Joshua R. Goldstein, "Kinship Networks That Cross Racial Lines: The Exception Or The Rule?" *Demography* 36, no. 3 (August 1999): 399–407.

23. Ibid., 399.

24. See for example, Stanley Lieberson and Mary Waters, *From Many Strands: Ethnic and Racial Groups in America* (New York: Russell Sage Foundation, 1988).

25. Anthony Marx, "Contested Citizenship: The Dynamics of Racial Identity and Social Movements," *International Review of Social History* 40 (1995): 159.

26. Among many examples, see William Julius Wilson, *The Declining Significance of Race: Blacks and Changing American Institutions* (Chicago: University of Chicago Press, 1987).

27. See for example, Patricia Hill Collins, *Black Feminist Thought: Knowledge, Consciousness, and the Politics of Empowerment* (New York: Routledge, 2000); and bell hooks, *Black Looks: Race and Representation* (Boston: South End Press, 1992).

28. See for example, Robert C. Smith, *We Have No Leaders: African Americans in the Post-Civil Rights Era* (Albany: State University of New York Press, 1996).

29. Doug McAdam, "Initiator and Spin-Off Movements," in *Repertoires and Cycles of Collective Action*, ed. Mark Traugott (Durham: Duke University Press, 1995): 219.

30. Sidney Tarrow, *Power In Movement: Social Movements, Collective Action, and Politics* (New York: Cambridge University Press, 1994), 85.

31. Doug McAdam, "Conceptual Origins, Problems, Future Directions," in *Comparative Perspectives on Social Movements: Political Opportunities, Mobilizing Structures, and Cultural Framings*, ed. McAdam, McCarthy and Zald (New York: Cambridge University Press, 1996), 27.

32. Carlos Fernandez, "Government Classification of Multiracial/Multiethnic People," in *The Multiracial Experience*, 23.

33. Ramona Douglass, personal interview, 14 June 1998.

34. Ramona Douglass, personal interview, 14 June 1998.

35. Susan Graham, personal interview, 6 April 1998.

36. Carlos Fernandez, "La Raza and the Melting Pot: A Comparative Look at Multiethnicity," in *Racially Mixed People in America*, ed. Maria Root (Newbury Park, CA: Sage, 1992), 133. Note, however, that "officially acknowledging racial mixture" presumes the existence of distinct racial groups.

37. My dissertation, *Boxed-In: The U.S. Multiracial Movement* (Cornell University, Dept. of Government, 2001) provides what is to my knowledge the first systematic

examination of currently active multiracial organizations across the United States. Many multiracial organizations assemble lists of similar groups across the country. I contacted as many groups as I could find via the Internet and through personal contacts, then I exhaustively compiled and compared the organizational lists of these groups in order to come up with a master list of all known multiracial organizations across the country. When preliminary attempts to contact some of these organizations failed, I then contacted multiracial activists whom I'd already identified to obtain contact information for the missing groups, and called, e-mailed, and sent out formal letters soliciting their participation in my survey. I also searched local telephone directories and search engines on the World Wide Web for information as to how I might find the missing groups/group leaders. This process went on for approximately one year before I administered my leadership survey. I originally started with a list of sixty-three multiracial organizations, but over time, I was able to verify that twenty-three of those groups had disbanded by the time I conducted my research. This left forty groups, and although I suspect that some of these groups are also defunct, I could not obtain information to definitively rule out this prospect. Thus, I am left with a total n of 40.

38. Regarding the solidarity marches, Ramona Douglass went on record with a posting to the (now defunct) Interracial Individuals Discussion List saying: "I believe the pen is mightier than the picket line . . . my demonstration days are numbered . . . the board room is where lasting decisions can be made—not in the streets. This isn't Selma in the sixties." From *AMEAPRES@aol.com*, posted on: 25 July 1995 <*http://soyokaze.biosci.ohio-state.edu/~jei/ii*>. But nevertheless, she attended both marches and spoke energetically on behalf of AMEA; for tactical reasons, she felt obliged to attend and participate.

39. AMEA Mission Statement, unpublished, no date listed.

40. Project RACE Mission Statement, unpublished, no date listed.

41. APFU Mission Statement, unpublished, no date listed.

42. Maria Root, "A Bill of Rights for Racially Mixed People," in *The Multiracial Experience*, 7.

43. Charles Taylor, *Multiculturalism and the Politics of Recognition* (Princeton: Princeton University Press, 1992), 25.

44. Doug McAdam, "Initiator and Spin-Off Movements," in *Repertoires and Cycles of Collective Action*, 219.

45. I thank Heather Dalmage for putting an apt name to this concept.

46. See for example, Root, *The Multiracial Experience*, xi.

47. Black-white marriages by gender in the United States from 1980–1998: white male–black female marriages represent 30 percent of the total; black male–white female marriages represent 70 percent of the total. Source: U.S. Bureau of the Census, "Marital Status and Living Arrangements," *Current Population Reports*, P-20-514 (March 1998).

48. Many of the questions asked in the leadership survey and case study questionnaire intentionally overlap. Thus, when I refer to "all respondents" I am referring to data compiled from both sources (n = 80).

49. Although no surveys existed at the time to gauge such sentiment directly, Ramona Douglass was not unaware of this circumstance. Just before she became

AMEA president in 1994, she noted the need for all three umbrella organizations to "share resources, information and strategies to combat the cynicism and skepticism both within and out of the interracial/multicultural community concerning the need for a multiracial category." AMEA President's Report (November 1994), unpublished.

50. See Anthony Marx, "Contested Citizenship: The Dynamics of Racial Identity and Social Movements" (1995).

PART II

DISCOURSES OF THE
MULTIRACIAL MOVEMENT

IN THIS SECTION each author addresses the way in which competing, contradictory, and often overlapping ideologies inform the politics of the Multiracial Movement. The practical goal of the Multiracial Movement has been
to force the official recognition of multiracial families and people through a
change in the way federal, state, and local agencies collect racial data. Arguments for changing racial categories have relied heavily on discussions of
the need for accuracy. Implicit in these conversations is an assumption that
race is essential, biological, and immutable; in short, that categories have
boundaries and the goal should be to better define those boundaries. The
theoretical goal has been to show the fallacies of race and thus change the
way people in the United States think about race. In this case, the discussion
has focused on the fact that race lacks a biological basis and is nothing more
than an myth enacted as reality. The myth plays out in the construction of
race in laws, the media, academic theorizing, and commonsense understandings of the world.

The Multiracial Movement is juggling the goals of shaping the practice
of race in society and the way multiracial family members think about themselves in society. Rainier Spencer argues that from a theoretical perspective
multiracialism can be used to undermine the concept of race in society; by
showing that racial categories are both permeable and fluid, thus bleeding

into each other, the strength of essentialist thinking is undermined. However, in practice, a demand for political recognition of multiracialism through the addition of a multiracial category undermines a powerful means for countering white supremacy by undermining racial categories. In short, the means for tracking discrimination and civil rights legislation is lost. Kerry Ann Rockquemore and Erica Chito Childs explore the attempt by some advocates in the Multiracial Movement to name and police the boundaries of acceptable and authentic multiracialism. Finally, Terri A. Karis explores racial discourses within multiracial families, specifically those of white mothers raising children of color, and shows that these women often default into color-blind discourse.

Each of the authors address the complexity of the discourse of the Multiracial Movement. Given the contradiction of racial thought and practice in the larger society, it is understandable that the Multiracial Movement is struggling to sift through and develop a racial politic that is concerned with social justice. Through an exploration of the insights, contradictions, and complexities of the discourse informing and shaping the Multiracial Movement, we will be better situated to redirect where necessary and develop the strengths needed to steer toward greater social justice.

FIVE

BEYOND PATHOLOGY AND CHEERLEADING: INSURGENCY, DISSOLUTION, AND COMPLICITY IN THE MULTIRACIAL IDEA

RAINIER SPENCER

Recommendations Concerning Reporting More Than One Race

- *When self-identification is used, a method for reporting more than one race should be adopted.*

- *The method for respondents to report more than one race should take the form of multiple responses to a single question and not a "multiracial" category.*

- *When a list of races is provided to respondents, the list should not contain a "multiracial" category.*

—Office of Management and Budget

IN OCTOBER 1997, the years-long drama concerning whether or not to revise the racial definitions utilized by the federal government so as to include a separate multiracial category came to a temporary halt. The nature of that halt was the decision of the Office of Management and Budget (OMB) to reject the idea of a separate multiracial category, and to also change the instruction on forms requesting racial designation from "mark one race only"

101

to "mark one or more."[1] This decision was the culmination of a four-year, multimillion dollar review of federal racial classification that included two sets of congressional hearings (totaling seven separate hearing dates over the four years), and numerous solicitations of public comment.

It was a formidable task undertaken with the utmost seriousness by the persons and agencies involved. Throughout the entire period of the review, the Statistical Policy Office of OMB's Office of Information and Regulatory Affairs consistently sought, collected, and considered the opinions and arguments of interested parties on all sides of the debate. OMB's ultimate decision—allowing for an expansion of the racial choices open to respondents by removing the instruction to "mark one race only," while avoiding the damage to civil rights compliance monitoring that would result from a separate multiracial category—was arrived at through considered judgment and informed debate.[2]

Yet, despite some initial applause at what was touted as a remarkable compromise, it was a decision that ultimately pacified some, angered a few, and truly satisfied none. In fact, not long after OMB's decision, the more vocal advocates of a separate multiracial category characterized OMB's judgment as being totally unacceptable. For instance, in spite of the new option to mark multiple categories, Jane Chiong remains critical of the government's rejection of a stand-alone multiracial category, lamenting that multiracial children continue to be the victims of "monoracial minority messages" being transmitted to them in schools.[3]

In fact, before the actual decision was rendered—when OMB's interagency committee for reviewing changes to federal race categories suggested the "mark one or more" solution—Project RACE (Reclassify All Children Equally), one of the most visible advocates of a multiracial category during the period of the review, quickly proclaimed its displeasure. Project RACE executive director Susan Graham criticized the interagency committee's recommendation by asserting: "We do not want to be the check-all-that-applies community. We want to be the multiracial community."[4] Within weeks, Graham again denounced the "mark one or more" compromise during one of the aforementioned hearings. Testifying before Congress on July 25, 1997, she offered her organization's assessment of the decision:

> I have been asked to come back today to address the Interagency recommendation to the Office of Management and Budget. The national membership of Project RACE expressed feelings of elation at the "mark one or more" part of the recommendation. For the first time in the history of this country our multiracial children will not have to choose just one race. It is progress. But after the elation came the sad truth. Under the current recommendation, my chil-

dren and millions of children like them merely become "check all that apply" kids or "check more than one box" children or "more than one race" persons. They will be known as "multiple check offs" or "half and halfers." You must understand that the proposal, in effect, says, multiracial persons are only parts of other communities; they are not whole. Let's be very clear: The compromise for "check one or more" without a multiracial identifier was not a compromise with the multiracial community. It was a compromise with the opponents of a multiracial category. I have brought short comments from Project Race members from across the country, of all races and ages, voicing their opinions about the recommendation and the need for the multiracial classification. I ask that they be entered into the record.[5]

An interesting side note to the foregoing commentary is the fact that although Project RACE had generally lobbied for a separate, stand-alone, federal multiracial category throughout the review period, there was a interval of time (from May to July 1997) during which the organization favored essentially the same "mark one or more" format that Graham subsequently denounced. During the May 22 hearings Project RACE expressly lobbied for the "mark one or more" option, going so far as to describe it as "clear," "precise, "and "accurate."[6] However, during the July 25 hearings, as shown above, Project RACE reversed itself and argued against the recommended "mark one or more" format. While the precise details fall outside the scope of this chapter, when examining the review period one finds that this kind of self-contradiction is not out of character for Project RACE.

Despite such contradictions, however, it remains clear that some people and organizations will continue the call for a separate federal multiracial category long past the 2000 census, the final preparations for which OMB's decision was timed to facilitate. It will be useful, then, in the space between the recent agitation for a federal multiracial category and the inevitable future agitation, to examine seriously the meaning of such a designation and the implications of its potential adoption. In order to do this in a useful and intellectually responsible way, however, it will be necessary to raise the level of the discussion significantly above the distinctly uncritical form that debates concerning multiraciality usually take, especially those found in the popular media.

THE PATHOLOGY TROPE

In this chapter I want to stimulate that dialogue-raising project by clearing a dialectical path that transcends the two most common approaches to the multiracial idea—namely, pathology and cheerleading. Most treatments of multiracial identity tend to fall into one or the other of these two camps. To begin with, on one side, there is the old and still lingering paradigm of pathology in which a so-called multiracial person is pathologized if she asserts a multiracial identity. In cases of black/white mixture, this view is usually expressed via assertions that the individual is engaged in attempting a futile escape from blackness, and should "just get over it" by accepting her true (black) identity.[7] This familiar, *tragic mulatto* trope has a long history, the essential features of which are encapsulated in Paul Spickard's description of that particular view of mulattoes as, "psychically divided, torn between the Blackness they were said to despise and the Whiteness toward which, it was said, they aspired and which was denied them."[8]

The resilience of this myth has been extraordinary, and its contemporary residue can be seen in the words of Leonard Dunston, president of the National Association of Black Social Workers, when writing about professional golfer Tiger Woods and the multiracial category debate: "But to the extent that there are people of African ancestry who do not value the importance of their history, and who want to escape the challenges which confront people of African ancestry, Mr. Woods and others like him will probably help move certain individuals toward the idea of the 'colored,' 'other,' or 'mixed' category that proved to be so disastrous in South Africa and other places, including Brazil, where it has been used to divide people of color and to keep them as an oppressed group."[9]

This is the new millennium version of the tragic mulatto myth. In Dunston's account, people of partial African ancestry who decline the ideological constraints of a unitary and monolithic black identity are seen as denying their blackness, and as being willing to harm other (authentic) blacks in the process. Unqualified loyalty to an ascribed black racial identity is constituted as the behavioral norm, and nonconformity is cast as a psychotic, or near-psychotic, deviation from that norm. As an example of this, Afrocentric theorist Molefi Asante describes African Americans who fail to toe that essentialist line (especially those who adopt a multiracial identity) as "inauthentic," "misoriented," "insane," and "in denial."[10]

Psychologist Thomas Parham proposes that psychologically healthy African Americans require a concept of self that "must contain a personal identity (self-portrait) which is rooted in one's blackness, a reference group orientation which recognizes one's connection and identification with other African people, a connectedness to an almighty supreme divine force, and a sense of esteem which radiates with pride and elation at one's cultural heritage."[11] This type of racially essentialist psychology owes much to the work of psychologist William Cross, who developed the idea of *nigrescence*, or the stages of black identity development.

These stages are said to be (1) pre-encounter, (2) encounter, (3) immersion-emersion, (4) internalization, and (5) internalization-commitment, and serve to explain "how *assimilated* Black adults, as well as *deracinated*, *deculturalized*, or *miseducated* Black adults are transformed by a series of circumstances and events into persons who are more Black or Afrocentrically aligned."[12] An important component of nigrescence is the concept of reference group orientation (RGO), a way of reifying the notion of biological race, to which Parham referred above. According to Cross: "Having a Black identity means that the RGO functions of one's identity *are grounded in one's Blackness*. Being Black has high salience to one's sense of well-being, one's purpose in life, one's sense of connection to other Blacks."[13] It is not difficult to see how the contemporary variant of the tragic mulatto myth is sustained by these kinds of essentialist psychologies and ideologies, all of which support the fallacious and racist notion of hypodescent, or, the one-drop rule.[14] If Americans of African descent are in a proper relation to themselves only when they invest psychologically in some sort of black frame of reference, then African Americans who identify as multiracial are, by definition, mentally ill. Saving racially mixed African American children from identity confusion and shattered lives then becomes an urgent rallying cry that is deployed against the idea of multiracial identity. Failure to heed the call is presumed to result in pathology.

With no small irony, multiracial activists have responded by developing a counter-paradigm in which the same person is pathologized if she does *not* assert a multiracial identity. On this view, the failure of mixed-race individuals to achieve a healthy multiracial identity will lead to "feelings of shame, emotional isolation and depression;"[15] "neurotic behavior;"[16] and a "conflicted, ambivalent, confused, and negative sense of identity."[17] Testifying at a congressional hearing, multiracial activist Marvin Arnold deployed the pathology paradigm when he warned that "racial identification is important for the Multiracial person because of the perceived psychopathology engendered as a result of his/her inability to identify with a specific racial category. Because he/she cannot identify with a specific racial group the conclusion is that dysfunction will ensue."[18]

Indeed, rather than criticize the nigrescence model of identity development as racially essentialist in addition to being a vehicle of hypodescent, some proponents of multiracial identity have explicitly appropriated portions of that particular format for their own arguments. Lynda Field relies on the aforementioned concept of RGO, enlarging Cross's formulation by postulating a bicultural RGO for multiracial teenagers.[19] James Jacobs suggests a three-stage process of multiracial identity development in black/white children: (1) precolor constancy: play and experimentation with color, (2) post-color constancy: biracial label and racial ambivalence, and (3) biracial identity.[20] Focusing on

Asian/white research subjects, George Kich also suggests three stages, consisting of (1) initial awareness of differentness and dissonance, (2) struggle for acceptance, and (3) self-acceptance of biracial identity.[21]

The result of the foregoing is an ever-escalating war of alleged neuroses and counter-neuroses in which each contingent deploys its own psychologists and social experts—the one side describing a multistage process of monoracial identity development that the multiracially identifying mixed-race person is in conflict with; and the other side describing a similar process of multiracial identity development in which the monoracially identifying mixed-race person is declared to be neurotic or confused. Unfortunately, each camp seems always more driven by group politics, whether monoracial or multiracial, than by any real concern for the personal development of the individuals in question.

THE CHEERLEADING TROPE

On the other hand, the phenomenon I characterize as cheerleading involves the rather simplistic theme of positing multiracial people as representing the best of both worlds. (Why not the worst of both worlds, after all?) Multiracial persons are said to be more attractive than monoracial persons (children, most especially), and to represent the personal embodiment of racial love and harmony. Typical of this rather naïve attitude is the outlook of one young multiracial person whom Kathleen Korgen reports as taking "comfort in the fact that she is a 'child of love'—the product of two people who had to overcome obstacles to be together because society disapproved of their relationship."[22]

In short, multiracial people are in themselves proffered as the solution to centuries of racial discord. Indeed, in Korgen's view, "biracial men and women possess a broader and more objective view of society than nonmarginal persons. Those who claim a biracial identity view race and our race-based society in general in a markedly different manner than the average monoracial American."[23] According to Korgen's research, not only do multiracial persons possess "the gift of objectivity," but they are also "more cosmopolitan," and "wiser than monoracial persons."[24] In like manner, Francis Wardle avers that the properly raised multiracial child "will have a very wide tolerance for differences and diversity," and "will not need to consider a child's racial label before she accepts him."[25]

Speaking at the 1996 Multiracial Solidarity March in Washington, D.C., Clarence Krygsheld, a past president of the Biracial Family Network of Chicago, offered a position he termed the "bi-cultural mulatto bridge." He explained this to mean that "the mixed-race person can be understood as the embodiment of harmony between the races."[26] However, in addition to its time-worn status as a familiar stereotype, this sort of condescending depiction is also quite patronizing. Krygsheld, like others before him, merely appropriates multiracial persons as the metaphoric sites of racial harmony, objectifying them and reducing their worth to the racial value of their parents' sex act.[27]

Among the most consistently glaring purveyors of the cheerleading approach are the popular media. Generally eschewing any hint of critical commentary, newsmagazine coverage of the multiracial identity debate overwhelmingly involves the labored use of language by writers endeavoring to illustrate the hipness of multiraciality (and likely their own as well), and what is more troubling—a propensity to publish, without editorial analysis, interview comments such as the following from *Newsweek*: "Mixed girls! That's the way to go! All the mixed girls I know are *fine*."[28] Throughout the recent public interest in the multiracial debate, *Time* for the most part demonstrated a similar level of journalistic insight.[29] As an example of this trend, one *Time* sidebar in a feature on mixed-race identity concludes with the following quotation that the editors saw no need to analyze or otherwise submit to scrutiny: "Those that are biracial and multiracial have a unique look" [at things]. "They see from both sides, and they try to be more just."[30]

There does exist something of a critical counterbalance to this brand of superficial romaticizing, as Lisa Jones, for example, captures in a concise way the cheerleading spirit in her critique of multiracial identity politics:

> Their [multiracial activists'] insistence on biraciality's unique status
> borders on elitism. They marvel at the perks of biraciality: That
> biracials have several cultures at their disposal. (Though don't we
> all as Americans?) They say things like "biracial people are free of
> bias because they embody both black and white." Can you fight
> essentialism with essentialism? Are we to believe that all biracials
> are chosen people, free of prejudice, self-interest, and Republican
> Christian fundamentalism? By proclaiming specialness aren't biracials
> still clinging to the niche of exotic other? "How could we not love
> them," boasted one white mother active in the census movement of
> her biracial children, "they're so cute."[31]

Mark Christian is another who is critical of the efforts of multiracial advocates to erect a racially superior identity that also necessarily ignores centuries of population mixture, characterizing a significant portion of the advocacy scholarship as "an attempt to produce an almost 'arty,' avant-garde, 'new people' for a twenty-first century U.S. that is devoid of the present endemic racism and racialised labeling."[32] In fact, far from multiracial identity bestowing harmony, wisdom, objectivity, or any other particular thing, it is in no sense clear that its meaning for individuals can be so easily captured.

Focusing on black/white multiracials, KerryAnn Rockquemore addresses and corrects the ways that multiracial identity has thus far been conceptualized inadequately:

> The voices of biracial people reveal that there are varying under-standings of what "biracial identity" means to individuals within this population. Individuals' selves have not one, but several ways in which they interpret and respond to biracialness. These divergent self-understandings are grounded in differential experiences, varying biographies, and crosscutting cultural contexts. This multiple mean-ing perspective breaks from the singular conception of Park's Mar-ginal Man, the assertions of multiracial advocates, and much recent research on the biracial population that rests on the unquestioned assumption that biracial identity has a singular and widely agreed upon meaning which an actor either does or does not understand.[33]

Notwithstanding the compellingness and intellectual rigor of the grow-ing body of critical multiracial scholarship of which Rockquemore's work is exemplary, the pathology and cheerleading approaches unfortunately remain the field's dominant modes of discourse. Nonetheless, it is imperative to displace naïve and essentialist appeals to an elitist, exotic, and "wiser" mul-tiracial identity in favor of a far more nuanced and intellectually demanding analysis. It is to a consideration of such a project that we now turn.

TRANSCENDING THE TROPES: THEORY

Any sophisticated discussion of a federal multiracial category must necessarily transcend both pathology and cheerleading, simplistic modes that serve only to hamper understanding by playing peoples' emotions against elementary concep-tions of biological racial identity. Since multiracial identity is based explicitly on the notion of biological racial mixture, central to any examination of a proposed multiracial category must be a consideration of those monoracial categories on which such a classification would by definition depend.

I shall begin my enquiry into the notion of a federal multiracial cat-egory with the presumption that race as a biological means of accurately classifying humans into three, five, or seventeen distinct and exclusive cat-egories is a complete fallacy. I take the same approach here as Kwame An-thony Appiah when he dismisses biological race by writing: "I announce this rather than arguing for it, because it is hardly a piece of biological news, being part of a mainstream consensus in human biology."[34] Racial skepticism, therefore, is the philosophical ground upon which I shall map the question of a federal multiracial category.

It is necessary to dismiss as well the increasingly popular assertion of race as a social, rather than a biological, reality. I want to be very clear here that I am not thereby dismissing the very tangible results of a still-virulent racism that is visited upon people every day. Rather, I am making the very important distinction between a thing that does not exist (biological race) and a thing that does (people's wrong-headed belief in, and actions based upon, the same). Where I depart from many of my colleagues is in my refusal to countenance the euphemistic notion of a social reality of race that bears no difference from the now-discredited biological construction. The effects of racism, which are made possible by an erroneous belief in biological race, are indeed a social reality; however, race itself is not.

If what is meant by the social construction (or social reality) of race is that people act as though race is real, and that therefore we should treat it as though it were real, then we merely acquiesce to ignorance. On such a view, one might as well argue that Earth in medieval Europe really was flat, since so many people acted as though it were. Alternatively, if what is meant by the social construction (or social reality) of race is that people believe in race, and that society is structured in accordance with that belief, then the term is in fact a misnomer. In this case it is not race at all, but belief in race, that is a social reality. The difference is not insignificant, since for so many people the assertion of race as a social reality allows them to maintain a comfortable belief in precisely the same racial categories that science long ago debunked.

Before proceeding, a few words are in order as well concerning the often misunderstood purpose of federal racial categorization. While race is a fiction that is supported to some extent by federal racial categorization, the issue is not so simple as merely doing away with all government racial statistics. These statistics remain our most potent weapon in the battle against covert and institutional discrimination, and simply doing away with federal racial categorization would seriously undermine civil rights compliance monitoring efforts. Federal racial statistics track discrimination against the five specifically defined groups (Asians, African Americans, Hispanics, Native Americans, and Pacific Islanders) that have historically suffered government-sanctioned oppression in the United States.[35] Because racists base their actions on a belief in biological race, these categories, however false, nonetheless reflect and capture the ways that racist ideologies are deployed through covert means and institutional structures.[36]

Until we are able to find an alternate means of tracking discrimination, the lesser of two evils is to continue government racial statistics keeping, even while we carry on with the project of debunking race generally. In this context, then, it becomes clear that consideration of a federal multiracial category—which would have everything to do with issues of self-esteem, and nothing to do with issues of historical, state-sponsored discrimination—is a weighty matter indeed. It is with this gravity in mind, therefore, that we undertake a critical analysis of the multiracial idea and of a federal multiracial category.

The general thesis I shall present in the remainder of this chapter is that the multiracial idea has the ability to either destabilize or support the idea of race, depending on how multiraciality is conceived. To see why this is so, we must consider the multiracial idea in two different aspects: one abstract, and the other practical; one theoretical, and the other applied. As I shall explain presently, this contrast is rooted in the difference between the freedom of conceptual thought, and the constraints imposed by race, especially as reified via the more practical matter of government regulations.

Race as it is understood in the United States refers to a system of classification based on a biological foundation (whether admitted consciously or not) in which each and every person belongs to one and only one racial group.[37] Since racial classification concerns people, and not rocks, reptiles, or clouds, it is important to deploy these classifications correctly. Biological race is not a reality, of course, but if it were real it would have to refer to distinct and exclusive categories in order to be a sensible concept at all. For the classifications to have any logical validity, races must be pure or else consistent classification is impossible since each racial group is by definition distinct from all the others. To allow that the categories are not distinct, or that people can fail to properly belong to one and only one category, is to immediately challenge the entire foundation of the race concept.

To see why this is so, let us accept for the sake of illustration the fallacious notion of biological race. By taking that initial step we must now allow either that racial categories are distinct and exclusive or that they are not. If they are distinct and exclusive, we can for the moment let that side of the question rest. If they are not distinct and exclusive, however, we are faced immediately with a serious logical problem revolving around the question of race mixture. For the sake of simplicity posit three different races— blue, green, and orange—that are not distinct and exclusive. However, what does their existence then mean if they have no boundaries, or if their boundaries are permeable?

Is bluish-orange still blue? Suppose a person's ancestry is mostly green, yet she appears bluish. Is she properly classified as green or blue? Would it make sense for the child of a green parent to not be green if the other parent were any other color, yet for the child of an orange parent to still be orange no matter what color the other parent might be? To travel down such a path would be to move from an objective and logical system of classification to a flawed and subjective one. Clearly, a logically valid system of racial classification would require exclusivity and distinctness, or else it would dissolve into meaninglessness. And it is critical to point out that this is not the same exercise as classifying rocks, birds, or insects, for we are dealing with sentient human beings who may have the inclination to challenge the racial classifications that might be assigned them.

In the absence of finite boundaries, the problem posed by racial mixture quickly becomes evident. The hypothetical child of an orange parent and a blue parent would be racially distinct from either parent, and if this child were to later procreate with a blue partner, the resulting child would be racially distinct both from its parents and grandparents due to the varying degrees of mixture. Already in merely two succeeding generations we have increased our number of distinct races from three to five, and we have only considered the intermixture of two of the original three types. Moreover, if we extend this kind of activity between all the types and the resulting crosses over a period of, say, five hundred years, the relation of our hypothetical case to the American context becomes evident. Ultimately, if we hold that racial boundaries are not distinct and exclusive, we are then forced to admit that there are actually as many distinct races as there are individual people on the planet.

Endeavoring to salvage the race concept, some may object here by invoking the example of the color wheel, and I want to devote some space to addressing this potential criticism. Such an objection would assert that there are varying hues we all agree by convention are blue, green, and orange, and that despite the fact that the range of a particular color may be broad or narrow most people would agree that this thing is red or that thing yellow. Drawing an analogy from the case of the color wheel, the argument is then made that there are racial types all people can agree on by convention even if precise boundaries are blurry.

However, the key word here is convention; and the key fact is that, properly understood, the color wheel makes quite the opposite point. The boundaries between different colors are conventions, useful for allowing humans to communicate thoughts about the world. The fact, however, is that colors actually merge seamlessly each into the other along a continuum, much the way that different phenotypic characteristics of human population groups meld geographically. Not only do the margins blend one color into another as red moves from orange and then to yellow, but the supposedly *pure* colors themselves are conventions, arbitrary in the sense that they are chosen by someone to represent true red or true yellow. Just as there is no particular hue that is true red in a natural or universal way; there is no characteristic or set of characteristics that prescribes true racial blackness or whiteness in a natural, universal, or biological way. Indeed, in both scenarios the acceptance of notions of purity and marginality allows the hegemony of misinformation to operate.

My point is not that we should refrain from using less-than-accurate conventions such as fixed color designations, or less-than-accurate terminology such as the "rising or setting sun," although either is certainly a philosophically defensible position however extreme it might appear. Rather, my point is that in the case of human beings it is fundamentally important that we resist the trap of using a framework so obviously false as race to classify them.[38] Saying that the sun is rising when in fact it is Earth that is revolving is a conventional inaccuracy about a thing. Asserting that this person is biologically Asian, this person biologically black, and that person biologically white is a fallacy that necessarily brings with it tremendous and significant inaccuracies about human nature and biological essences.[39]

One might, in support of biological racial classification, invoke Alice Brues's reply to the racial skeptic's dismissal of race: "I wonder what people are going to think when they hear this. They would have to suppose that the speaker, if he were dropped by parachute into downtown Nairobi, would be unable to tell, by looking around him, whether he was in Nairobi or Stockholm."[40] The point of Brues's example, of course, is to highlight her view that, in terms of race, *there is something there.*[41] I prefer a simpler and more compelling counterexample. The scenario I offer involves not parachuting, but the much less spectacular act of simply walking—walking from India to Malaysia via Iran, Saudi Arabia, France, Poland, Sweden, Russia, Korea, China, and Vietnam.

How many different races would one see along such a journey? Where would one race definitively stop and another begin? Rather than all the people our traveler might encounter looking as though they clearly belonged in one distinct racial category or another, she would instead find features of phenotype blending and changing along with features of geography. And of course, the foregoing example is limited to the Eurasian continent. Adding an excursion from Saudi Arabia through the Middle East and onto the African continent drives home the point with even more emphasis. Brues is wrong. It is not the case that *there is something there,* for there is no racial *thing* anywhere. All there is is endless variation on a human theme, variation that has been reified into the nonsense of biological race.

If one is going to defend the idea of biological racial groups with any real seriousness, one is necessarily relegated to accepting a framework that requires purity in order to be consistent.[42] White supremacists in particular have done this quite well.[43] Americans in general have sidestepped the nagging issue posed by centuries of population mixture by relying on hypodescent, which takes persons of African and European ancestry, and reallocates them to the black category. Hypodescent is vitally important in the United States since racial ambiguity threatens to distort the prevailing racial order by blurring the scientifically bankrupt distinctions that have been erected between the various racial groups, but most especially between ostensible whites and blacks. People in the United States have an almost narcotic need to place themselves and those around them in proper racial boxes. Robyn Wiegman writes about today's flawed understanding of race being the result of a move away from natural history, and toward biology—a move that situates racial difference as an immutable bodily essence:

> In the ascendancy of biology, as we shall see, the concept of "race" will undergo significant transformation, losing the kind of fluidity it achieved in natural history as a product of climate and civilization, as a variation within the human species, to become a rather stable and primary characteristic for defining the nature of the body, both its organic and ontological consistency. Natural history, in other words, was replaced by biology and in this, race was situated as potentially more than skin deep. As biology assigned to "man" a new sphere of specificity, the racial determinations wrought through this sphere produced not simply the constancy of race as an unchanging, biological feature, but an inherent and incontrovertible difference of which skin was only the most visible indication.[44]

Taking up the same theme, Samira Kawash also posits the modern notion of race as consisting in the certainty of essential bodily distinctions: "Race is supposed to be the truth of the body. In order for race to function smoothly to order relations, produce norms and expectations of behaviors, and regulate or restrict access to different forms of power and privilege, it must be produced as an irrefutable bodily marking."[45]

I should be clear in pointing out with Wiegman and Kawash that these are notions the scientific community has long since jettisoned, but that remain deeply held by the general populace. Knowing what race another person belongs to is therefore vitally important, and mistakes are critical transgressions of the highest order, especially mistakes made in regard to whiteness. It is important that people know what race they are, and that there be no questions of ambiguity. Thus, it is both a logical necessity and a matter of collective agreement that the lines be drawn clearly and distinctly if race is to perform its classificatory function properly.

The logical problem I want to propose for the race concept is the question of how to account for the offspring of parents of two different races in the context of race as a means of placing people into distinct and exclusive categories. As I have already noted, the primary avenue by which this is accomplished in the United States is via hypodescent. The practical purpose of hypodescent is to relegate persons with both African and European ancestry to the black group, thereby *appearing* to resolve the dilemma of racial mixture. This philosophically arbitrary process does not stand up to close scrutiny, however; and in many ways hypodescent is more a fervent wish than anything else.

Nonetheless, hypodescent facilitates the reproduction of the race fallacy along with the myth of white racial purity. The logical implication of hypodescent, whether one has consciously thought about it or not, is that whiteness cannot remain white if it is mixed with anything else, while blackness can remain black no matter what else it is mixed with. Perhaps the clearest illustration of the hegemonic power of hypodescent is to realize how easily and completely Americans accept the twin ideas that a white woman may give birth to a black child, but that it is a physical impossibility for a black woman to give birth to a white child.[46] Here is a doctrine of white superiority that, ironically, finds its most ardent support among African Americans. By uncritically accepting hypodescent, African Americans themselves assure that in this hegemonic arrangement whiteness remains the superior category, bounded and protected by illusions of purity and exclusivity.

Far from having any connection with biology or genetics, hypodescent is purely a means of mediating power via an arbitrary caste structure. Seeing hypodescent for the social instrument that it is, it should be clear that there is no more justification for placing a person of mixed parentage in one group than in the other. Biologically, genetically, such a hypothetical person must necessarily fall outside the distinct and exclusive boundaries of both racial groups that form her heritage. Her parents are members of their respective races because they are presumed to be pure and unmixed, and she—being mixed—cannot with any logical consistency be a member of either parental race.

In our hypothetical example, let us suppose further that one parent is black and the other white. Is the child resulting from this union white or black? For most Americans, of course, hypodescent provides the quick and easy answer unless two very specific things both occur. Unless our hypothetical individual receives no phenotypic characteristics at all from the black parent, *and* unless the black parent is not known publicly to be the parent, this individual will be considered black in the United States. Yet, the individual is certainly no more African than European, and as I shall offer presently, may even be more the latter in terms of biological heritage than the former.

Hypodescent fails to resolve the mixed-race problem precisely because it is an instrument of social hegemony, rather than a biological process. We can further problematize our scenario by noting that the black parent is in the first place not unmixed anyway, being the product of African, European, and possibly Native American admixture over the last several centuries. Moreover, it is altogether possible that this black parent's heritage is actually more European than African, depending on the particular genealogy in question. Here, the multiracial idea is the stimulus for exposing fissures in the logic of race. By recognizing that hypodescent is illogical and arbitrary in the case of the child, we are led to the same conclusion in the case of one of the parents. And of course, the same applies as we reach deeper into the family tree, until we come to the ostensible original points of mixture.[47]

It should be a commonplace that neither science nor logic provides a basis for assigning mixed-race persons to one race or the other. Any such assignment would be fully arbitrary. Thus, even if race were assumed to be true, and therefore to refer to biologically distinct and exclusive categories of human beings, the existence of children born of cross-racial unions would immediately invalidate that assumption. In other words, racially mixed people would in themselves be the proof of race's falsity. By simply existing, and challenging anyone to assign her to a race, our hypothetical individual single-handedly dismantles the entire theoretical structure. For as soon as a racial assignment is made, we must object that there is no more reason to assign her to this race than that one. As Naomi Zack puts it: "The facts of racial mixture, namely the existence of individuals of mixed race, undermine the very notion of race, which presupposes racial 'purity.' "[48] On the conceptual level, then, even whiteness thereby dissolves since it is a component (indeed, the primary component) of the racial superstructure.

Therefore, either races exist as pure and distinct categories or they do not exist at all. If they are taken to be pure and distinct categories, and if everyone is presumed to belong to one and only one race, then one must account for the categorizations of those whose parents belong to two different races—an accounting that cannot be given. Thus, in an abstract sense, the idea of the multiracial individual serves to delegitimize the notion of each person belonging to one and only one race. As we have seen, the critique of hypodescent illustrates its foundational inconsistency, its arbitrariness, and its basis in white supremacy. And once races are no longer taken to be distinct and exclusive categories, they can have no existence at all, for in that case there may as well be as many different races as there are people in the world. This is the insurgent quality inherent in the multiracial idea. By its even being thought it works to dissolve the idea of distinct and exclusive racial categories. However, of necessity, it then dissolves itself as well; for by dismantling the idea of distinct races it thereby dismantles the precondition of its own existence.

So in the abstract sense the multiracial idea can be a powerful tool against the continuing fallacy of biological race. A person who is the product of parents of supposedly different races respectively, and who challenges being assigned to one race or the other, by that very act invalidates the notion that race exists and that each person belongs to only a single racial category. This is a powerful conceptual insurgency, and at the level of logical reasoning it works a priori to undermine the possibility of classifying people into distinct and exclusive racial groups. Such persons, then, are living, personal counterexamples to assertions of race as a reality. They are not a new racial type, but are instead proof that no racial boundaries and no racial (or multiracial) types actually exist. But it is critical to keep in mind the fact that once the multiracial idea has done its conceptual work, it necessarily must dissolve itself as well, leaving us without the fallacies of either monorace or multirace.

Through a priori reasoning, then, it becomes possible to lay bare the flaws and inconsistencies of the American racial paradigm. In sum, if the proposition is offered that race consists of distinct and exclusive categories, then the multiracial idea invalidates the proposition via a simple, yet devastating, *reductio ad absurdum* argument. If, on the other hand, the proposition is offered that race does not after all consist of distinct and exclusive categories, then all racial categorization is immediately suspect as being arbitrary and compromised, for without exclusivity and firm boundaries racial assignment is meaningless. In either case, racial purity (and therefore race itself) is impossible to maintain. At the conceptual level the multiracial idea is insurgent, corrosive, and ultimately self-destructive, exposing the illogic of biological monoracial groups as well as anything that might be erected upon that foundation.

TRANSCENDING THE TROPES: PRAXIS

But at a different level, at the level of concrete application, the multiracial idea acts in an entirely different way. Any corrosive effect the multiracial idea has on the concept of race in a theoretical sense would not be transferable to practical application should a multiracial category be established alongside the present federal racial categories. To see why this is so we must consider the difference between the abstract and practical realms under consideration.

In terms of practical application, the multiracial idea is expressed through multiracial advocates lobbying for a federal multiracial category. The world of government forms and check-boxes is a far different place than the world of a priori thought, however. In the former, there is an important kind of power that is invoked by race terms merely appearing on a printed piece of paper—Asian, Black, Native American, Pacific Islander, White—especially one used for government purposes. Here, there is not much introspective thought regarding the unreasonableness of racial classification. Rather, by virtue of their appearance on government-mandated forms, the race categories receive validation rather than critical examination.

The introduction of a separate multiracial category into the practical realm has the opposite effect than the multiracial idea does in the theoretical realm. In its abstract form, the multiracial idea can operate in an a priori fashion to problematize and dismantle the idea of race. It is an independent idea that is free to challenge the superstructure. In the practical world, on the other hand, it would reify explicitly those other racial categories on which it necessarily would depend for its own existence. It is important to recognize that in its abstract state the multiracial idea is a *reductio ad absurdum*, while in its instantiated form it would derive legitimacy—at least as much legitimacy as is possessed by the current racial categories.

David Goldberg's analysis is that " 'mixed race' may *seem* to capture in the most adequate fashion prevailing demographic heterogeneity, but it does so only by silently fixing in place the racializing project."[49] In Goldberg's view, the multiracial idea necessarily "reimposes the hegemony of racial duality—of blackness and whiteness—as the standard, the measure, of mixedness."[50] Jayne Ifekwunigwe echoes Goldberg's point when she asserts that "an intermediate 'multiracial' or a 'mixed ethnic category' perpetuates false ideologies of 'racial' purity and 'racial' pollution within social contexts such as the United States wherein most African Americans already have at least partial White American or Native American ancestry."[51] The practical price of establishing a multiracial category would be the loss of all the corrosive, subversive, theoretical energy inherent in the multiracial idea—resulting in what, in other venues, has been called collaboration or co-optation.

Far from challenging the current racial paradigm, a federal multiracial category would in fact be fully complicit with the false idea of biological race. If a federal multiracial category were adopted it would not cause people to question the logic of the available racial choices. Most people don't begin to question them now, dutifully complying instead with the self-categorizations requested. By appearing on the form itself, those erroneous choices are thereby validated, and a multiracial category would receive the same validation.

That validation includes the reification of the biological construction of race, appeals to social reality notwithstanding, and surely does not represent the path toward deconstruction. As Heather Dalmage asserts: "Biologically based arguments rehash simplistic understandings of race that historically have been used to maintain white supremacy. A multiracial category and an officially recognized community would create greater divisions, and society would not necessarily be pushed to think more critically about race and racial identities."[52] Moreover, Dalmage argues: "The myth of white racial purity, based on a biological notion of race, is indeed the foundation upon which the U.S. racist system was constructed. Yet a multiracial category will not challenge purity as the basis for whiteness."[53]

Lisa Tessman considers the same issue, and ultimately reaches the same conclusion. In doing so, she supports the thesis I have been advancing regarding the operation of the multiracial idea in theory as opposed to in practice:

What does seem promising about mixed-race racial identification—
and promising in terms of its antiracist potential—is that if there
can be a sense of collective identity around mixed-race peoples, it
is an identity that is impure. Since racism rests on notions of racial
purity—white superiority is premised on white purity—one can
challenge racism with the assertion that the process of racialization
masks the impurity of the "races" that it creates. However, it is not
clear that identifying as mixed race or multiracial does this, since
one could read the introduction of a multiracial category as implying that all the other categories, in contrast to the multiracial
category, are pure.[54]

A federal multiracial category would in fact further cement the idea of
race in the United States, thereby making it that much more difficult to
excise its cancerous effects from our social body. Indeed, by asserting their
desire for a multiracial category, multiracial advocates demonstrate that they
accept and are fully complicit with the fallacy of biological race. There is no
denying this important conclusion, for even though supporters of a federal
multiracial category claim they are working toward the destablilzation of
race, it nonetheless remains the case that multiracial identity is not even
conceivable without parents or more remote ancestors who are supposedly of
different biological races.

In a sense, then, multiracial advocacy involves a step backward into a
benighted ignorance we have been trying to crawl out of, rather than a step
forward into enlightenment, as Dalmage describes: "Some multiracial family
members have even evoked essentialist imagery and language in their claims
that multiracial people are biologically distinct from others. Those searching
for spaces of comfort and those advocating for a separate multiracial category
may unwittingly reproduce the color line and reinforce white supremacy."[55]

Not to be forgotten is the purpose of federal racial categorization I
mentioned earlier. In addition to the problem of further cementing in place
the idea of biological racial groups, a federal multiracial category could in no
sense serve legitimately as the signifier of populations that have suffered
historical, government-sanctioned oppression. Its very adoption would belittle those people whose tremendous sufferings were the rationale for the
federal categories in the first place. Removal and extermination, slavery,
dispossession of lands, restricted immigration, internment—these are the
government acts whose legacies still haunt their victims' descendants.

Far from dealing with anything of this magnitude, multiracial advocacy
is concerned instead with self-esteem and with federal validation of personal
identity choices, neither of which have any relevance to the critical work of
civil rights compliance monitoring.[56] As Juanita Lott correctly observes: "[I]t

is the policy relevance of racial and ethnic data that makes [federal racial categorization] salient, not its possible use for identifying every population group that would like federal recognition," since "in discrimination cases, the relevant factor is how a victim of discrimination is perceived by the discriminator regardless of how an individual self-identifies."[57] To the extent that a federal multiracial category would—by disrupting the historical continuity of the statistical database gathered over the past quarter-century—confuse or otherwise damage current efforts to track discrimination, it must be rejected in the strongest possible terms.[58]

CONCLUSION

Clearly there is real frustration among those who feel that neither current monoracial categories nor the "mark all that apply" option fit their self-identification needs; however, the manner in which that frustration is directed—the call for a federal multiracial category—is wrongheaded to say the least. It would be better to devote our energies toward challenging and dismantling the racial fallacy that serves as the parent of the multiracial myth. Instead, supporters of a federal multiracial category legitimize what is no more than scientific nonsense, reifying and valorizing the idea that biological race is a meaningful method of classifying the incredible diversity of the human race. In this regard, it is important to recognize that a federal multiracial category would be every bit as *racial* as the monoracial categories its supporters want it to join.

A good many sincere people have been caught up in the Multiracial Movement, and the pain that the racial fallacy has caused them is palpable. Because asserting a multiracial identity requires them to assent to a belief in biological race (whether explicitly or implicitly acknowledged), and because they believe they are the embodiments of two or more distinct racial essences, multiracial advocates are bound to experience pain, frustration, and disappointment. I want to be clear that this is not an instance of the pathology trope; in fact it is no more and no less than the inevitable result of championing a fallacy. Suspension of critical thought is not the answer to the problem posed by the American racial paradigm. The only possible answer lies in adopting a critical and skeptical attitude toward the idea of biological race itself, eschewing both it and the multiracial myth it makes possible.

As we await the next round of arguments over a federal multiracial category, we must maintain our goal of debunking the idea of biological race, while ensuring that we do not undermine civil rights compliance monitoring in the process. These are the real issues at stake in the multiracial category debate, not uninformed displays of pathology and cheerleading. We must continue walking toward the light; for Earth is not flat, it is not the center of the universe, and neither race nor multirace have a shred of reality on this world.[59] This is the scientific and logical truth. As intellectuals and scholars, we have a professional obligation to spread, rather than ignore, that truth.

NOTES

Executive Office of the President, Office of Management and Budget, "Recommendations From the Interagency Committee for the Review of the Racial and Ethnic Standards to the Office of Management and Budget Concerning Changes to the Standards for the Classification of Federal Data on Race and Ethnicity," by Sally Katzen, *Federal Register* 62, no. 131 (July 9, 1997): 36937. These were among the recommendations presented to OMB in July 1997 by the interagency committee it fielded to review potential changes to the federal race categories. OMB accepted the recommendations three months later.

1. Executive Office of the President, Office of Management and Budget, "Revisions to the Standards for the Classification of Federal Data on Race and Ethnicity," by Sally Katzen, *Federal Register* 62, no. 210 (October 30, 1997): 58786.

2. For a detailed discussion of civil rights compliance monitoring, federal racial categorization, and the potential effects of a separate multiracial category, see Rainier Spencer, *Spurious Issues: Race and Multiracial Identity Politics in the United States* (Boulder: Westview, 1999), chaps. 2 and 4.

3. Jane A. Chiong, *Racial Categorization of Multiracial Children in Schools* (Westport: Bergin and Garvey, 1998), 111–12.

4. Quoted in Steven A. Holmes, "Panel Balks at Multiracial Census Category," *New York Times*, July 9, 1997, A8. Graham's use of the term *we* when speaking of the purported multiracial community is somewhat curious since she identifies herself as white.

5. House Subcommittee on Government Management, Information, and Technology of the Committee on Government Reform and Oversight, *Hearings on Federal Measures of Race and Ethnicity and the Implications for the 2000 Census*, testimony by Susan Graham on July 25, 1997, 105th Cong., 1st sess., April 23, May 22, and July 25, 1997, 547.

6. House Subcommittee on Government Management, Information, and Technology of the Committee on Government Reform and Oversight, *Hearings on Federal Measures of Race and Ethnicity and the Implications for the 2000 Census*, testimony by Susan Graham on May 22, 1997, 105th Cong., 1st sess., April 23, May 22, and July 25, 1997, 291.

7. Race terms in this chapter are always a reference to people's belief in the illogical system of racial categorization in the United States. Given that my topic concerns the notion of racially distinct and racially mixed people in the United States, my use of such terms in some instances is necessary as I endeavor to engage the current racial paradigm in considering the multiracial idea. Race terms in this chapter—including the adjectives *mixed-race* and *multiracial*—should always be read as if preceded by the words *so-called*.

8. Paul Spickard, *Mixed Blood: Intermarriage and Ethnic Identity in Twentieth-Century America* (Madison: University of Wisconsin Press, 1989), 329.

9. Leonard Dunston, "Black America and Tiger's Dilemma," *Ebony*, July 1997, 32, 138.

10. Molefi K. Asante, "Racism, Consciousness, and Afrocentricity," in *Lure and Loathing: Essays on Race, Identity, and the Ambivalence of Assimilation*, ed. Gerald Early (New York: Penguin, 1994), 139–43.

11. Thomas A. Parham, *Psychological Storms: The African American Struggle for Identity* (Chicago: African American Images, 1993), 74.

12. William E. Cross, *Shades of Black: Diversity in African-American Identity* (Philadelphia: Temple University Press, 1991), 190.

13. Ibid., 217.

14. Theoretically, hypodescent operates in socially stratified societies to always place the offspring of two different groups in the lower-status group. In the United States it comes into play primarily in cases of black/white mixture, ensuring that regardless of one's European ancestry any known or detectable African ancestry renders one black. Hypodescent is a racist implement because it operates on the presumption of white racial purity and black racial impurity.

15. Dorcas D. Bowles, "Bi-Racial Identity: Children Born to African-American and White Couples," *Clinical Social Work Journal* 21, no. 4 (Winter 1993): 427.

16. Ruth G. McRoy and Edith Freeman, "Racial-Identity Issues Among Mixed-Race Children," *Social Work in Education* 8, no. 3 (Spring 1986): 166.

17. Elaine Pinderhughes, "Biracial Identity—Asset or Handicap?" in *Racial and Ethnic Identity: Psychological Development and Creative Expression*, ed. Herbert W. Harris, Howard C. Blue, and Ezra E. H. Griffith (New York: Routledge, 1995), 83.

18. House Subcommittee on Census, Statistics, and Postal Personnel, Committee on Post Office and Civil Service, *Hearings on the Review of Federal Measurements of Race and Ethnicity*, testimony by Marvin C. Arnold on June 30, 1993, 103rd Cong., 1st sess., April 14, June 30, July 29, and November 3 1993, 162.

19. Lynda D. Field, "Piecing Together the Puzzle: Self-Concept and Group Identity in Biracial Black/White Youth," in *The Multiracial Experience: Racial Borders as the New Frontier*, ed. Maria P. P. Root (Thousand Oaks, CA: Sage, 1996), 214, 217.

20. James H. Jacobs, "Identity Development in Biracial Children," in *Racially Mixed People in America*, ed. Maria P. P. Root (Newbury Park, CA: Sage, 1992), 199–203.

21. George K. Kich, "The Developmental Process of Asserting a Biracial, Bicultural Identity," in *Racially Mixed People in America*, ed. Maria P. P. Root (Newbury Park, CA: Sage, 1992), 305.

22. Kathleen O. Korgen, *From Black to Biracial: Transforming Racial Identity Among Americans* (Westport: Praeger, 1998), 74.

23. Ibid., 79.

24. Ibid., 77, 79.

25. Francis Wardle, *Tomorrow's Children: Meeting the Needs of Multiracial and Multiethnic Children at Home, in Early Childhood Programs, and at School* (Denver: Center for the Study of Biracial Children, 1999), 7.

26. Clarence Krygsheld, speech delivered at the Multiracial Solidarity March, Washington, D.C., July 20, 1996.

27. Moreover, as with all people, there is a portion of rape, incest, abuse, and failed marriages within this population (and among its parents) as well, so that they

are no more the "embodiment of harmony between the races" than are white-identifying persons the embodiment of harmony amongst whites.

28. Quoted in Lynette Clemetson, "Color My World: The Promise and Perils of Life in the New Multiracial Mainstream," *Newsweek*, May 8, 2000, 74.

29. I specifially exclude *Time* writer Lise Funderburg from the foregoing criticisms. Hers are perhaps the only newsmagazine articles on multiracialism that possess intellectual merit.

30. Quoted in Jack E. White, " 'I'm Just Who I Am,' " *Time*, May 5, 1997, 34.

31. Lisa Jones, *Bulletproof Diva: Tales of Race, Sex, and Hair* (New York: Doubleday, 1994), 58–59.

32. Mark Christian, *Multiracial Identity: An International Perspective* (New York: St. Martin's Press, 2000), 5.

33. Kerry Ann Rockquemore, "Between Black and White: Exploring the 'Biracial' Experience," *Race & Society* 1, no. 2 (1998): 202.

34. Kwame A. Appiah, "But Would That Still Be Me?," in *Race/Sex: Their Sameness, Difference, and Interplay*, ed. Naomi Zack (New York: Routledge, 1997), 78.

35. Whites are also included in these statistics although they are most often used as a reference group. In other words, one must know the numbers of white and black children in a particular school, for instance, before one can make comparative analyses of students who have been ability-tracked or placed in remedial programs. Additionally, although Hispanics are not considered a race by the federal government, when the combined race and ethnicity format for collecting these statistics is used, they become a de facto racial group in that particular analysis.

36. I want to be clear that I am not here endorsing the idea of race as a social reality, but am instead honestly attempting to grapple with the effects of massive belief in race. Far from accepting race a social reality, I am advocating, in a very limited and specific way, the continued use of federal statistics, given that the alternative of foregoing them would result in an inability to track racism.

37. It remains to be seen whether OMB's "mark all that apply" decision will have any effect at all on the general monoracial paradigm in the United States, especially given the fact that OMB has instituted a complex tabulation algorithm to redistribute multiple responses to single categories. Executive Office of the President, Office of Management and Budget, "Guidance on Aggregation and Allocation of Data on Race for Use in Civil Rights Monitoring and Enforcement," Bulletin No. 00–02 (March 9, 2000).

38. I stress again that the only exception to this must be the case of federal racial classification, which serves to track racial discrimination by statistically using the language of the racist. The goal remains to find a way to move beyond such classification without undermining civil rights compliance monitoring.

39. I am not referring here merely to racist assumptions about groups. The very act of assigning people to racial groups, even absent any connotations of superiority or inferiority amongst those groups, is wrongheaded. It is not just racist baggage that is the problem, as many people assert, but rather that race itself is the problem.

40. Alice M. Brues, "The Objective View of Race," *NAPA Bulletin* 13, *Race, Ethnicity, and Applied Bioanthropology* (1993): 78.

41. Ibid.

42. Or, at least, white purity. Although I won't pursue the matter here, one could also posit an alternative system consisting of a pure white race along with various pure and impure nonwhite races. Such an arbitrary system would have no logical force, however, and would still fall victim to the destabilizing conceptual power of the multiracial idea, which I will describe shortly.

43. For an excellent analysis of the connections between racial purity and white supremacy see Abby Ferber, *White Man Falling: Race, Gender, and White Supremacy* (Lanham, MD: Rowman and Littlefield, 1998).

44. Robyn Wiegman, *American Anatomies: Theorizing Race and Gender* (Durham: Duke University Press, 1995), 30–31.

45. Samira Kawash, *Dislocating the Color Line: Identity, Hybridity, and Singularity in African-American Literature* (Stanford: Stanford University Press, 1997), 130, 148.

46. Perhaps in vitro fertilization would overcome the latter rule, but even this is far from certain.

47. I am referring here only to mixture on American soil, of course. Some sub-Saharan Africans transported via the transatlantic slave trade had European and other admixtures even before their arrival here, which further discredits the idea of blacks as a biological race.

48. Naomi Zack, "Mixed Black and White Race and Public Policy," *Hypatia* 10, no. 1 (Winter 1995): 126.

49. David T. Goldberg, "Made in the USA: Racial Mixing 'n Matching," in *American Mixed Race: The Culture of Microdiversity*, ed. Naomi Zack (Lanham, MD: Rowman and Littlefield, 1995), 243.

50. Ibid.

51. Jayne O. Ifekwunigwe, *Scattered Belongings: Cultural Paradoxes of "Race," Nation, and Gender* (New York: Routledge, 1999), 180.

52. Heather M. Dalmage, *Tripping on the Color Line: Black-White Multiracial Families in a Racially Divided World* (New Brunswick: Rutgers University Press, 2000), 149.

53. Ibid., 151.

54. Lisa Tessman, "The Racial Politics of Mixed Race," *Journal of Social Philosophy* 30, no. 2 (Summer 1999): 289.

55. Dalmage, *Tripping on the Color Line*, 133.

56. In the case of multiracial complaints of discrimination, they reduce overwhelmingly to bigoted reactions against some portion of a person's ancestry, rather than against any mixture per se. The likelihood is that the bigot is operating with such crude conceptions of racial identity that the victim's self-identity choice, even if known, would be irrelevant.

57. Juanita T. Lott, *Asian Americans: From Racial Category to Multiple Identities* (Walnut Creek, CA: AltaMira Press, 1998), 56–57.

58. Also significant here is the fact that some multiracial category supporters advocate not filling out the racial check-boxes used to track discrimination, or filling them out incorrectly (marking all the boxes, or marking one that has no relation at all to the respondent, for instance), so as to purposefully frustrate the statistics-keeping

effort. That such selfish actions serve only to aid racists escape detection places the multiracial movement in a decidedly less flattering light.

59. It is worth making the point again that I am certainly not blind to the debilitating effects of racism in the United States. However, I maintain that we must distinguish the reality of racism and the reality of actions based on the misguided belief in race from the unreality of biological race itself. It is because I acknowledge the material outcomes of racial thinking that I favor continued use of federal racial categorization until some alternative means of monitoring compliance with civil rights laws is developed.

SIX

DECONSTRUCTING TIGER WOODS:
THE PROMISE AND THE PITFALLS OF
MULTIRACIAL IDENTITY

<hr>

KERRY ANN ROCKQUEMORE

THE COLLECTION OF ACTIVISTS, parents, and support groups that make up the Multiracial Movement were seemingly given a "gift from heaven" in April 1997 in the form of Tiger Woods. At twenty-two, Woods won the Masters Golf Tournament and quickly became a media superstar. Shortly after his win he appeared on the Oprah Winfrey show and announced to the American public that he was, in fact, *not* black, but "Cablinasian." In one fell swoop, the Multiracial Movement, which had been working diligently at the grassroots level for the previous decade to get a particular multiracial agenda into public consciousness, had an unsolicited and unexpected poster child for multiracialism. On the surface, Tiger Woods seems to be the ideal symbol of multiracialism in the United States, representing all of the hopes and desires of various wings of the movement. This chapter will scratch that surface in order to problematize the symbol of Tiger Woods, the discourse surrounding his refusal to accept a black identity, and his attempts at racial self-identification.

Multiracial celebrities make numerous choices about their racial identity. In fact, their varied racial identities reflect the multifaceted nature of multiracialism. While Tiger Woods may be the most visible, and the one

125

most frequently cited by many multiracial activists, he is by no means the only multiracial celebrity, nor is his choice of racial identity the only choice that multiracial people make. Therefore, it is necessary to first explore what is known about how mixed-race people understand their racial identity in the United States. After a brief explanation of the various choices that multiracial people make, I will focus on Tiger Woods specifically to illustrate the ways in which some racial identity choices among multiracial people are privileged above others and explore why the Multiracial Movement has embraced some multiracial celebrities as standard bearers while virtually ignoring others. Tiger Woods is of interest, not only because he has become the symbol of multiracialism to the American public, but more importantly, because of his particular choice of racial identification. The media frenzy that followed his statement of identification illustrates both the grand possibilities of multiracial identity and the enduring pitfalls that make a narrowly defined multiracialism an utter impossibility in the current climate of race relations in the United States.

HOW DO BIRACIAL PEOPLE UNDERSTAND THEIR RACIAL IDENTITY?

Social science researchers studying the multiracial population have sought, both conceptually and empirically, to answer how multiracial people understand their racial identity. Using in-depth interviews, surveys, and case studies, researchers have explored the multifaceted and complex ways that multiracial people understand themselves and their place in the United States' racial system. And yet, many Multiracial Movement activists, as wells as members of the media, tend to paint multiracial identity in a simplistic, monolithic, and narrow manner. I will briefly review what is known about the racial identity choices that biracial[1] individuals make, highlighting celebrity cases that illustrate each identity option. The celebrity cases are used here to underscore the selective attention that has been given to Tiger Woods by the multiracial community, in spite of the numerous other individuals who make very different choices about their racial identity.

BIRACIAL AS A SINGULAR IDENTITY: EXCLUSIVELY BLACK

Some biracial people understand their racial identity in alliance with only one of their birth parents. Racial identity for these individuals is typically exclusively black (as opposed to exclusively white).[2] The singular black identity is far more prevalent than a singular white identity because of the one-drop rule and the myth of white racial purity, each with its roots in slavery. The one-drop rule took on legal codification after the Civil War when many states adopted laws articulating specific definitions of who is black.[3] Legal statutes were gradually dropped from state law books, but their legacy has remained in the de facto application of the one-drop rule.[4] Because of this long-standing pattern of racial categorization, the singular black identity has historically been the only identity "option" available to multiracial people with one black parent. So deeply embedded was this cultural norm that it was not even conceptualized as an option, nor would most individuals have considered any other racial identity. Root refers to the singular black identity as a multiracial person's "acceptance of the identity society assigns."[5] Because of the historical, ideological, and cultural persistence of the one-drop rule, the singular black identity option has been heavily studied and is still assumed to be the primary identity choice for multiracial individuals.

As a cultural norm, the one-drop rule has profoundly informed research on the multiracial population. The assumption of a singular black identity as normative is firmly grounded in the empirical and theoretical literature as numerous scholars have used conceptual models of black identity to assess multiracial people.[6] These projects assume that the singular black identity is the only "healthy" response for multiracial people—those who do not follow this developmental trajectory are assumed to be consigned to a life of tragic uncertainty and social malaise.

Numerous celebrities who have one black and one nonblack parent identify themselves as exclusively black, including Halle Berry, Lenny Kravitz, Rain Pryor, Giancarlo Esposito, and Jasmine Guy. Lenny Kravitz is representative of the comments made by these celebrities who opt for a singular black identity. In an interview in the mid-1990s he stated:

> Luckily, I was not one of those children [with insecurities about my racial identity]. I knew lots of them who were mixed "am I black? am I white? what am I?" I used to see kids at school who were fair like me or even more fair. They wanted to be white; they didn't want to be black because it's too hard being black. And then the white kids are like, "you're black, so get away from us," and the black kids are like, "you're white." I never had that. My mother had taught me: "your father's white, I'm black. You are just as much one as the other, but you are black. In society, in life, you are black." She taught me that from day one you don't have to deny the white side of you if you're mixed, accept the blessing of having the advantage of two cultures, but understand that you are black. In this world if you have a spot of black, you are black. So get over it.[7]

Kravitz's nuanced statement about his racial identity reveals his political and social consciousness. He is aware of both the racial stratification system in the United States and the one-drop rule-based categorizations that evolve from that hierarchy. At the same time, he differentiates culture from race, by acknowledging the uniqueness of interracial family life. In doing so, he enables the possibility of biculturalism, while simultaneously declaring an exclusively black racial identity. His self-understanding represents a balance between individual experience and social constraints.

In addition to the multitude of celebrities who choose a singular black racial identity, the popular press has recently been flooded with autobiographical accounts of individuals with one black and one white parent who identify themselves exclusively as black including Lisa Jones's *Bulletproof Diva*, James McBride's *The Color of Water*, Judy Scales-Trent's *Notes of a White Black Woman*, and Gregory Williams's *Life on the Color Line*.[8]

The common thread among each of the autobiographical accounts parallels Kravitz's assertion that irrespective of parentage, the one-drop rule remains the classification norm. The persistence of the one-drop rule, ideologically and in its social ramifications of white privilege and continued racial inequality, has led black community leaders and civil rights activists (as well as some multiracial family members) to challenge the Multiracial Movement. They contend that while individuals may perceive themselves as multiracial, they will experience the world, and be considered by others, as black.[9]

BIRACIAL AS A BORDER IDENTITY: EXCLUSIVELY BIRACIAL

Differing from the singular black identity, the border identity conceptualizes biraciality as a new and separate category, one that is neither exclusively one race, nor another, but a blending of all an individual's racial backgrounds.[10] Root characterizes this new identity by the "ability to hold, merge, and respect multiple perspectives simultaneously."[11] Daniel refers to this option as a "blended identity" and describes it as one that "resists both the dichotomization and hierarchical valuation of African American and European American cultural and racial differences."[12] Such an identity represents a break with the paradigmatic reliance on the one-drop rule to understand the multiracial experience.

Illustrative of that paradigmatic shift is Taylor-Gibbs's reference to the singular black identity as an "overidentification with the black parent."[13] This statement is reflective of recent transformations in multiracial identity research, where the singular black identity, once the goal, is now pathologized. In more recent research, the border identity is viewed as the only "appropriate" and "healthy" identity for multiracial individuals. This contemporary research reflects a variety of social changes including declining structural barriers for minority group members, increasing numbers of interracial marriages (and corresponding increases in the multiracial population), and the growing presence of multiracial researchers among social scientists studying racial identity. All of these trends have combined to result in a new branch of identity work that has introduced the border identity (unaccepted prior to the mid-1980s) as a legitimate racial identity option for multiracial people.

The shift in acceptable racial identities can also be seen in the growing number of multiracial celebrities who claim border identities. Mariah Carey, Paula Abdul, Derek Jeter, and Tiger Woods are the most prominent examples. In 1994, Carey (whose father is black/Venezuelan and mother is Irish) described her racial identity in the following way:

> I am very much aware of my Black heritage, but I'm also aware of the other elements of who I am. And I think sometimes it bothers people that I don't say "I'm Black" and that's it. But it's not true. I have a mother who is 100 percent Irish who raised me from birth and who is my best friend. So if I were to say that I'm Black only, that would be negating everything she is. So when people ask, I say I'm Black, Venezuelan and Irish because that's who I am. I can only be all the things that I am. I cannot be one out of three.[14]

Derek Jeter responds similarly to questions about his racial identity by stating, "I'm biracial. People ask if I'm black or white. I'm both. I'm not one race. No matter how you look at it, I can't pick one or the other group because I'm part of both."[15] One similarity in both responses is the perception of an inability to disentangle the mixture of culture, race, and the social influences of both parents, and the acceptance that something unique and separate emerges from that blending. Because the border identity is, in many ways, a newly emergent phenomenon, celebrities who claim this particular option of self-identification tend to receive a great deal of press coverage for their refusal to accept a singular identity. For this reason, the public tends to be much more familiar with their racial identity choice, than the choices of those who opt for the singular identity. The border identity is also the option that is privileged by the Multiracial Movement because it provides the ideological framework around which the movement defines itself and its politics.

PROTEAN IDENTITY: MULTIPLE IDENTITIES

Multiracial identity may also be interpreted as the protean capacity to move between and among several racial identities that are interchangeable.[16] Individuals may move fluidly among black, white, and/or multiracial identities, using whichever identity may be situationally appropriate for a specific interactional context. The term *integrative identity* has also been used to describe this identity option, implying that multiracial people who choose the protean strategy may have the capacity to reference themselves *simultaneously* in various communities while functioning as an insider within these differing social groups.[17]

As unusual as the protean identity option may seem, one particular celebrity case provides a concrete illustration of how it is lived. Vin Diesel is an up-and-coming Hollywood actor whose professional career epitomizes the protean existence. His racial fluidity is not only a matter of personal perception, but exemplified by the various roles he has played in different films. In *Saving Private Ryan*, Diesel played an Italian American soldier; in the science fiction film *Pitch Black*, his character was African American; and in the film *Knockaround Guys*, he portrayed a Jewish gangster. So ambiguous and fluid is the actor that he tends to refer to himself "multifacial" as opposed to multiracial. Diesel provides an excellent example of individuals who understand being multiracial as a protean identity, not only because of his fluid movement in and out of these roles, but also because of his acceptance by others in these various manifestations. Strangely, however, this identity option is neither accepted nor promoted by the Multiracial Movement. It seems that the protean identity would be an ideal example of the way in which race, and therefore racial categorizations, are fluid due to their social construction. The very idea that an individual can move freely between racial identities delegitimzes both the existence of mutual exclusivity between races and the biological reality of racial categories. At the same time, it is unclear what political ramifications (much less census categorizations) would emerge from this self-understanding. It is precisely the complexity of the protean option that makes it the most challenging to the logic of the existing categorization system, yet it is so challenging, that it was incompatible with the Multiracial Movement's political goal of establishing a multiracial category on the 2000 census.

A TRANSCENDENT IDENTITY: BEYOND RACE

One final way that multiracial individuals understand their racial identity is by refusing to have any racial identity whatsoever. In other words, some mixed-race people claim to have "transcended" racial categorization altogether.[18] This approach to multiracialism is reminiscent of Park's Marginal Man where, by virtue of his in-between position, the social actor discounts racial categorizations completely.[19] Failing to fit within the rigidly defined groupings of the existing system, transcendent individuals disregard race as a master status altogether. This identity allows individuals to have an objective perspective on the subjective, socially constructed phenomenon of race.[20]

While empirical research documents the existence of the transcendent identity option, it is difficult to find a single multiracial celebrity that has chosen this identity. Several possibilities exist to explain the absence. First and foremost, black-appearing multiracial celebrities may choose a transcendent racial identity; but because they are assumed to be black by the media they are never explicitly asked about their racial identity. The same could be said for white-appearing multiracial celebrities who are assumed to be white, but in fact, have chosen a transcendent identity. Another possibility is that there are multiracial celebrities that feel social and economic pressure to declare either border or black identities, and do so, not as a reflection of their own self-understanding, but to protect their celebrity status.

MULTIRACIAL IDENTITY: SELECTIVE PERCEPTIONS AND POLITICAL AGENDAS

Having established that multiracial people make various choices about their racial identity, we are forced to ask why some racial identity options are celebrated and legitimized by multiracial activists while others are ignored. In other words, if multiracial people actually understand their racial identities in at least four different and radically distinct ways, why then did the Multiracial Movement embrace Tiger Woods and not Halle Berry or Vin Diesel as the "correct" personification of what it means to be multiracial?

In order to answer this question, it is necessary to contrast the racial identity typology previously described with the narrow definition of multiracialism put forth by activists. Specifically, many movement activists assume that individuals who have parents of different races understand their racial identity exclusively as a border identity. Based on this limited understanding, the Multiracial Movement had, as a central goal, official governmental recognition through a stand-alone category. This narrow definition of multiracialism created a political and symbolic void that can only be filled by individuals who understand being multiracial as a border identity. Thus, those choosing the singular, protean, or transcendent options could not serve as symbols of the movement because their varied racial identities did not overtly support the political goal of adding a multiracial category to the 2000 census. In addition to this political reality that disallowed singular, protean, or transcendent identifiers from being the voice of the movement, there are several additional factors that contributed to Tiger Woods, specifically, becoming the symbol of multiracial identity.

First and foremost, Tiger Woods won the Masters Golf Tournament at a time of fevered lobbying by multiracial advocates. The year was 1997, the same year that the Office of Management and Budget would hand down its final verdict on the addition of a multiracial category to the 2000 census. Shortly after his dominating win, Woods became a media superstar. However it was in an interview on the Oprah Winfrey show that he set off a racial firestorm that brought a narrowly defined multiracial message to the American public and enshrined him as the symbol of the Multiracial Movement. Winfrey asked Woods if it bothered him, the only child of a black American father and a Thai mother, to be labeled "African American." He replied, "Yeah it does. Growing up, I came up with this name: I'm a 'Cablinasian.'" Tiger Woods went on to explain that "Cablinasian" was an acronym, created to reflect the fact that his background is actually one-eighth Caucasian, one-fourth black, one-eighth American Indian, one-fourth Thai, and one-fourth Chinese.

This brief and spontaneous interchange had profound and lasting effects. Woods's answer to Winfrey's question, an act of racial self-definition, amounted to a wholesale endorsement of multiracialism as a border identity. In addition, his personal childhood name—Cablinasian—provided a memorable acronym for his complex identity that seemed to embody all the blending, bending, and burden of being multiracial. His public testimonial, on one of America's most popular daytime television programs (stating that he was *not* black, was bothered by being described as African American, and truly considered himself Cablinasian) fully corresponded to the argument put forth by multiracial advocates. He corroborated the Multiracial Movement's tenet that mixed-race people truly understand themselves and experience the world as multiracial. At the same time, Tiger Woods became the role model that so many parents in the Multiracial Movement were seeking for their children—an accomplished celebrity who openly acknowledged his multiracial identity. As former AMEA president Ramona Douglass stated shortly after Woods's Masters win, "[W]hether he wants to or not, he is sort of becoming the poster person for multiracial identity."[21]

Tiger Woods's unplanned and unconscious endorsement of the Multiracial Movement on the Oprah Winfrey show, while a celebrated moment for multiracial activists, was not the only reason he became a symbol of the movement. Clearly, many individuals in the past have publicly declared their racial identity as a border identity. The difference was that Tiger Woods was *Tiger Woods*. In other words, he was the handsome, charming, young man that had turned the upper-crust white world of golf on its head by executing a dominant win at the Masters Tournament. He was, therefore, not just a celebrity. Instead, he was a superstar, not unlike professional basketball player Michael Jordan, who was so thoroughly dominating at his sport that he was almost universally respected by the American public. But even more than Michael Jordan, the combination of this youth, his race (or races), his charm, and his dominating performance, captivated the world's attention. Many may have wanted to be "like Mike," but the children in Nike ads now transcended like-ness of Jordan in order to declare, "I *am* Tiger Woods." Needless to say, there could be no better ambassador of multiracialism, bringing the story of mixed-race people to the masses.

Multiracial activists and politicians were quick to capitalize on the media coverage of Tiger Woods's multiracialism (and the ensuing public debate) in order to move legislation forward. Representative Tom Petri's bill (H.R. 830) mandating that a freestanding multiracial category be added to the 2000 census became known the "Tiger Woods Bill," using the symbol and celebrity of Tiger Woods to move the multiracial agenda into public discourse. Tiger Woods, of course, had no personal input into this legislation, at no time publicly expressed support for it, nor even provided permission for his image to be used in conjunction with the bill. That, however, was unimportant to either activists or politicians. His public statement that he was not black but Cablinasian was an implicit endorsement of their agenda and permanently lodged the essence of the Multiracial Movement in the public's, especially the white public's, consciousness. Who could deny the loveable, charming, and all-admired Tiger Woods—and by extension, any other person like him—the right to define himself in any way he saw fit?

As with any political movement, the public facade of multiracial activism hides a number of important and contentious issues. Peering behind that facade provides a more comprehensive perspective on the purposive framing of issues, the meaning of the discourse, and the privileging of the stories used by multiracial activists. When considering Tiger Woods as the emblem of multiracialism and an icon attached to legislation to broaden bipartisan and public appeal, a number of factors are easily overlooked. Primary among them are Tiger Woods's utter political apathy. While he may consider himself Cablinasian, and feel "bothered" by others' attempts to describe him with the singular African American label, he has expressed neither a desire nor a willingness to serve as the political spokesperson for the Multiracial Movement—or any other movement.

In his political apathy, Tiger Woods seems to want to be "like Mike" who has persistently avoided making even the vaguest statements that could be interpreted as political. For instance, Jordan infamously responded to criticism of his failure to support a Democratic challenger to Republican senator Jesse Helms (a former segregationist) by stating: "Republicans buy shoes, too."[22] Similar to Jordan's apolitical stance, Woods continues to play golf at men-only clubs, has refused to acknowledge Thai Nike workers' requests for his help to improve sweatshop-like working conditions, and broke a Screen Actors Guild strike in order to film a commercial for General Motors. In fact, he has been described in the press as "an apolitical, non-boat-rocking, portfolio-protecting social humanoid."[23] Given Tiger Woods's political apathy, it comes as no surprise that Petri's "Tiger Woods Bill" had neither his official support, nor approval for the use his name.

In addition to Tiger Woods's apathy, there remains the fact that there currently exist many multiracial celebrities who identify themselves exclusively as black. In short, it is seemingly unacknowledged by the multiracial community that Tiger Woods is the *exception*, not the rule, among mixed-race celebrities, particularly among those who have one African American parent. While Tiger Woods may be the most prominent individual to publicly assert a multiracial identity, we are forced to ask about the even greater number of multiracial people that choose other racial identities. Those who do not choose a border identity are still multiracial by ancestry. However, their choices of racial identification are not only ignored by multiracial advocates, but the community's silence on the legitimate existence of alternative racial self-understandings has the effect of simultaneously privileging the border identity, and delegitimizing all other identity options. The border identity is the easiest for many to understand and fits with the push for a separate multiracial category. In other words, the *idea* that multiracial people may have multiple ways in which they identify themselves is a complex reality that is incompatible and inconsistent with a singular push for separate status as multiracial.

One final, unspoken tension is the interconnected effects of power and celebrity on racial identity choice. Tiger Woods is a wealthy and well-known presence in the media and thus has the capacity, the space, to define himself. His social power is beautifully illustrated by his use of Cablinasian, a term that has no previous existence or meaning in the American lexicon. Yet, after being introduced by Tiger Woods on the Oprah Winfrey show, Cablinasian has become a socially accepted term of self-understanding: for Tiger Woods. Indeed, from the moment he declared his self-identity, the media's fascination with the new term began. However, Cablinasian has not become a universal category of identification. Instead, it is a term specific to Tiger Woods, a term that is used by the media at his request, and a term that pertains to him and him alone. It is, in essence, the quintessential example of how social and economic power enables individuals to define their reality and the ways that others will thus perceive them. Clearly, no average citizen could state that they were Cablinasian, or any other self-created term, and have that fiction be immediately and widely used as a legitimate term of self-description. Ultimately, Tiger Woods, because of his fame, may define himself on the Oprah Winfrey show in any way he wants and she, as well as the majority of Americans, will readily accept it.

THE PROMISES AND PITFALLS OF A
NARROWLY DEFINED MULTIRACIALISM

There were various subtle, and not so subtle, reasons that Tiger Woods became the public face of multiracial identity celebrated by multiracial activists. At a broad level, he represents both the promise and pitfalls of a Multiracial Movement that is focused, at one end of the spectrum, on developing a new category of racial identification and, at the other, of removing racial categories entirely.

The promise that is inherent in Tiger Woods's self-declared multiracialism is that he, as an individual, has created a blended racial identity that he considers to be an authentic expression of his true self-understanding. In this way, the twin themes of individual freedom and self-determination are combined on the lips of a wildly popular sports celebrity. Many Americans support an individual's desire to break out of the straitjacket of rigid racial categorization, and look askance on the government's practice of collecting racial data. For those in the Multiracial Movement who want separate categorization, Tiger Woods represents the possibility that one enormously popular individual's refusal to be put into a singular racial category may lead to "multiracial" becoming an additional and legitimate category of racial understanding. In other words, Tiger Woods represents many multiracial activists' desire to insert the idea of multiracial identity into the American psyche. This desire is reflected in the statement of Project RACE's executive director, Susan Graham: "Tiger Woods could not have come at a better time. The public can now see a face of what it means to be multiracial."[24]

At the other end of the ideological spectrum within the Multiracial Movement lie activists and groups that wish to do away with racial categorization entirely. For those activists, Tiger Woods represents an even more profound promise embedded in the multiracial idea. Because they desired the dissolution of all racial categorization, they saw in Woods a multiracialism that would be the means to explode and condemn the myth of race as a biological reality. To this wing of the movement, Tiger Woods represents the futility of racial categorization. His self-designation as Cablinasian highlights the meaninglessness, and the absurdity of racial categorization as we know it.

While the intention of some multiracial activists is to dismantle racial categorization as a logical extension of the civil rights agenda, they have been joined by others who shared their goal of dismantling racial categories, if not their politics. This wing of the movement was the first to reach out to, and form coalitions with, conservative Republican politicians who favored the addition of a multiracial category to the 2000 census as a means of dismantling all racial categorization. Neoconservative Newt Gingrich himself stated "our goal is to have one classification—American."[25] Those seeking to explode the myth of race made convenient, if not odd, bedfellows with those seeking to dismantle civil rights gains by eliminating the government's capability to monitor compliance with that legislation. Interestingly, this coalition tapped into a somewhat unspoken sentiment within the general white mainstream audience who, by and large, believe that racism is a thing of the past, that racial inequalities no longer exist, and that the government perpetuates the race problem by the continued collection of racial data. The message that multiracialism is a step toward a race-less society, implying that the time has come for Americans to move beyond race, resonated with various constituencies across the political spectrum.

What is clear is that for those in the Multiracial Movement, irrespective of goals or ideology, Tiger Woods's act of self-definition was a watershed event, a moment pregnant with possibilities, yet rife with reality. While the symbol of Tiger Woods brought both attention and support to the movement, it also highlighted the enduring pitfalls of a narrowly defined multiracialism. For multiracial activists seeking separate status, the reality of racial polarization set in quickly in the form of a black backlash. Tiger Woods's public statement that he was not black but Cablinasian was immediately interpreted by African Americans as rejection at best, and antiblack sentiment at worst. Reflecting on Woods's self-definition, the Reverend Jesse Jackson had the following to say:

> The other dilemma for Woods is that his decision was perceived quite differently by Blacks and Whites. And so the politics of it is that he runs the risk of making Black people feel that he is disassociating himself from Black people and that he is uncomfortable with Black people. On the other hand, if he comes from a position that he makes Blacks feel that he does not belong to us and/or our circumstances—and he does belong to us, because he's been called n----r, because he's been the object of race-bait jokes—but if he's seen as rejecting Blacks and not being totally accepted by Whites in these circles, that leaves him in the Twilight Zone—too Black to be White, too White to be Black.[26]

Jackson's statement is representative of sentiments expressed by African American leaders in the wake of the Oprah interview. Woods's assertion of a border identity caused a great deal of tension within the black community and mobilized generations-long suspicions that mixed-race people consider themselves, and desire to be officially designated, as something "beyond black." Many African Americans were uncomfortable with his insistence on differentiation, or the mere suggestion that as a result of his racial mixture, he was somehow distancing himself from the black community. In fact, the perceived negativity in Tiger Woods's declaration that he is *bothered* by being described as African American overrode his stated indebtedness to legendary black golfers during his acceptance speech after the Masters Tournament win.

While Tiger Woods's identification as Cablinasian revealed the pitfalls of racial essentialism, there were even greater obstacles to face for those who viewed him as the means to abolishing all racial categories. The reality of racism quickly set in, illustrating that individuals, regardless of their desire to be viewed by others as authentic human beings, continue to be stereotyped and differentially treated. Not only are people categorized by others, but they are assumed to have basic behavioral traits that accompany that categorization. As quickly as Tiger Woods became a golfing legend at the Masters Tournament, his race became an immediate issue. Not only in the way that the media framed his achievements (paralleling them to Jackie Robinson's), but more pointedly, in the now infamous comments made by fellow golfer Fuzzy Zoeller. When asked by a CNN reporter, on camera, to comment on Woods's performance, he responded: "That little boy is driving well and he's putting well. He's doing everything it takes to win. You pat him on the back and say congratulations and enjoy it and tell him not to serve fried chicken next year, got it." After snapping his fingers, he turned to walk away from the camera and then added, "Or collard greens or whatever the hell they serve."[27]

Zoeller's comments, for which he later apologized, were quickly and overwhelmingly denounced by the media as racist. And yet, the comments highlighted both the impossibility of self-generated racial identities and the irrationality of a color-blind ideology in the context of a racially stratified society. Clearly, Zoeller understood Tiger Woods as black, not as Cablinasian. His reference to the twenty-two-year-old, six-foot-tall Woods as "that little boy" was demeaning. His invocation of "fried chicken" and "collard greens" reveals his categorization of Woods as African American. The most significant segment of the statement, however, is the final clause "or whatever the hell *they* serve," where *they* clearly signifies a cognitive distinction for Zoeller.

In Zoeller's mind, Tiger Woods is a member of a separate racial group that has well-known characteristics, behaviors, and food preferences. The true nature of his comment lies precisely in his use of "they" in designating a group of people who are different than Zoeller, to whom Woods belongs, and who (in Zoeller's mind) can be made fun of for their collard green and fried chicken–eating ways. What he did *not* say is as revealing about how he views Tiger Woods, and the racial hierarchy in the United States, as what he did say. Indeed, his failure to mention food stereotypically associated with any other elements of a Cablinasian identity simply reiterate his assumption that Tiger Woods is African American.

What is critical to understanding Zoeller's comments is that, from his perspective, he was not making a racist remark and, in fact, considers himself color-blind. He stated the following, still baffled and bewildered by the media's characterization of his comment as racist: "My biggest problem, is I don't see black and white. I never have. Because I've played sports all my life and the people I played with were my friends, it didn't make any difference to me if they were black or white. If they played well, I'd pat them on the back and get on with it. I still feel that way today."[28] This sentiment is typical of many

Americans who espouse a "color-blind" ideology because at the surface level, Zoeller claims to make no distinctions between races; yet at a deeper level, the reality of his belief in categorical group distinctions is profoundly and directly reflected in his comments.

Ideally, self-definition and/or the creation of an additional category of racial identity seemed to be realized by Tiger Woods's assertion of his Cablinasian identity. However, racial identity, as an interactionally validated self-understanding, is an ongoing process of mutual agreement between an individual and others in their social environment. This negotiation does not occur at the abstract level of census categorization, but at the spontaneous individual level of interaction. It is in the supermarkets, gas stations, and front yards of America that individuals interact with one another and where their racial identities are instantaneously determined based on a longstanding schema of mutually exclusive categorizations. While the promise of multiracialism is to either add to or do away with that schema, the social reality is that the meanings underlying those categories are deeply embedded in both the structure and culture of our society.

TIGER WOODS: AN ICON OF PARADOX

Tiger Woods as the embodiment of multiracial identity is more complex than a single individual's desire to be understood as Cablinasian. The timing of his athletic achievements and his public refusal to be categorized as African American dovetailed perfectly with the Multiracial Movement's final push for inclusion of a separate multiracial category on the 2000 census. His personal support was unnecessary because his fame and his unusual act of self-definition framed the public's perception of multiracial people as struggling against the oppression of racial categorization, while simultaneously framing civil rights leaders as monoracial category-pushing, power-seeking bullies, incapable of seeing the outdated nature of their schema. However, the reality of Tiger Woods as the symbol of millennial multiracialism is problematized in three ways. First, Woods never personally endorsed the addition of a multiracial category to the census, making the "Tiger Woods Bill" a manipulative illusion. Secondly, as a multiracial celebrity who identifies as "multiracial," he is the exception and not the rule. Indeed, most multiracial celebrities make a variety of choices about their racial identities with most choosing the singular option. Finally, Woods's status as a wealthy celebrity enabled some level of self-definition that is simply unattainable by the average citizen. Most people will never exercise a similar level of power over their own identity and instead will be categorized within historically and culturally dictated parameters. Ultimately, even Woods's self-definition was limited, because some (such as Fuzzy Zoeller) refused to accept his multiracial identity and continued to think of him as black.

At one level, Tiger Woods is an incomplete and even misleading icon for the complex reality of multiracial people's lives. We know from existing research that multiracial people choose between at least four different racial identity options. Some identify exclusively as one race, some as multiracial, some use different racial identities at different times, and still others claim to have no racial identity whatsoever. The elevation of Tiger Woods, Halle Berry, or Vin Diesel as emblematic of multiracialism denies the empirical reality that racial identity for mixed race people is *multidimensional, complex, and varied*.

At a deeper level, Tiger Woods may paradoxically be the ideal icon of multiracialism, embodying both its grand idealism and profound shortcomings. His desire to assert a border identity, and the political aftermath, provide an accurate reflection of the schizophrenic state of American race relations. His very existence enables us to see the fallacy of biologically pure, mutually exclusive, racial categorization. Yet his experiences simultaneously provide a window into how race continues to affect not only the opportunities of people of color, but the most intimate of day-to-day interactions, by shaping the way that people categorize and make assumptions about one another. In other words, Tiger Woods exists—as America currently exists—in a fractious space in which race is both socially real and biologically unreal, where the system is sagging to the breaking point under the weight of its own insanity, yet continues to influence individuals' attitudes and behavior, limiting opportunities and life chances.

NOTES

1. In the context of this chapter, the term *biracial* is used to denote individuals having one black and one nonblack parent. The term *multiracial* is used to describe those with any other combination of racial ancestries. While these narrow definitions of the terms are not ideal, there does not currently exist a widely used lexicon in the social sciences to describe various combinations of racial mixture.

2. Maria Root, "Resolving 'other' status: Identity Development of Biracial Individuals," *Women and Therapy* 9 (1990): 185–205; Maria Root, "The Multiracial Experience: Racial Borders as Significant Frontier in Race Relations," in *The Multiracial Experience: Racial Borders as the New Frontier*, ed. M. Root (Thousand Oaks, CA: Sage, 1996); Kerry Ann Rockquemore and David L. Brunsma, *Beyond Black: Biracial Identity in America* (Thousand Oaks, CA: Sage, 2001); Debbie Storrs, "Whiteness as Stigma: Essentialist Identity Work by Mixed-Race Women," *Symbolic Interaction* 23 (1999): 187–212. For a description of biracial individuals choosing a white racial identity see Rockquemore and Brunsma, *Beyond Black*.

3. Charles Staples Mangum, *The Legal Status of the Negro in the United States* (Chapel Hill: University of North Carolina Press 1940).

4. John Blassingame, *The Slave Community: Plantation Life in the Antebellum South* (New York: Oxford University Press 1972); F. James Davis, *Who Is Black? One Nation's Definition* (University Park, PA: Pennsylvania State University Press 1991).

5. Root, "Resolving 'Other' Status": 188.

6. Dorcas Bowles, "Bi-Racial Identity: Children Born to African-American and White Couples," *Clinical Social Work Journal* 24 (1993): 417–28; A. W. Boykin and F. Toms, "Black Child Socialization Framework," in *Black Children: Social Educational and Parental Environments*, ed. H. P. McAdoo and J. L. McAdoo (Beverly Hills: Sage, 1985); W. Cross, "The Negro-to-Black Conversion Experience: Toward a Psychology of Black Liberation," *Black World* 20 (1971): 13–27; Roger Herring, "Developing Biracial Ethnic Identity: A Review of the Increasing Dilemma," *Journal of Multicultural Counseling and Development* 23(1995): 29–38; R. Miller and B. Miller, "Mothering the Biracial Child: Bridging the Gaps Between African-American and White Parenting styles," *Women and Therapy* 10 (1990): 169–80; J. Morten and D. Atkinson, "Minority identity development and preference for counselor race," *Journal of Negro Education* 52 (1983): 156–61; E. Porterfield, *Black and White Marriages: An Ethnographic Study of Black-White Families* (Chicago: Nelson-Hall, 1978); W. Carlos Poston, "The Biracial Identity Development Model: A Needed Addition," *Journal of Counseling and Development* 69(1990): 152–55.

7. Lynn Norment, "Lenny Kravitz: Brother with a Different Beat" *Ebony*, June 1994, 29.

8. Lisa Jones, *Bulletproof Diva: Tales of Race, Sex, and Hair* (New York: Doubleday, 1994); James McBride, *The Color of Water: A Black Man's Tribute to His White Mother* (New York: Riverhead Books, 1996); Judy Scales-Trent, *Notes of a White Black Woman* (University Park: Pennsylvania State University Press, 1995); Gregory Williams, *Life on the Color Line: The True Story of a White Boy Who Discovered he was Black* (New York: Dutton, 1995).

9. Rainier Spencer, *Spurious Issues: Race and Multiracial Identity Politics in the United States* (Boulder: Westview, 1999).

10. Gloria Anzaldua, *Borderlands/La Frontera: The New Mestiza* (San Francisco: Spinsters/Aunt Lute Foundation, 1987); Bowles, "Biracial Identity"; Philip M. Brown, "Biracial Identity and Social Marginality," *Child and Adolescent Social Work Journal* 7(1990): 319–37; G. Reginald Daniel. "Black and White Identity in the New Millennium: Unsevering the Ties that Bind," in *The Multiracial Experience: Racial Borders as the New Frontier*, ed. M. Root (Thousand Oaks, CA: Sage, 1996); Lynda D. Field, "Piecing Together the Puzzle: Self-concept and Group Identity in Biracial Black/White Youth," in *The Multiracial Experience: Racial Borders as the New Frontier*, ed. M. Root (Thousand Oaks, CA: Sage, 1996); Christine Hall, *The Ethnic Identity of Racially Mixed People: A Study of Black-Japanese* (unpublished doctoral dissertation, University of California, Los Angeles, 1980); Herring, "Developing Biracial Ethnic Identity"; Deborah Johnson "Developmental Pathways: Toward an Ecological Theoretical Formulation of Race Identity in Black-White Biracial Children," in *Racially Mixed People in America*, ed. M. Root (Newbury Park, CA: Sage, 1992); C. Kerwin, J. G. Ponterotto, B. L. Jackson, and A. Harris, "Racial Identity in Biracial Children:

A Qualitative Investigation," *Journal of Counseling Psychology* 40(1993): 221–31; George Kich, "The Developmental Process of Asserting a Biracial, Bicultural Identity," in *Racially Mixed People in America,* ed. M. Root (Newbury Park, CA: Sage, 1992); Poston "The Biracial Identity Development Model"; Kerry Ann Rockquemore, "Between Black and White: Exploring the Biracial Experience," *Race and Society* 1(1999): 197–212; Root, "Resolving 'Other' Status"; Jewelle Taylor Gibbs, "Biracial Adolescents," in *Children of Color: Psychological Interventions with Culturally Diverse Youth,* ed. Jewelle Taylor Gibbs and Huang Larke-Nahme (New York: Jossey-Bass 1997); Barbara Tizard and Ann Phoenix, "The Identity of Mixed Parentage Adolescents," *Journal of Child Psychology and Psychiatry* 36(1995): 1399–1410.

11. Root, "The Multiracial Experience."

12. Daniel, "Black and White Identity in the New Millennium": 133.

13. Taylor Gibbs, "Biracial Adolescents."

14. Lynn Normant, "Mariah Carey: Singer Talks About Storybook Marriage, Interracial Heritage, and Sudden Fame," *Ebony,* April 1994, 56.

15. Rob Parker, "Jeter Doesn't Choose Sides," *Newsday,* July 20, 1998, 44.

16. Daniel, "Black and White Identity in the New Millennium"; Robin L. Miller, "The Human Ecology of Multiracial Identity," In *Racially Mixed People in America,* ed. M. Root (Newbury Park, CA: Sage, 1992); Rockquemore, "Between Black and White"; Rockquemore and Brunsma, *Beyond Black;* Root, "Resolving 'other' status"; Root, "The Multiracial Experience"; Cookie Stephen, "Mixed-Heritage Individuals: Ethnic Identity and Trait Characteristics," in *Racially Mixed People in America,* ed. M. Root (Newbury Park, CA: Sage, 1992); Tizard and Phoenix, "The Identity of Mixed Parentage Adolescents."

17. Daniel, "Black and White Identity in the New Millennium"; Rockquemore, "Between Black and White"; Rockquemore and Brunsma, *Beyond Black.*

18. Daniel, "Black and White Identity in the New Millennium"; Rockquemore and Brunsma, *Beyond Black.*

19. Robert Park, "Human Migration and the Marginal Man," *American Journal of Sociology* 33(1928): 881–93.

20. Daniel, "Black and White Identity in the New Millennium"; Naomi Zack, *Race and Mixed Race* (Philadelphia: Temple University Press, 1993).

21. Spencer, *Spurious Issues,* 192.

22. DeWayne Wickham, "Jordan's Assist Won't Help Bradley Score," *U.S.A Today,* February 15, 2000, D1.

23. Tim Guidera, "Decision to Take a Stance Bigger than What Serena Said," *Savannah Morning News,* April 16, 2000, C1.

24. Spencer, *Spurious Issues,* 192.

25. Jerelyn Eddins. "Counting a 'New' Type of American: The Dicey Politics of Creating a 'Multiracial' Category in the Census," *U.S. News* (1997), 23.

26. "Black America and Tiger's Dilemma," *Ebony* (1997), 28.

27. J. Mead, "Zoeller out-of-bounds with remarks about Woods," *Fayetteville Observer Times,* April 23, 1997, C1.

28. Jack O'Leary, "Fuzzy," *Senior Golfer,* April 15, 2000, 16.

SEVEN

MULTIRACE.COM:
MULTIRACIAL CYBERSPACE

ERICA CHITO CHILDS

THROUGH THE INTERNET, multiracial individuals and families who have negotiated the segregated neighborhoods and schools that mark the U.S. racial terrain can meet other multiracial family members just by clicking and typing. This cyberspace has created an "imagined" community where most of the members may never meet, though "in the minds of each lives the image of their communion."[1] Type "multiracial" in a search engine such as MSN, Google, Yahoo, or Excite and hundreds of results will be given, identifying the varied websites that exist. Surfing through these sites from individual webpages of interracial couples to larger sites such as *Interracial Voice* [2] or *The Multiracial Activist,*[3] it becomes clear that these sites are not detached and separate but rather form an intricate web, connected by links. Furthermore, these websites are an instrumental part of the Multiracial Movement because of the ability to reach large numbers of people.[4]

Unfortunately this Internet community reinforces the color line. Moreover, most multiracial websites simply reproduce the racial hierarchy by further demarcating a separate multiracial community and vilifying blackness. While families are turning to these multiracial websites for information, resources, and support, they are also discovering an underlying discourse about multiracial group boundaries and racial politics.

In this chapter, I explore the significance of these multiracial websites, the ideologies they support, the images and ideas they project about multiracialism and racial politics, and their role in the Multiracial Movement. Specifically, I will address the ways these websites attempt to construct a multiracial community and promote a particular type of multiracial identity. Unfortunately, the discourses that thread through these various websites are problematic on a number of levels, simultaneously denying the importance of race and the racial hierarchy that exists while emphasizing multiracial as a separate and distinct racial category. Despite the positive functions that these sites serve in creating a sense of community, beyond the poetry and chat rooms is a larger political agenda forwarded by those running the websites.

METHODS

Using four different search engines,[5] I conducted advanced searches on "multiracial," "Multiracial Movement," "interracial," and "biracial." My initial search yielded hundreds of matches, yet after removing web addresses for websites that no longer exist and pornographic websites, I grouped the remaining websites into six categories based on their type and size: large multipurpose cyberspace sites; webpages of multiracial organizations;[6] sites that sell products geared toward multiracial families;[7] Internet magazines;[8] interracial dating services;[9] and individual web pages of interracial couples and/or multiracial individuals that are linked to these larger websites.

Despite the relatively large number of websites, the website "hits" or the amount of visitors these sites receive varies greatly. Search engines such as MSN, along with many of the websites themselves, track how many hits a website receives, with some averaging thousands of hits per day to those sites that have had only a few hundred hits ever. Therefore, based on information from the search engines and my review of the various categories of websites, I chose to analyze a large multipurpose cyberspace site, The Multiracial Activist (TMA),[10] edited and published by James Landrith, and an Internet magazine, Interracial Voice (IV), edited and published by Charles Michael Byrd. These sites are two of the largest and most prominently featured and, more importantly, they are exclusively cyberspace communities. The webpages of multiracial organizations such as Association of Multi-Ethnic Americans (AMEA) and Project RACE also receive a large number of visitors yet they are attached to organizations that were founded and built outside of cyberspace, therefore I chose not to include them. The other categories of websites, such as the interracial dating sites, sites that sell products geared to multiracial families, and personal webpages of multiracial families, were not included primarily because they are smaller, specialized, and lack an overt political agenda. Though both TMA and IV will be the main focus, the discourses and ideologies found in these sites are characteristic of the large cyberspace multipurpose sites, and the Internet magazines devoted to multiracial issues that are increasingly found on the Web.

Since I am interested in documenting discourses and images, I primarily drew from ethnographic content analysis[11] and critical cyberculture studies.[12] In general, like the transcript of an interview, the language and images of the websites were read and reviewed for content and meaning, including the social, cultural, and political interactions that take place online.[13] Through content analysis, the meaning and significance of the discourses and images of the Multiracial Movement found on these websites were documented and analyzed as "social products in their own right, as well as what they claim to represent."[14] Drawing from the methods of ethnographic content analysis, which argues that the researcher should "interact" with the materials that they are studying in order to understand the social context,[15] I have monitored the websites for two years, and have visited them daily for a six month period from September 2001 to May 2002. Both editors/publishers, Charles Michael Byrd and James Landrith, were asked (via e-mail) general questions about the history of the sites, and encouraged to provide any comments or information they thought relevant. Also, I sat in on listserves, group e-mail lists, and chat rooms to get an "inside" sense of these sites, including the dating sites. I have spent more than fifty hours analyzing the information contained on these websites in an effort to critically discuss the meaning or significance of these websites, and, more importantly, the discourses and imagery that are commonly used. Since discourse analysis is interpretative and explanatory, there are always multiple interpretations and explanations depending on the reader (or web browser), therefore extensive quotes and examples from the websites are used to support the arguments.

THE MULTIRACIAL ACTIVIST

The Multiracial Activist represents the largest and most frequently visited multiracial site, averaging three thousand unique hits a day, as well as one of the most comprehensive and all-encompassing of information pertaining to the Multiracial Movement, covering a wide range of topics and issues related to multiracialism. According to editor/publisher James Landrith, TMA was founded in April 1997 "originally as an outlet to post links to the large amount of articles, essays, legislation"[16] that he had compiled on the Multiracial Movement, interracial families, and transracial adoption. Also, it was "founded as an outlet for individuals to contact their local, state and federal representatives in government for the purpose of lobbying for a 'multiracial' category . . . and included a downloadable lobbying kit[17] that could be used for this purpose as well as a sample letter to be customized for the legislator receiving the kit."[18]

Currently, TMA self-identifies as "an activist journal covering social and civil liberties issues of interest to individuals who perceive themselves to be 'biracial' or 'multiracial,' 'interracial' couples/families and 'transracial' adoptees."[19] The home page features the mission statement, "hot news" relevant to the multiracial community, "advocacy activity," which documents letters and views on specific political issues, and essays about relevant topics. Beyond this, there is a "library," which contains news, reader's letters, essays, a newsletter, "research papers," statistics, and a "Hall of Shame"/"Legislative Hitlist" that identifies those who oppose or have expressed oppositional views to a multiracial category or the views of TMA.

There is also a large interactive section, which allows the visitor to contact TMA, a forum/chat room, sign-up for a "multiracial.com" e-mail address, listings of research projects of people who have contacted the site looking for interviews or answers, and a link to Interracial Voice. A significant part of the website is the extensive links to other "multiracial related links," which includes categories such as transracial/intercultural adoption, multiracial celebrities/historical figures, interracial children/youth, multiracial clubs/forums, multiracial organizations, multiracial web publishers, and interracial personal websites.

As a part of the Multiracial Movement, TMA argues for the "right to self-identify in any racial category or instead choose NO racial identity and instead shed race as an identity altogether." TMA also takes a stand on various political and social issues, such as supporting transracial adoption and opposing the collection of racial data in financial transactions. One of the main goals of the website is "to educate our community about the need to be vigilant against the racism that still targets people of mixed heritage and those involved in interracial relationships." TMA identifies as racist individuals and groups of all races who are viewed as oppositional toward interracial and multiracial individuals and families.

INTERRACIAL VOICE

Interracial Voice was founded by Charles Michael Byrd in September 1995 and self-identifies as "an independent, information-oriented, networking newsjournal, serving the mixed-race/interracial community in cyberspace." It is one of the most prominent multiracial Internet publications, averaging 1,300 unique hits a day. Furthermore, the editor/publisher Charles Michael Byrd is a primary figure in the Multiracial Movement. For instance, he organized the Multiracial Solidarity March in 1996 in Washington, D.C., to petition the government for a multiracial category on the 2000 census and bring national attention to issues of multiracialism. He recently published an online book titled *Beyond Race: the Bhagavad-gita in Black and White*, which includes commentaries from his IV editorials and he regularly gives lectures on multiracial issues at universities and other venues. Details of his own activism, speeches, and writing are prominently featured on IV.

Interracial Voice mainly consists of interviews with and essays written by members of multiracial families and "notable opinion-leaders from within the mixed-race, multiracial community."[20] This site includes regularly updated sections on the census, letters to the editor, e-mail links, live-chat, news media, resources, research, other sites, poetry, and book reviews. Information is also available on the numerous interracial advocacy groups in America. Like TMA, IV advocates "universal recognition of mixed-race individuals as constituting a separate 'racial' entity and wholeheartedly supported the initiative to establish a multiracial category on the 2000 Census." Through the essays and guest editorials, which are the major part of the site, IV advocates for the right to identify as multiracial, opposes the "one-drop rule," and maintains that multiracial people are victimized by both white communities and communities of color. IV's editor Byrd also takes a political stand, describing IV as "stepping away from the traditional leftist positions that others within the 'Multiracial Movement' cling to."[21] Within IV, Byrd expands on this position in a response to a letter he received:

At the risk of someone accusing me of engaging in sweeping generalizations, "liberals" are inclined to embrace a neo-Marxist philosophy where people are kept in groups, where group rights outweigh individual liberties. Thanks to this country's "liberals" you cannot, for example, opt out of identifying "racially" on Census forms and those of other government agencies . . . though I have not yet opted for official Republican status. (I did vote for George W. in 2000, though.) I am totally fed-up with the Democrats, and I believe the only way race-based policies will eventually fade from the landscape is with more and more moderate-to-conservative justices appointed to the various courts across this land. If the Democrats regain the White House, you can rest assured this race nonsense will continue unabated, as only liberal-to-moderate jurists will be appointed. Actually, I rarely use the term "liberal," because the word really means open-minded and tolerant. What groups, however, were most opposed to any form of a multiracial classification for the 2000 Census? Answer: The "liberal" groups. That's why I prefer to use the terms "leftist" or "socialist" as they more accurately describe these groups' political ideologies.

It is evident that through IV and TMA distinct views on multiracial politics, multiracialism, and multiracial identity are expressed. In the next section, I will explore the perspectives shared by these two sites and discuss the pitfalls and contradictions.

TMA AND IV: CREATING A MULTIRACIAL COMMUNITY

TMA and IV have similar perspectives and both undoubtedly contribute to the Multiracial Movement by fostering the sense of a multiracial community through the dissemination of information, outlining of goals, providing of services and ideas, and the creation of a shared history. TMA and IV have also allowed many more people to feel connected on some level to the Multiracial Movement by providing a space for multiracial family members to correspond with each other. Yet once at these sites multiracial family members are reminded of the unique discrimination they face and the need to speak and act out against it. In other words, these sites are creating a "multiracial us" by defining the outgroup and laying parameters of community boundaries. For example, TMA argues:

> [B]iracial/multiracial people, interracial couples/families, and transracially adopted individuals have unique needs that cannot or will not be met by traditional civil rights groups who tend to brush off our community or denigrate us. We need to handle our own affairs. Join The Multiracial Activist in taking charge of our community!

DEFINING MULTIRACIAL IDENTITY AND COMMUNITY

In many respects, one of the goals of these sites is to define multiracial identity. For example, TMA outlines its strong belief and support for "the right to self-identify in any racial category or instead choose NO racial identity and instead shed race as an identity together" and the "abolition of all the divisive, unconstitutional racial categories." Similarly, IV "advocates universal recognition of mixed-race individuals as constituting a separate 'racial' entity and wholeheartedly supported the initiative to establish a multiracial category on the 2000 Census." Despite statements on TMA and IV which advocate for the abolishment of the concept of race entirely, each consciously creates and works for the interests of a multiracial community. Thus, a new multiracial category of "us" is advocated for, blacks and whites are lumped together as "they," and racial inequality is ignored.

A major part of the TMA and IV websites is the creation and promotion of communities of multiracial family members. In the IV Letters to the Editor section, individuals and families write in asking about local multiracial groups in their area, which the editor provides.[22] Within both IV and TMA, there are extensive links to multiracial support/advocacy groups (IV's "Resources" and "Other Sites"; TMA's "Links Directory"). The overwhelming majority of the social organizations that are linked and/or featured prominently on TMA and IV emphasize creating multiracial social networks and communities. For instance, *Swirl, Inc.*[23] is "an organization that aims to build a mixed race community in New York City while providing support to mixed families (including families who have trans-racially/culturally adopted), along with mixed individuals and inter-racial/cultural couples to celebrate and explore their heritages." By offering a space where multiracial individuals and families can feel included and surrounded by others who are similar, these websites (and organizations) are helping to create a multiracial community, with a distinct set of beliefs and consciousness. This social framework used by TMA/IV provides a broader reach as well as a facade for their political agenda.

Another contradiction inherent in these two sites is the numerous links to interracial dating websites, which are devoted to individuals interested in dating someone of another race specifically. Many of the dating services that TMA links to use a color-blind discourse, such as Salt and Pepper singles,[24] which describes itself as "an interracial Mecca where love is color-blind," or Interracial Singles,[25] which states one can "find a love that transcends color." Yet if race and "color" are insignificant then why is interracial dating or dating certain races being marketed on TMA and IV through their links to these dating sites?

CONSTRUCTING THE MULTIRACIAL EXPERIENCE

Beyond the resources and links they provide, TMA and IV provide references and information on multiracial family members, particularly the discrimination they face within many realms of society, which creates the sense of a "shared past or history." TMA and IV also document and archive relevant news stories, articles, essays, and commentaries about multiracial issues, multiracial individuals/families, and events. Each site contains a history of the Multiracial Movement complete with a telling of the struggles that others have encountered, legal battles fought,[26] and social problems continuing to face the multiracial community, as well as celebratory stories of multiracial family members and events. TMA even has a section titled "Multiracial Celebrities and Historical Figures," in which individuals with mixed parentage are highlighted regardless of how the individual identified or identifies. The idea of a shared experience is further marketed through links to "businesses/professional services provided by the multiracial community," including companies that sell multiracial products such as multiracial wedding cake figures, and multiracial greeting cards.

TMA and IV link individuals through their common experiences, and provide the opportunity for multiracial individuals and families to communicate, however the information, encouragement, and support is filtered through a discourse on what constitutes an "authentic" multiracial identity. The IV editor Byrd, in particular, posts letters he receives, often followed by his response, which provides an opportunity to further promote his version of multiracial identity and community as exemplified in the following excerpt from the "Letters to the Editor" section of IV:

> I am a 29-year-old (black and white) mixed female. My white father wasn't around much at all growing up. My mom raised me. Naturally, I identify more with my black culture. I was in a relationship with a man mixed with black and puertorican . . . I got into a relationship with a man who is ethnic Mon (sino-tibetan chinese etc) from Myanmar . . . My family is not happy that I am with . . . what they keep calling him . . . "foreigner" . . . This relationship has gotten to be extremely serious. We have both discovered that we really are in love with each other . . . I heard this site may really be good with resources and information on the subject. I feel sort of alone sometimes . . . If you could please help me with information . . . on people who are in the similar situation. Or how to seek them out. I have heard that on this site, there are people like me. How do I find them? I need to hear what they have experienced and . . . what it's been like for ones who have decided to have children . . .

Byrd responded,

> So much I could talk about here. A 'mixed' woman who still identifies solely as 'black' who lets others influence her because she is involved with a 'foreigner.' *SIGH!* He's a human, and so are you, and I say to hell with racial/ethnic/cultural identity politics . . .

Despite the woman's request for support, the editorial response is critical. Even though she is biracial and involved interracially, her views clash with that of Byrd. Through his response, Byrd is defining the boundaries of acceptable multiracialness. In other words, multiracial authenticity and community boundaries are at stake. While providing a space where multiracial family members come together, the only way to be included within these community boundaries is to subscribe to the same discourses and beliefs about multiracialism and race as those espoused by IV, TMA, and their followers. The narrowness of their definition of multiracial can be very alienating, especially for those multiracial family members who live in segregated communities where they already feel like outsiders. Byrd and Landrith act as gatekeepers who speak for all multiracial people, and carefully patrol the multiracial border, keeping out or shunning all individuals and groups who do not agree with their ideas of authentic multiracialism.

WHO SPEAKS FOR THE MULTIRACIAL COMMUNITY?

This is especially problematic since these websites are often used as representative of the entire multiracial population. For example, on both TMA and IV there are sections where individuals conducting research or seeking information can post requests. A large number of high school students, undergraduate students, Ph.D. students, and even professors use these research posts to locate individuals or families to interview for their studies on interracial marriage, biracial identity, and transracial adoption. As Rockquemore and Brunsma argue, asking those who belong to a multiracial organization (or frequent multiracial websites) about their identity and using it to represent all multiracial people can be misleading because those who don't join a group or participate in an organization may think and define themselves much differently.[27] The news and media also turn to these websites for assistance when covering multiracial issues. When census hearings were held to determine whether a multiracial category should be added to the 2000 census, a large number of individuals selected to speak to the committee were drawn from members of these multiracial organizations and circles.[28] Still, on a regular basis news reporters contact groups often through these sites for stories they are writing on multiracial issues. For example TMA's publisher James Landrith has been interviewed for and mentioned on national and local television news and media outlets on numerous occasions, as he states in his bio on TMA. Also, IV's Byrd is often asked to speak on multiracial issues such as the "mixed-race perspective," on college campuses.

Therefore, despite the fact that many multiracial family members may not agree with the views espoused on TMA and IV, these websites and their spokespersons are often sought to speak on *the* multiracial perspective. Many of the essays and commentaries that are featured on TMA and IV are presented as scholarly works, yet are highly opinionated and not necessarily based in research. For example, on IV a number of the featured articles are reviews of academic books dealing with multiracial issues, yet the critiques offered are based on whether or not the author agrees with the views espoused on the websites, not the merit of the study. This is especially problematic if researchers and reporters, students and families are turning to these sites for the "facts" or further information about multiracial issues.

Moreover, Byrd and Landrith identify themselves as official spokespersons for the multiracial community. For example, in a 1999 letter written by Byrd and Landrith to the board of governors of the Federal Reserve System in response to the Equal Credit Opportunity Act, which dealt with the collection of racial information in financial transactions, they wrote:

> The constituencies we represent consist of people who already have
> a heightened awareness of the concept of race and how they are

viewed by society in general. We would personally be loath to hon-estly answer any question regarding race on any form related to financial services. The only color that should matter with regard to financial transactions is green. As our constituencies have rebelled against Census classifications, so shall it against these types of invasive classification questions . . . we, as representatives of constituencies this proposal is designed to protect, urge you not to implement it.

They clearly identify themselves as speaking for the multiracial community, and advocate their brand of racial politics and ideology in the name of their multiracial "constituency." Yet the multiracial community that TMA and IV have helped create is limited; remarkably absent are any coalitions with groups or organizations (or links to websites) devoted to racial justice issues especially those groups or organizations that hold divergent views.

WHERE IS THE "RACE" IN MULTIRACIAL?

Though there is an acknowledgment of websites that more generally address issues of race, the majority of the content on TMA and IV websites focuses on multiracial couples and families, and issues that directly effect multiracial families. For example, there are various links to what TMA calls "Race Related Links" (which is separate form "Multiracial Related Links"), which are categorized as Aboriginal/Native People; Afrocentric/African American Organizations and Websites; Asian/Asian American Organizations and Websites; Hispanic/Latino Organizations and Websites; and multiculturalism and ethnicity.[29] Still, the broader issues of racism, discrimination, and social justice are shadowed behind discussions of the ways that multiracial indi-viduals and families experience racism and discrimination from monoracial communities. Also, only those websites that advocate a similar view on multiracial issues are promoted positively; groups such as the NAACP are mentioned only as organizations that wrongly oppose multiracial identity and the Multiracial Movement.

Relatedly, the essays and articles on IV and TMA clearly identify the enemy or outgroup as traditional racial and ethnic communities, further demarcating boundaries and promoting particular views on multiracialism. For example, on IV, James Landrith has an article entitled, "Daddy's House, or Knowing who Your True Friends Really Are." He discusses the issue of a multiracial category, and uses the essay to criticize the NAACP, the National Council of La Raza, and "white Members of Congress" for their opposition to a multiracial category. He ends with a message for multiracial individuals:

> You are of age. Declare your racial independence and move out of Daddy's house. He's only keeping you around for the tax deduction

anyway. Sure, he might get angry, he'll certainly call you names, he already has, but in the end you'll be able to call yourself by your own name—multiracial.

This essay clearly defines multiracial identity and how one must distance oneself from other racial communities and other multiracial family members who don't follow the same definition.[30] Some multiracial family members even write in to the website to question this lack of affiliation with larger racial communities. For example, in this letter to the editor on IV one woman writes,

> As a super-duper mixed-race woman who has been forced to identify as "Black" by a white power establishment that persecutes difference, I question the ways in which you attack Black people on your web site. You do not attack whites, who created the system of racism. We "colored" folks are just doing the best we can to live under this oppressive system—even as we live with and love our white relatives. Some of your points are well-taken, but you come off as a person of color who has internalized white racism and believes that Black people are the folks keeping you down.

Yet even critical responses such as this are used to further espouse the discourse on authentic multiracial identity, as evidenced in the letter written in response by A. D. Powell, a frequent contributor to IV and vocal figure in the Multiracial Movement:

> Here's another "one-dropper." Sorry, kid. I despise the term "people of color" and I am certainly not one. Why not just go to "Aryan" and "non-Aryan"? As a system of "racial" classification, it's just as good as the one you're using. As for these mythological all-powerful "white" people (Multiracial whites have been "white" for a long time, and we can tell you there are no "whites" as Negroes use the word) and helpless slave "colored" (also a mythological people), let's put it this way: If you have to break out of a prison, do you spend your time cursing the long dead architects who designed it, or do you get past the guards who are dedicated to keeping you in? The "guards" are all black-identified. This was proved beyond a shadow of a doubt when "black" organizations led the fight to stop the multiracial census option, and still lead the fight to keep hypodescent alive along with its twin myth of white racial "purity."[31]

This response embodies the central discourses found on the websites. The question of what constitutes multiracial identity is clearly answered, with any multiracial individual who does not identify multiracially labeled derisively a "one-dropper." TMA's editor and publisher, Landrith, states that one of TMA's functions is "to work to help those stuck in a 'one-drop' or 'racialist' mindset to understand that 'racial' lines can be blurred" and to address how "the population at large is in denial about how mixed the average so-called 'white,' 'black' or American Indian really is in this country."[32] As Landrith states, he "looks forward to the day that we as a people can shed 'racial' identities in favor of individual identities."[33] Even more problematic is the emphasis on the ways that the black community hinders multiracials, and the critical views of the black community, as Powell argues in her prison metaphor that imagines black communities as more responsible for the discrimination against multiracials and denial of multiracial rights. Whites are described as "long dead architects" implying that whites may have created a racist system but they no longer enforce it. These types of statements reflect a denial of the ways that race impacts the lives of members of historically excluded racial groups such as African Americans. Remarkably absent is any discussion of institutional racial inequalities that exist against all people of color, and an acknowledgment that any opposition is rooted in the systemic racism that permeates America.

IDENTIFYING THE ENEMY

Therefore, despite fostering a sense of community and place of acceptance for multiracial individuals and families, a sense of "us versus them" is created, pitting the multiracial community against the "enemy," who is readily identified as people of color who identify with traditional racial and ethnic communities. TMA has an entire section entitled "Hall of Shame" which criticizes those individuals or groups who have publicly opposed interracial relationships or biracial/multiracial identity in any way. For example, TMA states that it opposes blind allegiance to traditional civil rights groups who've abandoned our community in the pursuit of more political power and resources. These same groups are the ones battering self-identifying multiracials as "running from their blackness" and calling them "Uncle Tom" as well as belittling and demeaning interracial marriages. This type of behavior is clearly not to be supported or excused.

Within TMA's list of individuals and groups who have expressed "repugnant view(s) of multiracial identity/interracial relationships through their words and deeds," they specifically and repeatedly argue that white and black opposition is the same. The power and privilege of whites inherent in the racial hierarchy of American society is rarely discussed. As TMA states,

> The Multiracial Activist believes in fighting hatred and bigotry regardless of the color of the bigot. The racism of Kweisi Mfume,

Maxine Waters, Louis Farrakhan, Al Sharpton and Diane Watson is no less dangerous than the racism of Matt Hale and Don Black.

Another example is the criticism of the African American singer Jill Scott on TMA where she is cited for her song, "Do You Remember," which suggests that African Americans who become involved interracially may be doing it for the wrong reasons. In response TMA states:

> We are led to believe that Ms. Scott is not against "interracial" marriages/relationships, but is instead, only questioning the intent of some involved. Do not be deceived, this is the same sorry garbage that is spouted by "white" racialists. If it is not acceptable coming out of the mouth of a "white" person, why is it okay for Ms. Scott to espouse it? Ms. Scott should be ashamed and so should (people) who make excuses for her bigotry.

Any questioning or opposition to interracial relationships and/or multiracial identity is criticized. This represents a denial of the politicized nature of multiracial identity and interracial relationships, a lack of awareness and understanding of why others may have opposition, and a refusal to acknowledge that white and black opposition are not the same.

Though TMA and IV make the argument that racial categories are divisive, throughout the websites, the essays written are divisive and critical of other groups (often racially identified) whose beliefs are in opposition to what are viewed as the best interests of the multiracial community. TMA describes black organizations' opposition to a multiracial category as "assisting in their lust for power and privilege at the expense and safety of biracial/multiracial individuals and interracial couples/families." Similarly, IV argues:

> Contemporary advocacy of a mixed-race identifier is the largest and most meaningful assault on the mythical concept of white racial purity/supremacy—an idea lustfully embraced, unfortunately by political leaders "of color" generally and by black "leaders" specifically—to come down the pike in many moons. Consequently, the group most able to help this society bridge the gap between the race-obsessed present and an ideal future of racelessness is the mixed-race contingent.

Therefore, beyond criticizing other racial groups there is also a privileging of those who are multiracial or in an interracial family. According to IV's Byrd in the introduction to his online book *Beyond Race: The Bhagavadgita in Black and White*, "individuals of mixed racial backgrounds quickly begin searching for a higher spiritual truth, something that allows them to make sense of the madness behind lumping human beings into separate and distinct 'racial' groupings."[34] The rhetoric espoused by IV and TMA, particularly, tends to assume that somehow multiracial individuals and families are the only ones capable of understanding and correctly dealing with race. As Landrith states, "for those who've progressed and reached that level, The Abolitionist Examiner exists to help TMA move these individuals onto the understanding that false belief in 'race' as an entity is paramount to the formation of 'racist' concepts and belief systems." So any groups that take a different view of multiracial identity or race, such as black civil rights organizations, are labeled racist. Great importance is placed on a recognized multiracial category and the idea that multiracial people share certain experiences, yet the idea that other racial groups may have valid reasons for their policies and beliefs is dismissed.

In a speech given at the Multiracial Solidarity March (and archived on IV), IV's Byrd stated:

> [A]nd the question we as multiracial Americans have to ask is where are we supposed to position ourselves: amongst segregationist whites or amongst separatist blacks?. . . . No principled multiracial can endorse separate but equal. How can we? We are the living, breathing antithesis of separatist and racist dogma. We cannot be separated!

Byrd defines multiracial identity, and clearly states what multiracial is not. Therefore, while TMA and IV support the view that racial categories should be abolished and should not play a role in redressing racial injustices, there is no problem with constructing multiracial individuals and families as separate and different from groups and communities that identify "monoracially," thereby promoting the creation and maintenance of a multiracial community. By emphasizing particular ideologies and beliefs, TMA and IV consciously *do race, and more specifically multiracialism* in certain ways. On these sites the message is clear that individuals should be free to self-identify as long as the identity they choose is multiracial. Within the numerous essays and articles featured on TMA and IV, certain discourses of the multiracial movement are marketed.

MARKETING A PARTICULAR BRAND OF MULTIRACIALISM

Beyond the actual services, information, and products provided, a significant piece of these websites is devoted to promoting the agendas of the multiracial movement (and its leaders). Specifically, the sites petition government officials about laws that are viewed as disadvantageous to multiracials, call for boycotts of public figures who have oppositional views to interracial couples, or who do not identify as multiracial, and encourage joining multiracial organizations or buying multiracial products, especially in the case of Byrd's self-promotion of his on-line book and TMA's on-line store.

It becomes a question of who can belong, and as much as there is an argument made that other "monoracial" groups don't accept them, these multiracial websites can be seen as engaging in their own form of exclusion, especially in defining what is multiracial identity (for example, to have one black parent and one white parent and claim a black identity is viewed negatively) and who has the ability to transcend race (in many ways, it seems only multiracials). Within the discourses that are commonly espoused on these websites, rather than simply celebrating diversity, it is a particular type of diversity that is privileged. Multiracial is misleading because rather than bringing individuals of different races together, the emphasis is on bringing *multiracial* people together, creating a safe and accepting atmosphere for multiracial family members.

While advocating a color-blind ideology, these sites place a distinct emphasis on a multiracial community and the right to claim a multiracial identity. TMA describes racial categories as "breeding" racism rather than fighting it. Yet if race and racial categories don't matter and shouldn't matter, then why the importance placed on a "multiracial" category? Moreover, if race is unimportant, then why is so much emphasis placed on fostering a "multiracial" community, and even bringing together multiracial families, or helping people date interracially? In short, underlying ideologies paint a picture in which color and race are both everything and nothing. The discourses used on these websites cling to both essentialist views of race and denying race altogether, even the ways race (as a social construction) shapes everyday experiences.

CONCLUSION

Overall, these sites provide valuable services and support, especially for multiracial individuals and families who may be struggling with a lack of acceptance and problems in the larger society. The information databases that they have compiled, as well as the extensive links between the various multiracial organizations, events, and groups is useful and provides documentation of issues involving or affecting the multiracial community. Yet beyond these functions, the websites reproduce certain racial ideologies that do more to separate us by race than to bring us all together.

While playing into the desires of multiracial families to escape discrimination and to live in a society that is "blind" to their racial differences, these attempts to form a multiracial community do not challenge racism, but rather allow those who are in it to escape from the racism of the larger society. Also, simply seeking out other multiracial individuals and families only reinforces the idea that those of the same race, or in this case "multirace," form distinct groups. These websites are primarily, if not exclusively geared toward multiracial family members. Rather than promoting inclusion of all people, it is a project of exclusion that targets only members of multiracial families who identify multiracially. There is virtually no alignment with other racial communities. They are ignoring the racial hierarchy, and ignoring the white power structure, by claiming that blacks are racist and arguing that there is no difference between white and black opposition to a multiracial category. By pointing fingers at black civil rights organizations and publicly shaming these groups for their "mistreatment" of multiracial individuals and families, it gives support to the argument that all people are racist and undermines the argument against white supremacy. There is no acknowledgment of the historical circumstances that have created opposition within black communities and the reasons why some black groups oppose multiracial identity. The emphasis is placed on how multiracial individuals and families are discriminated against and not allowed to identify as they choose, yet there is no acknowledgment of how multiracial individuals and families may occupy a more privileged position due to color stratification and the white privilege of family members. Instead, a generic color-blind ideology is given.

Most importantly, this distancing from black and other racial groups, and in essence other racial identities, serves to solidify the collective identity of the multiracial movement by enforcing boundaries between black (or any other racial group) and multiracial. To sustain a multiracial movement, a collective consciousness about what it means to be multiracial and share experiences, opportunities, and problems is essential. The fight for a multiracial category, and the creation of an "us versus them" dichotomy ("them" being all racial groups that do not support a multiracial category), is part of the process of negotiation to ensure representation for multiracial individuals and families. Unfortunately, rather than challenge the color line there is an attempt to be formally recognized as existing on it, or bypassing it altogether.

NOTES

1. Benedict Anderson, *Imagined Communities: Reflections on the Origin and Spread of Nationalism* (New York: Verso, 1991).
2. Interracial Voice is found at www.interracial voice.com.
3. The Multiracial Activist is found at www.multiracial.com.
4. David Gauntlett, *Web.Studies: Rewiring media studies for the digital age* (London: Arnold, 2000).
5. Yahoo, MSN, Excite, and Google were used.
6. Sites for organizations such as Association of Multi-Ethnic Americans, Interracial Family Circle, and Project Race.

7. Sites such as iMeltingPot.com and Blindheart.com.

8. Sites include Interracial Voice, Mavin, and the New People Interracial Magazine.

9. These sites are either general interracial dating sites such as www.interracialsingles.com, interraciallink.com, mixedfeelings.com or directed at certain racial combinations such as whitewomenblackmen.com.

10. According to the MSN rating of direct hits to multiracial websites, *The Multiracial Activist* is the most frequently visited "multiracial" website.

11. David L. Altheide, *Qualitative Media Analysis*, Qualitative Research Methods Series 38 (Thousand Oaks, CA: Sage, 1996).

12. David Silver, "Looking Backwards, Looking Forwards: CyberCulture Studies 1990–2000," *Web.Studies: Rewiring media studies for the digital age*, ed. D. Gauntlett, 19–30 (London: Arnold, 2000).

13. Ibid.

14. Altheide, 1996.

15. Ibid.

16. Landrith, personal e-mail correspondence 2002.

17. This lobbying kit was based on the Project RACE model for a "multiracial" category. See Project Race website at www.projectrace.com.

18. Landrith, personal e-mail correspondence 2002.

19. All quotes, unless otherwise identified, are taken directly from the website.

20. IV website.

21. Byrd personal email correspondence 2002.

22. For a recent example see IV's Letters to Editor, May 14, 2002.

23. Swirl Inc. can be found at www.swirlinc.com.

24. www.saltandpeppersingles.com.

25. www.interracialsingles.com.

26. According to James Landrith, the editor and publisher of TMA, they are also looking to "establish a referral relationship with a legal aid society for those individuals frequently visiting the site looking for legal assistance" (Landrith, personal e-mail 2002).

27. Kerry Rockquemore and David Brunsma, *Beyond Black: Biracial Identity in America* (Thousand Oaks, CA: Sage, 2002).

28. Rockquemore and Brunsma, *Beyond Black*.

29. TMA includes certain sites in their featured Website Program, and gives them a more prominent display, if that website puts a link to TMA on their website.

30. Also the language used implies a patriarchal system, which along with the racial ideologies only serves to reproduce a white patriarchal society. There is virtually no discussion of gay/lesbian issues within these two websites and the discourses on the websites are overwhelmingly heterosexist, which is an avenue for future research.

31. The use of "kid" implies the writer is less experienced, immature, and in need of Powell's perspective.

32. Landrith, personal e-mail 2002.

33. Landrith, personal e-mail 2002.

34. Byrd's online book *Beyond Race: The Bhagavad-gita in Black and White* can be found at http://www1.xlibris.com/bookstore/bookdisplay.asp bookid=14201.

EIGHT

"I PREFER TO SPEAK OF CULTURE":
WHITE MOTHERS OF MULTIRACIAL CHILDREN

TERRI A. KARIS

IN THIS CHAPTER, I look at the racial discourse of white mothers of multi-racial children and the social justice implications of their practices. In focusing on how white women think about, talk about, and construct race within multiracial families, I am following Hartigan's lead: "In order to think differently about race we need to pay attention to the local settings in which racial identities are actually articulated, reproduced, and contested, resisting the urge to draw abstract conclusions about whiteness and blackness."[1] Hartigan draws attention to the family as "perhaps the most critical site for the generation and reproduction of racial formations" and as the location "that generates a great degree of variation in how racial categories gain and lose their significance."[2] He notes that the meanings given to race depend in large part on whether individual families reproduce heterogeneous or homogeneous racial categories, making multiracial families a rich site in which to explore how race is constructed, and how racial categories are inhabited and transformed.

My chapter draws on a qualitative research study of seventeen white middle-class women who either are, or previously had been, in interracial relationships with black men, and who are the mothers of biracial children. The ways in which these women constructed race varied widely. Their stories reveal not only the heterogeneity within the category of white women in multiracial families, but also discontinuities within individual women's accounts. In their attempts to make sense of the differences and similarities that mattered in their lives, women's racial constructions were fluid and unstable, shifting in response to different situations and relationships.

While some of these women embraced their racial border crossing as a political opportunity to challenge racism and normative whiteness, they were not the norm among women in my study. More commonly, women claimed that there was nothing political about their interracial partnerships or their family lives, or offered complex and sometimes contradictory accounts in which they acknowledged awareness of the political implications of their own seemingly individual choices, yet backed away from linking that awareness to political commitments. I am particularly interested in exploring these contradictory accounts, as a means of understanding the obstacles that reduce the likelihood that women will translate knowledge into action.

The very existence of multiracial families challenges practices of white racial bonding that prescribe white racial solidarity and loyalty, yet this social location may also impede women's political action. Despite increased racial awareness, white women draw on the normative white practices of individualism and racial innocence, in part as a means of dissociating themselves and their family relationships from pathologizing stereotypes. Unfortunately, women's efforts to distance from whiteness lead to color-blind approaches to race, and make it less likely that they will translate their personal experiences into political commitments and strategies that challenge racism.

WHITE WOMEN IN MULTIRACIAL FAMILIES

The social location of white women in multiracial families mediates the ways that white women construct race in general, and whiteness in particular. Frankenberg (1993) defines whiteness as having at least three dimensions: the structural advantage and privilege of whites; the "standpoint" of whiteness as a location from which to view oneself and others; and a set of taken for granted cultural practices, a white way of life that might often be considered "normal" or "American."[3] Whites are positioned to take their racialness for granted because whiteness is transparent as the universal norm, and issues of race often are not considered relevant to their day-to-day lives. Being in a racially mixed family means that whiteness loses some of its taken for granted status and privilege, and that white women face situations in which they no longer have the option to ignore race. For instance, when in public, a woman may be treated differently depending on whether she is alone or with her family.[4] Experiencing this difference heightens a woman's awareness of previously unnoticed racial privilege.

At the same time, because of their relationships with black men, white women may be viewed by other whites as "less than white." While these women still have white skin, the privilege and status of whiteness are mediated by racialized gender prescriptions. Moon argues that whiteness, like other identities, is developed through a "complex enculturative process that begins in the family/home," and leads to the production of "good *white* girls" who embody the respectability of white womanhood.[5] Because interracial sexual relationships are viewed as a threat to white identity[6] and to the property interests of white men,[7] a white woman's privilege is contingent on her acceptance of the expectation that she maintain her racial chastity by partnering only with white men.[8] Winddance Twine calls attention to "the contingent nature of racial privilege for white heterosexual women who violate codes of respectability that require them to establish familial and caretaking alliances solely with white men."[9]

Some have conceptualized white women in multiracial relationships as "outsiders within":[10] while they still have white skin and its accompanying privileges, being in intimate family relationships with people of color potentially subjects them to discrimination, prejudice, and racism that "rebound" onto them,[11] something not experienced by white women in monoracial white families. As an "insider" within dominant white culture, the same system that privileges a white woman excludes her nonwhite partner and children as outsiders. Because her experience of race and racism is rooted in her relational connections, as well as in the skin color she embodies, she is partially exempt from the oppression faced by those she loves. At the same time, because she sees how racism hurts the people she loves, racism becomes consciously relevant in her life.

The ambiguous racial position of being an outsider-within can lead to profound changes in a woman's public and private identities, and in her negotiation of the public realm.[12] White women may grapple with the tension between their whiteness becoming increasingly salient, as they are consistently characterized as a "white woman with a black man," and a growing sense of feeling different from many other whites.[13] Many white women in multiracial families have specific language for naming racial identity shifts that reflect their dual positioning of being a racial insider and an outsider-within. Women name racial identity shifts using metaphors such as masquerading as white in public,[14] being white but not quite,[15] being white with a black soul, and being a spy.[16] The terms that women use reflect their experience of the discrepancy between their white physical characteristics and their daily racial interactions, and lend support to Luke's assertion that white women in multiracial families live double lives, resulting in the "composite dual position of insider-outsider, visible-invisible, and doubly 'other.' "[17]

Based on these experiences, one might conclude that white women in multiracial families are more likely than others to move beyond essentialist and color-blind racial paradigms[18] to a highly developed racial awareness that would support antiracist political action. When women talk about their lives, however, their stories reveal the coexistence of increasing awareness of the racial privilege they had previously taken for granted, a movement away from an "epistemology of ignorance"[19] regarding the racial realities experienced by their nonwhite family members, and unconscious normative white racial practices. It is common for women's narratives to reflect a contradictory blend of racial paradigms, moving from sophisticated awareness of racial privilege to drawing on simplistic racial stereotypes.

Although women's accounts regularly demonstrate that the structural advantage and privilege of whiteness have become less transparent, they continue to be under the influence of taken-for-granted practices of whiteness that make antiracist political commitments less likely. In this chapter I will look at two interrelated aspects of normative whiteness that shape women's racial constructions: the ideology of individualism, with its accompanying assumption that nonwhites are members of racial groups, while whites are simply individuals; and whiteness as innocence. The ways that white mothers talk with their multiracial children about race illustrate how normative whiteness may inform not only women's practice of mothering, but also their disinclination to take political action.

INDIVIDUALISM AND INNOCENCE

One way that white women dissociate themselves and their relationships from racial realities is by drawing on the belief that their relationships started from a clean slate, based on being "just individuals," one human to another, outside of a historical and social context. Women who are interracially partnered often emphasize that they did not marry "a black man," but simply "the person I loved."[20] They highlight their ordinariness as a couple,[21] a practice that makes sense given reductionist stereotypes that pathologize interracial relationships by viewing them as racially and sexually deviant.

When white women view themselves and their relationships through the lens of individualism, however, it allows them to maintain the innocence of normative whiteness, and to sidestep their own experience of being members of a racial group. For many white women, it is not apparent that "[w]e all may be individuals, but none of us are just individuals."[22] Even as they display a deepening awareness of how racial oppression impacts their nonwhite family members, white women do not necessarily see the ways in which systems of oppression structure their own ways of knowing and being in the world.

The approach that some white mothers take regarding the subject of black history offers one example. Many white mothers of multiracial children enthusiastically support their children in learning black history. Frequently, white mothers report taking a more active role than their children's black fathers in activities such as getting black history books from the library and taking their children to Afrocentric cultural events. White mothers also may express their desire to learn about black history, *for the benefit of their children*, believing that their children need them to have this knowledge. What white mothers often don't see is that this knowledge is essential for them, too, if they want to have a more accurate view of the world in which they live. In the following example, Claire[23] includes black history as one of the things she "should" know more about:

> I should know what Kwanzaa is. And I should be able to celebrate it. I don't even think I can say the word. I should know how to do [my daughter's] hair so that it looks nice for her, and doesn't break or fall out. I should know more cultural stuff and history stuff. And I don't. And I maybe never will. . . . I think I should know it because my kids will have questions. I think I should know it because I suspect other folks think I should know it. And because . . . I want to be able to talk about it with [my kids] so they can be proud of it.

When women are unaware of how normative whiteness has structured their ways of knowing, black history, or racial knowledge in general, is considered optional for whites, and primarily relevant for those who are nonwhite. This may explain why a number of white mothers report feeling guilty because, despite their stated desire, actually learning black history remains an obligatory "should" that they haven't followed through on.[24]

DISTANCING FROM WHITENESS

In order to distance themselves from association with the white racial category, white mothers use a number of strategies, two of which will be highlighted in this chapter: retreating from race, and locating race outside of the family in the public domain. Retreating from race includes three related approaches: not directly discussing whiteness, talking in terms of culture and ethnicity rather than race, and promoting color-blind thinking that minimizes the significance of racial differences. By defining differences as cultural or ethnic, and by locating race in the public sphere, white women are able to detach from pathologizing racial stereotypes, but in the process they also distance themselves from knowledge about normative whiteness.

Retreating from Race

Many of the white women in my study prefer to describe their families as "multicultural" rather than "multiracial," and to define themselves using the language of culture and ethnicity, rather than racial terms. While being in a multiracial family can lead to increased opportunities for a more sophisticated racial understanding, this social location may also, in some ways, inhibit white women's awareness of their own whiteness. In the following two examples, white mothers retreat from race by sidestepping discussion of whiteness, and instead focus on culture and ethnic heritage.

> Terri: Well I'm curious, what have you said to your girls about being white?

> Mary: At one point (my daughter) said something like, "The only thing I know about Polish is Polish sausage." So, okay, I think we need to talk about this. I mean I've done some family history, and talked to them some about my parents. We're connected with my family a lot too. . . . So I think what I've done is more sort of that genealogy and family history. But not a lot.

> Annie: I know that I am white, and that someone from the outside would classify me as European American. I doubt that I would classify myself that way. I would more want to be identified by my whole family and seen in that context, rather than as European American. I wouldn't be exactly proud to be only European American . . . . I would say I'm a woman in a multiracial family, or a multicultural family, because I don't really believe in race . . . the thing that we have in common is the humanity and not the color.

One interpretation of Mary's complete evasion of any reference to whiteness is that it is a form of what Moon calls "hyperpoliteness," a way of using language that is ahistorical, decontextualized, and attentive to an etiquette that privileges form over content.[25] From this perspective, just to notice race would verge on impoliteness. If she does not "see" race, Mary's own racial innocence is maintained, and her position as a white person is obscured.

Mary's reluctance to speak in terms of race reflects the historical norm of whiteness as the invisible standard against which all groups are judged. Her account illustrates that, despite increasing racial awareness, she does not consider whiteness to be an important aspect of her identity.

At the same time, white women's preference for the color-blind language of culture and ethnicity may stem, in part, from their experience that race functions differently within the family sphere than at the public or group level. "A politicized view of race as a contest between two absolute collectives, one dominant and the other subordinate,"[26] does not fit how women experience their family relationships, and thus, they tend to distance themselves from racial discourse.

In Annie's case, identifying as "a woman in a multicultural family" might be understood as a move away from narrow essentialist racial categories that cannot accommodate her ambiguous racial position as an outsider-within, or the increased racial knowing that results from that position. By defining herself as a woman in a multicultural family, Annie emphasizes commonality and unity among family members, rather than her separateness as the only family member who is white. At the same time, however, Annie's acknowledgment that she "wouldn't be exactly proud to be only European American" might be viewed as a means of distancing from the privileges of whiteness, or distancing from being seen as racist. Separating from racial discourse may result in less awareness of normative whiteness, and a reduced chance that white women will move beyond racial innocence toward racial accountability.

One way to understand Annie's preference to "be identified by my whole family" is that it is a means of distancing from objectifying stereotypes about interracial relationships that emphasize sexual deviancy, and irreconcilable racial differences. While there is a stigma attached to being the white mother of multiracial children, the stigma is largely a reflection of the negativity associated with images of white women and black men. Claiming an identity that is connected to one's family, or to one's role as a mother, may help to highlight, and to reinstate, a white woman's respectability.

Both women's accounts reflect confusion about the concepts of race, ethnicity, and culture. These terms are defined in numerous, sometimes overlapping ways, and in everyday discourse, they are often used interchangeably. Annie's preference to define her family in terms of culture rather than race illustrates a common error in racial thinking. By arguing that she doesn't "really believe in race," Annie is dismissing race as an illusion that doesn't have social reality. Moreover, her preference for culture misses the point that it too is a social construction, and that cultures, like races, are structured by relations of power.

Based on my research, when white women, such as Annie, use the word *culture*, they seem to draw on a definition "whereby culture is taken to mean values, beliefs, knowledge, and customs that exist in a timeless and unchangeable vacuum outside of . . . racism."[27] This understanding of culture obscures power relations, and implies that it is possible to learn the correct cultural rules, and to develop cultural sensitivity, so that "with a little practice and the right information, we can all be innocent subjects, standing outside hierarchical social relations."[28] Sensitivity to cultural differences, while useful, does not necessarily lead to an understanding of the workings of normative whiteness. Individualistic thinking, which locates difference in persons rather than in social relations, allows white women to maintain racial innocence, and to develop awareness about how race impacts their nonwhite family members, without seeing how their own ways of being in the world are shaped by race.

Mary's halfhearted attempts to connect with her ethnic heritage may be an example of what Bailey calls "unreflective detours to white ethnicity,"[29] one strategy that whites use to avoid addressing white privilege. Mary's relationship to her ethnic identity seems to reflect a tentative, symbolic attachment rather than one that is characterized by "commitment" and "salience."[30] Ethnicity, like race and culture, is a fluid, unstable category,[31] and Mary's ethnic identity provides an example of the common experience among "white ethnics, [that] ethnicity is not something that influences their lives unless they *want* it to."[32]

Because ethnicity is viewed as a primarily positive attribute that is voluntary, a focus on ethnicity may obscure the fact that whiteness is not really about ethnicity, but is about race and racial privilege. Haney Lopez argues that although a European American ethnic identity seems to provide a white identity that is independent from the oppositional construction of whiteness and nonwhiteness, it is, in fact, still an identity constituted in hierarchical opposition to identities imposed on racial minorities.[33]

Although blackness has both racial and cultural aspects, whites and blacks are not simply parallel cultural groups. The development of whiteness has been founded on access to privilege and property, relative to those who were defined as nonwhite, rather than on common white cultural experiences.[34] White mothers, such as Mary and Annie, may have an investment in accentuating the common ground and equity in their relationships with black partners, leading them to emphasize ethnicity and avoid discussion of how race functions in their day-to-day lives. While family members might safely discuss race in political and historical terms, they are likely to highlight cultural aspects of blackness, such as food or music, because there are comparable cultural traditions in the white parent's heritage.

One approach used by multiracial families to communicate about race is to "affirm the multiethnic experience."[35] While some families prepare their multiracial children for interactions in society by teaching them to identify as black, parents who use the multiethnic approach believe that children "should be raised with the identity of the totality of both birth parents' heritages."[36] Even though this approach includes a commitment to promote black history and social consciousness, it also includes a belief that endorsing blackness should not be "at the expense of denying the presence of other parts of one's cultural heritage."[37] In an attempt to maintain equitable acknowledgment of each parent's cultural heritage, white mothers may completely sidestep talking about whiteness, and instead emphasize their own ethnicity. When white mothers talk in terms of ethnicity or culture rather than race, they are then not in a position to help teach their children about racial realities or themselves. In Veronica's family, as in many multiracial families, this task was then left to the children's black parent.

And the fact that they are black and that's what they're going to be seen in society as—Demetrius [the children's father], especially for my boys, he knows something on a much deeper level than I'll ever know, that he needs to teach them. And I had to learn how to get out of the way. I really did. I had to learn how to get out of the way and let something occur that I know they're going to deal with and that they need to know how to deal with and that they need to know how to stand up to in the future. Because they're going to be part of that black society and they need to know that. And as a white Caucasian woman, I don't have any of those tools to teach them that.

Veronica's account illustrates how unexamined normative whiteness leads to disengagement from the topics of race and racism, with Veronica, in effect, saying that these subjects have little to do with her. Her narrative provides an example of "Whitespeak" a "racialized form of euphemistic language in which what is not said . . . is often far more revealing than what is said."[38] Although Veronica seems to be talking about race or racism (it's not clear which), she never specifically names them. They are implied as something her children "need to know how to deal with" and "know how to stand up to." This passivity maintains Veronica's racial innocence, and makes it less likely that she will take responsibility for directly addressing racial issues.

Another reflection of Veronica's lack of awareness of normative whiteness is her comment that her children will need racial information "because they're going to be part of that black society." While it is important that multiracial children embrace their blackness, Veronica seems to imply that it is blackness, rather than racism, that makes racial knowledge so necessary for her children. Her emphasis misses the point that the hierarchical construction of whiteness and blackness within a racially stratified culture is what makes racial information essential, not being part of a "black society."

Although Veronica, as a white woman, cannot draw on the same experiential knowledge as her black partner, it does not necessarily follow that she has nothing to teach her children on the subjects of race and racism. Veronica's view reflects what Awkward labels an "interracial epistemology," which assumes that racial knowledge comes only from experience, and that it is impossible for whites to ever understand the experience of nonwhites.[39] Combining this epistemology with normative white assumptions that race is only about nonwhites, and that racial differences are located in individuals, rather than in social relationships, Veronica concludes that she is not an authoritative knower on the topic of race. Consequently, she is not positioned to teach her children, and must leave racial discussions to her black partner.

While Veronica may be an "outsider" with respect to racial oppression, she is an "insider" regarding gender oppression. Her willingness to defer to her male partner as the authoritative knower offers one example of the complex intertwining of race and gender identities.

DRAWING A LINE BETWEEN THE PRIVATE FAMILY SPHERE AND THE PUBLIC SPHERE

A second strategy that white women in multiracial families use to distance from whiteness is to draw a definitive line between the racially stratified public world where race matters and the privacy of their own families where it is not considered relevant. This recurrent theme, that race does not matter within the privacy of multiracial families' homes, draws on a distinctly American construction of public and private as separate spheres, a construction that has been fundamentally shaped by race and gender.[40]

Historically, the white male public domain of work and politics has been considered separate from the white female private domain of family and domesticity. As private property, enslaved Africans occupied a unique position. Having no rights of citizenship, they were excluded from the public sphere. At the same time, because they lacked rights to privacy, they remained inside the public sphere. Collins argues that "family constituted the ultimate private sphere for Whites only. It regulated multiple dimensions of social organization, including sexuality, gender relationships, citizenship rights, racial classification, and property relations."[41]

When white women draw a distinction between separate spheres, it might be an unconscious protective response to stereotypes about interracial relationships that conceptualize racial difference in oppositional terms, making love across racial lines unimaginable. It also might be an articulation of their white privilege, and of their lack of awareness of the ways in which normative whiteness shapes all family life, for monoracial families, as well as for those that are multiracial.

The following example illustrates how one white mother located race outside the family and used a color-blind approach to teach her multiracial children about racial identities.

> I guess it's like if you had a pallet [sic] with paint on it and you lifted out white. I would say I'm not white any more because I have been touched with gold and brown and purple and other colors. So I try and stay really away from the white and black thing. I teach my children that there's a world out there that talks white and black. "That's okay. It's their problem. But you are not black and you're not white." I said, "I'm not white. If you look at me, I'm peach. If

I look at you, you're gold. And if I look at your father, he's brown. So I don't really see very many black people. And I really don't see very many really white people. Albinos are white." I talk to them that way because I want them to have a sense of realism about what they're talking about and not to get pulled into those stereotypes out there that are going to hurt them. So my daughter will come and say, "Who's that peach lady?" That's how she talks. Or, "Who's that brown guy?" We don't talk in white and black in here. But I know that they have to deal with it out there. My older son who's fifteen, he talks in that white and black because he's very aware of it now.

Despite her attempt to draw a line between public and private spheres, Veronica's account illustrates the impact of nonfamily power structures on the creation of family identities.[42] In her effort to protect her children, and to resist the racial categorization that creates "those stereotypes out there that are going to hurt them," she may, although unwittingly, be reinscribing whiteness as the universal unmarked norm.

In conflating the paint palette of colors with the socially significant differences between black and white, Veronica accents the sameness within her family and seems to adopt the view that race should not mean anything. Because all of their colors can be found on the palette, the privilege connected with whiteness is rendered invisible, and Veronica is not situated as separate from her nonwhite family members. Frankenberg notes that many white women are caught in this either/or thinking about racial difference, thinking that either it implies hierarchy, or it does not, or should not, mean anything.[43]

As an individual, Veronica does not have the ability to single-handedly change systems of racial categorization. The significance of race does not rest only on an individual or attitudinal level, but functions based on its collective significance.[44] Through the lens of individualism, a white person may conclude that her racial identity is not personally meaningful, and thus, race is irrelevant. In a racially stratified culture, however, only those who are not subjected to others' racial categorization have the privilege to claim that race doesn't matter.

Given the injustices that have been facilitated by racial categorization, and Veronica's desire to accentuate family togetherness, there is intuitive appeal in the ideals of color blindness that she seems to be embracing. When race is only about someone or something outside their homes, white woman can maintain their racial innocence, and their view that they, and their family members are simply individuals. Veronica's color-blind strategy is not an effective method for reaching the ideal, because the reality of racial subordination is not dislodged by obscuring it.[45] Moreover, she conceals the ways in which she continues to be under the influence of normative whiteness, and leaves little room for accountability. Although Veronica wants to protect her children from the racial stereotypes that they are subjected to, her unwillingness to talk in racial terms means that she can't offer her children "a sense of realism," and doesn't have an avenue for discussing the social realities of racism with them.

SOCIAL JUSTICE IMPLICATIONS

When white women in multiracial families draw on the individualism and innocence of normative whiteness, it follows that they will be less likely to make connections between their own seemingly individual choices and antiracist political commitments. The social location of being in an interracial relationship, or in a multiracial family, has political implications, but individuals in this location will not have a political voice unless they have a vision of belonging to a community that shares political commitments. White women who define themselves as "just individuals," portray their relationships as "ordinary," and distance from race by locating it in the public sphere, are not constructing race in ways that contribute to building a community of multiracial families who might engage in public political efforts.

While Killian argues that interracial couples "represent a site of social and political resistance to larger social forces and institutions,"[46] many white women do not embrace the opportunity offered by their racial border crossing. Because race is socially constructed and not an essential difference, we are able to connect "across racial lines" and create loving multiracial family relationships. Having already moved away from some aspects of normative whiteness, white mothers of multiracial children are uniquely positioned to rearticulate whiteness as an oppositional racial category. By looking at the ordinary and everyday ways that we draw on whiteness, we have the opportunity to use our increased racial knowledge to challenge and transform white racial dominance. As we become aware and name the ways in which race impacts our lives, even within our most intimate relationships, we extend the possibilities for conscious choices, authentic moments of connection, and strategies that move away from normative whiteness toward social justice.

NOTES

1. John Hartigan, *Racial Situations: Class Predicaments of Whiteness in Detroit* (Princeton: Princeton University Press, 1999), 4.
2. John Hartigan, "Locating White Detroit," in *Displacing Whiteness: Essays in Social and Cultural Criticism*, ed. Ruth Frankenberg (Durham: Duke University Press, 1997), 184.

3. Ruth Frankenberg, *White Women, Race Matters: The Social Construction of Whiteness* (Minneapolis: University of Minnesota Press, 1993).

4. Carmen Luke, "White Women in Interracial Families: Reflections on Hybridization, Feminine Identities, and Racialized Othering," *Feminist Issues* 14 (1994): 49–72.

5. Dreama Moon, "White Enculturation and Bourgeois Ideology: The Discursive Production of 'Good (White) Girls,'" in *Whiteness: The Communication of Social Identity*, ed. Thomas Nakayama and Judith Martin (Thousand Oaks, CA: Sage, 1998), 178.

6. See Abby Ferber, *White Man Falling: Race, Gender and White Supremacy* (Lanham, MD: Rowman and Littlefield, 1998).

7. See Cheryl Harris, "Whiteness as Property," *Harvard Law Review* 106 (1993): 1706–91.

8. Current discourse against interracial relationships is founded on stereotypical notions of racialized masculinities and femininities, and of sexual deviancy. White women who choose relationships with black men transgress cultural proscriptions and are viewed in sexual terms: as promiscuous, as unsuccessful with white partners, or as sexually radical. See Frankenberg, *White Women, Race Matters: The Social Construction of Whiteness* (Minneapolis: University of Minnesota Press, 1993): 71–72, 77.

9. Frances Winddance Twine, "Transracial Mothering and Antiracism: The Case of White Birth Mothers of 'Black' Children in Britain," *Feminist Studies* 25 (1999): 744.

10. Carmen Luke borrowed this term from Patricia Hill Collins, *Black Feminist Thought: Knowledge, Consciousness, and the Politics of Empowerment* (Boston: Unwin Hyman, 1990).

11. Frankenberg, *White Women, Race Matters*, 112.

12. Despite being in multiracial families white women continue to have racial privilege. At the same time, it is important to note that white racial privilege is situationally and relationally constructed. Because of the intersections of race and gender, white women do not share the same racial privilege as white men. White women in interracial relationships are uniquely positioned to experience the contradictory juxtaposition of privilege and marginalization. As women, as whites, and as heterosexual partners of black men, they are objects of sexist and racist ideologies. (See Luke, "White Women.") At the same time, they are active subjects, constructing multiple, sometimes conflicting or contradictory aspects of themselves.

13. Ibid.

14. Maureen Reddy, *Crossing the Color Line: Race, Parenting and Culture* (New Brunswick: Rutgers University Press, 1994).

15. Hettie Jones, "Mama's White," *Essence*, May 1994, 151.

16. Terri A. Karis, "Racial Identity Constructions of White Women in Heterosexual Black-White Interracial Relationships" (unpublished doctoral dissertation, University of Minnesota, 2000).

17. Luke, "White Women," 68.

18. See Frankenberg, *White Women, Race Matters*, 11–15.

19. Charles Mills, *The Racial Contract* (Ithaca: Cornell University Press, 1997), 18–19.

20. Karis, "Racial Identity Constructions," 5.

21. See Paul C. Rosenblatt, Terri A. Karis, and Richard D. Powell, *Multiracial Couples: Black and White Voices* (Thousand Oaks, CA: Sage, 1995): 24–39.

22. john a. powell, "The Color-blind Multiracial Dilemma: Racial Categories Reconsidered," *University of San Francisco Law Review* 31 (1997): 799.

23. In order to protect the confidentiality of research participants, all names have been changed.

24. Karis, "Racial Identity Constructions," 234.

25. Moon, "White Enculturation," 192.

26. Hartigan, *Racial Situations*, 61.

27. Sherene H. Razack, *Looking White People in the Eye: Gender, Race, and Culture in Courtrooms and Classrooms* (Toronto: University of Toronto Press, 1998), 58.

28. Ibid., 10.

29. Alison Bailey, "Despising an Identity They Taught Me to Claim," in *Whiteness: Feminist Philosophical Reflections*, ed. Chris Cuomo and Kim Hall (Lanham, MD: Rowman and Littlefield, 1999), 89.

30. Richard D. Alba, *Ethnic Identity: The Transformation of White America*, (New Haven: Yale University Press, 1990).

31. Cheryl Hyde, "The Meaning of Whiteness," *Qualitative Sociology* 18 (1995): 87–95.

32. Mary C. Waters, *Ethnic Options: Choosing Identities in America* (Berkeley: University of California Press, 1990), 7.

33. Ian Haney Lopez, *White by Law: The Legal Construction of Race* (New York: New York University Press, 1996).

34. David R. Roediger, "Is There a Healthy White Personality?" *The Counseling Psychologist* 27 (1999): 239–44.

35. Mark P. Orbe, "Communicating About 'Race' in Interracial Families," in *Communication, Race, and Family: Exploring Communication in Black, White, and Biracial Families*, ed. Thomas. J. Socha and Rhunette C. Diggs (Mahwah, NJ: Lawrence Erlbaum Associates, 1999), 175.

36. Francis Wardle, "Tomorrow's Children," *New People: The Journal for the Human Race* 2 (1991): 5.

37. Orbe, "Communicating About 'Race,' " 176.

38. Moon, "White Enculturation," 188.

39. Michael Awkward, *Negotiating Difference: Race, Gender, and the Politics of Positionality* (Chicago: University of Chicago Press, 1995).

40. Patricia Hill Collins, *Fighting Words: Black Women and the Search for Justice* (Minneapolis: University of Minnesota Press, 1998).

41. Ibid., 16.

42. Myra M. Ferree, "Beyond Separate Spheres: Feminism and Family Research," *Journal of Marriage and the Family* 52 (1990): 866–84.

43. Frankenberg, "White Women."

44. john a. powell, "The 'Racing' of American Society: Race Functioning as a Verb Before Signifying as a Noun," *Law and Inequality* 99 (1997): 99–125.

45. Haney Lopez, "White by Law."

46. Kyle D. Killian, *What's the Difference: Negotiating Race, Class and Gender in Interracial Relationships*, (Paper presented at the annual conference of the National Council on Family Relations, Arlington VA, 1997).

PART III

LESSONS FROM THE

MULTIRACIAL MOVEMENT

THE CENTRAL QUESTIONS of the Multiracial Movement have been: How do we want to name our experiences and ourselves? In addition, how can we shift the meaning of race in society? Central to the goals of the Multiracial Movement then, has been the process of naming experiences publicly. Yet, "while individuals or groups may assert names for themselves, governments have the power to create categories of people."[1] The tension between self-naming and being named is at the heart of both the promise and pitfalls of the Multiracial Movement. The process of self-naming is a social and political act played out in the lives of individuals. It is at this level that the Multiracial Movement holds promise because it has pushed individuals in society to rethink the meaning of race. Yet, wrapped up in the promise is its pitfall. For many in the Multiracial Movement, pushing the boundaries of race thinking has meant little more than making claims to race as an illusion, something created in the context of human interaction, imposed on others and sold as reality. For these individuals, the goal is to disrupt the imposition of race, by undermining the role it plays in daily life, by forwarding a color-blind agenda, and by working to eliminate race-based initiatives and legislation. In doing so, they believe, individuals will be better served because society will have policies to protect individual rights, rather than policies that are built around "identity constraining" categories.

175

The authors in this section will argue that a struggle on behalf of individual rights in the context of a society structured around institutional, group-based discrimination will do little to shift the balance of racial power. A white supremacist society will not be challenged by moving the discourse to the level of the individual, that is, making claims to individual rights, racism as an individual pathology, rugged individualism, and postmodern fragmentation through which community building and solidarity are painted as impossibilities. Instead, the authors will argue, we must acknowledge historical contexts, systemic or institutional injustice, and interlocking discourses that perpetuate injustice. Rebecca Chiyoko King-O'Riain illustrates the importance of understanding the historical context of racial formation before making claims about a broad-based Multiracial Movement. Through her study of multiracial Japanese Americans, she explains why these individuals are choosing to work from *within* Japanese American communities to redefine community boundaries rather than creating a separate multiracial community. Barbara Katz Rothman urges us to examine larger social structures to avoid falling into the trap of examining social problems, in this case, transracial adoption, at the level of the individual. Through her interviews with white members of multiracial families, Heather Dalmage shows the discourses of individualism that whites in multiracial families draw upon to maintain their privileged positions and sense of racial comfort. Finally, Eileen T. Walsh explores the need to understanding interlocking discourses of domination and privilege so that the movement avoids the pitfalls of narrow and contradictory racial reasoning. Multiracial activists need to be mindful of this discourse to avoid reinscribing white privilege, even as they attempt to distance themselves from it.

NOTES

1. Karen Rosenblum and Toni Michelle Travis, *The Meaning of Difference: American Constructions of Race, Sex and Gender, Social Class, and Sexual Orientation,* 3rd ed. (New York: McGraw-Hill, 2002), 8.

NINE

MODEL MAJORITY? THE STRUGGLE FOR IDENTITY AMONG MULTIRACIAL JAPANESE AMERICANS

Rebecca Chiyoko King-O'Riain

THE MULTIRACIAL MOVEMENT has been mired in essentialism (often used by liberals) and illusionism (often used by conservatives), both of which tend to remove the conceptualization of "multiracial" from its social and political context. This is because the Multiracial Movement itself, and analysis of it, has taken place in a predominantly black/white context. If we look closely at the racial politics of multiracial identity in another context, the Japanese American community, we find alternative and, at times, conflicting notions of racial essentialism and illusionism where multiracial identities are transforming themselves, community, and racial politics from within the Japanese American community at large.[1] In fact, for historical and demographic reasons, Japanese Americans are both inclusive and exclusive of multiracial people as community members in distinctly different ways to the black/white multiracial experience.

In the Japanese American community, highlighting racial constructionism offers a way out of the illusionary bind by positing that multiracial identity is shaped by the interaction of the racial projects of groups of color and by forces external to those groups, therefore multiracial people won't look the same in all groups. Given the unique histories of multiracial people and the construction of whiteness, opportunities for building solidarity around multiraciality *within* traditional groups of color have been rare. Multiracial people in the Japanese American community are only in recent times being welcomed into established groups with their multiracial agendas honored. Traditional Japanese American groups are now willing to entertain and enact racial change based on multiracial members but only under certain conditions. I examine historical understandings of race in the Japanese American community, demographic pressures such as gender dynamics associated with interracial marriage rates, and the rising socioeconomic status of Japanese Americans. Further, I illustrate how Japanese Americans have developed their understandings of race and seemingly positive orientations toward multiraciality in the present time.

Many Japanese Americans have gained middle-class standing, thus increasing their contact with white people. In fact, claims have been made that Japanese Americans may be "outwhiting the whites."[2] While some multiracial Asians, and particularly multiracial Japanese Americans, may identify as white, this is clearly not the case for all Japanese Americans.[3] An examination of the cultural images of multiracial Japanese Americans, their, at times, lightened skin color (through mixing), and their middle-class status can lead to the conclusion that multiracial Japanese Americans are "white." However, such a conclusion essentializes assimilation instead of recognizing the complexities of racial renegotiation that are going on presently in Japanese American communities, particularly in California and Hawaii. Moreover, the assumption of assimilation focuses on intermarriage and multiracial children as evidence of cultural decline in the Japanese American community. Moving beyond blaming multiracial Japanese Americans for the fate of the community, I show how some multiracial Japanese Americans (and later other multiracial Asian Americans) are in fact building on historical notions of race from within the Japanese American community to widen definitions of Japanese Americanness to include themselves. Structural factors such as demographic pressures are forcing traditionally monoracial Japanese American community groups in turn to deal with multiracial Japanese Americans as a last-ditch effort to sustain their organizations. There is a nuanced and complex nature to multiracial identity in the Japanese American community where shifting notions of Japanese Americanness do not follow the historical pattern of acceptance or essentialism of multiracial experiences in the Native American, Latino, or black communities.[4] These communities have long histories of mixing, some continued immigration, and high cultural retention even in the face of high out-marriage rates. Japanese Americans, like many Asian groups, have, by contrast, arrived more recently, sustained less out-marriage initially, and registered low immigration numbers in recent years.

HISTORICAL PATTERNS OF RACIALIZATION

The Japanese American community has its own history with racialization. Initially, Japanese immigrants brought with them from Japan strict ancestry rules that implied that most true Japanese were assumed to be descended directly from the emperor of Japan.[5] In practice, then, this was a new twist on the one-drop rule used for/by African Americans. It wasn't that you were Japanese if you had one drop of Japanese blood, but instead you were "other" if you had even one drop of blood that wasn't Japanese. Only pureblooded Japanese could claim authenticity, and multiracial people were considered *gaijin* (foreigner).[6] Therefore, negative attitudes exist in Japan toward "nonpure" racial groups such as the *Burakumin*, who are thought to be descended from Koreans and who don't fit notions of racial purity in Japan.[7] Bringing strict bloodline and ancestry dependent racial ideologies across the sea to the United States, Japanese immigrant notions of race played into a racialized capitalist system in their settlement areas, such as the plantation system in Hawaii where there were differential wages for each racial/ethnic group. Some historical accounts explain how this system actually rewarded and justified the higher economic position of Japanese plantation workers over others such as Filipinos by paying Japanese more, which allowed them to have families on the plantation.[8] These racial attitudes combined with racially motivated legal restrictions on immigration (Gentlemen's Agreement 1907/8), land ownership (Alien Land Law 1913), and interracial marriage (antimiscegenation laws in California until 1948) meant that Japanese American interracial marriage rates were less than 1 percent in the early years and only 10 percent for the Nisei (second generation) in the 1930s.[9] In Hawaii, home to the largest Japanese American community, those rates were even lower, with only 4 percent of all Nisei men and 6 percent of all Nisei women interracially married in the 1930s.[10]

These low rates of interracial marriage meant that there was not a large multiracial Japanese American population at the time of internment. Nonetheless, the government used blood quantum rules in the guidelines for the internment of Japanese Americans during World War II. Jeffery Bulton and his colleagues note:

> Even though the justification for the evacuation was to thwart espionage and sabotage, newborn babies, young children, the elderly, the infirm, children from orphanages, and even children adopted by Caucasian parents were not exempt from removal. Karl Bendetsen, Assistant Chief of Staff in Charge of Civilian Affairs of the Western Defense Command, was quoted as saying, "I am determined that if

they have one-drop of Japanese blood in them, they must go to camp."[11]
In fact, anyone with 1/16th or more Japanese blood was included.[12]

In addition, there was a gendered notion of culture reflected in the
War Relocation Authority's regulations that allowed Japanese American
women married to white men and their children early exit from the camps.
For instance, in 1944 Carey McWillaims noted the government position:

> The ban on the West Coast should be lifted gradually, not only for
> the protection of the evacuees, but to guard against a possible mass
> return. Nisei soldiers are now permitted to return on furloughs; and
> the wives of Caucasians have been permitted to join their families.
> New categories should gradually be added to the list.[13]

Ironically, these governmental racial rules did not agree with many of the
racial understandings internal to the Japanese American community, which
assumed that those fathered by whites were white.

After internment, Japanese Americans were scattered geographically
and discouraged from coming back to the west coast of the United States.
This geographic dispersal, along with job training programs and a culture of
hyperassimilation, made many Japanese Americans ashamed of being Japanese American, and they tried to be 110 percent American.[14] Their orientation toward upward mobility through education, work, and marriage
dovetailed nicely with the growing focus on assimilation and proving what
"good Americans" Japanese Americans were. During and after the war, the
Japanese American Citizen's League (JACL) played a prime role in encour-
aging assimilation by trying to ostracize draft resisters within the internment
camps and by colluding with the U.S. government to encourage compliance
and assimilation into mainstream society. It is no surprise, then, that the JACL
supported early attempts to overturn antimiscegenation laws and encouraged
interracial marriage, primarily with whites.[15] The improvement in socioeconomic status and increases in interracial marriages were explained to be an
outcome of assimilation.[16] The acceptance of mainstream racial views, such as
the notion that whiteness meant success or access to power, was deeply ingrained in both the individual Nisei and their organizations, such as the JACL.
Only recently has the JACL issued an apology to draft resisters whom they
ostracized during the war and even then, the apology caused controversy.[17]

When the civil rights movement, and more specifically the Asian Power
Movement came along in the 1970s, Japanese American Sansei, as third-
generation newly identified Asian Americans, were in politically, education-
ally, and economically more secure positions than some of the more recently
arrived Asian immigrants, which allowed them a leading role in the Asian

Power Movement.[18] As a small minority group, and having been racially targeted during internment, Japanese Americans understood the need to join other Asian and Pacific Islander ethnic groups in order to form a more powerful political bloc. In *Asian American Panethnicity*, Yen Espiritu explains how Japanese and other Asian ethnic American groups joined together to bring attention to issues specific to the civil rights of Asians in the United States, such as the racist war in Vietnam, the closing of the International Hotel in San Francisco, and political underrepresentation.[19] The Asian Power Movement, like the Chicano Power Movement, did not see their specific issues reflected in the larger civil rights movement. The legacy of being a large group within the Asian American community, but small compared to the overall community is still present today in Japanese Americans' orientation to racial politics. For example, Japanese American leaders recognize that their numbers are shrinking today compared to other Asian ethnic groups and that they are losing their political voice within the Asian American community.

Japanese Americans have historically experienced being a small minority group, that has had to join with other Asians to gain a political voice. However, among Asian Americans they were once large and powerful. More recently, with increasing immigration of other Asian ethnic groups, Japanese Americans are losing that demographic power and are thus anxious over the future of the community. Two recent conferences, The Ties that Bind (1998) and Nikkei 2000, responded to this anxiety by addressing two central questions: What is the basis of the Japanese American community? Moreover, what is the future of the community? Multiraciality figured prominently in this discussion as one of the main issues facing the Japanese American community today. From espousing purist racial notions brought from Japan, to being the target of racial discrimination during World War II, to learning more American forms of racialization in the 1970s, and now struggling to define who is Japanese American, Japanese Americans have had a long and contentious history of developing racial understanding, which places them in a unique context and position to understand multiraciality.

DEMOGRAPHIC PRESSURES

Structural demographic pressures such as group size and rate of intermarriage have also shaped the racial discourse around multiraciality for Japanese Americans. In this section, I use data for Asian Americans and where I can, I abstract information about Japanese Americans. In the 2000 census, Asian Americans made up only 3.6 percent of the total population and Japanese Americans only 0.3 percent of the total population. In 1994, 70 percent of Asian Americans were in same-race couples and 28.7 percent were with white partners. More-over, as noted in a Hapa Issues Forum (HIF) News Release:

> New census data show that over one in ten Asian Pacific Islanders (APIs) in California are multiracial, or of mixed-race heritage. According to these Census 2000 data, over 500,000 Hapas (multi-racial APIs) reside in the state. Indeed, the API community is pro-portionately more multiracial than the African American, Latino, and White communities.[20]

Moreover, rates of intermarriage are higher in the Asian American community than these other communities. Within the Asian American com-munity, Japanese American out-marriage rates are among the highest.[21]

In 2000, in the Asian American community 1,655,830 people (or 13.9 percent) indicated that they were of multiracial ancestry, that is, they checked Asian and some other race.[22] In addition, 18.2 percent of Asian Pacific Islander kids are recognized as being of a different race than one or both parents, while the percentage was only 6.3 for black multiracial children.

Not surprisingly, then, the Office of Management and Budget's Racial and Ethnic Target Test of 1996 found that Asian Americans were the group most affected by the addition of the multiracial category to the census. In addition, "the National Research Council estimates that by 2050, a fifth of all Americans—36 percent of Asians and 45 percent of Hispanics—would be of multiple ancestry."[23] Asian Americans then will continue to be one of the racial/ethnic groups most affected by the addition of multiracial representation on the census, as well as multiraciality in community and cultural spheres. In the Japanese American community, this shift is based largely on increasing rates of interracial marriage (50 percent or higher) and a larger number of multiracial people. Unlike the black community, the Japanese American com-munity does not have a long history of mixing. As a result, multiracial Japa-nese Americans are concentrated in the younger age groups. These younger multiracial Japanese Americans seem more likely to participate in multiracial student groups than in family groups, and have been actively engaging the Japanese American community in discussions of racial identity.[24]

For African Americans, the National Association for the Advance-ment of Colored People (NAACP) established a clear racial ideology toward multiracial people that rejected their claims to representation on the 2000 census. The NAACP has little incentive to change their ideology. Initial rejection of multiraciality within the Japanese American community could not be sustained in the face of shifting demographics. Moreover, unlike black Americans, Japanese Americans historically did not recognize or accept multiracial individuals as Japanese American. Yet, there were pressing incentives to change and incorporate more members into the community, and the cost of inaction was reckoned to be high. The combination of these factors created a unique political opportunity for multiracial Japanese Americans to work from within the Japanese American community to create racial change.

GENDER AND CULTURAL REPRODUCTION

The historically and demographically specific politics of racialization among Japanese Americans is further reinforced by tremendous gender differences and dynamics in relation to intermarriage. In 1980, 28.7 percent of Asian/white marriages had an Asian husband and white wife whereas 71.3 percent of all interracial marriages in the Asian community had a white husband and an Asian wife.[25] These gender dynamics have produced certain racial/gender discourses and orientations toward culture. Images of Asian American women (and men) as feminine[26] may also be a key factor in the gender dynamics of Asian/white interracial couplings where the woman tends to be Asian and the man white.

This gender difference may also shape the way that multiracial people see themselves culturally and in their relation to symbolic and material culture. Within the Japanese American community, men have not always been seen as the bearers of culture, despite assumptions underlying the creation of the War Relocation Authority in the 1940s. Some studies find that it is in fact the white male culture that is pervasive in defining Asian/white children as white.[27] However, these data are often based primarily on parents' (often the white dads') identification of their children. If the Asian mother happened to be filling out the form identifying their multiracial child, she might identify them as Asian, not white. In the end, parental identification is NOT self-identification and many multiracial kids may not grow up to "fit" their parents' racial labels. Children may be identified as white, and surely, this may have an impact on their identity development, but that is not the same as the impact of their own identity choices as an adult. Hence, it is important to analyze how multiracial people identify themselves and not just how others identify them.

In the Japanese American community mothers are typically seen as language and cultural teachers, which may mean that they have closer associations with racial/ethnic community organizations. This is supported by findings of 2000 survey data from within Japanese American community organizations, which found that Japanese American grandmothers are bringing their multiracial Japanese American grandkids to cultural events.[28] White mothers of black/white multiracial children may bow out of racial discussions in their families[29] and may flock to multiracial organizations[30] instead of black ones. Some white mothers may feel that they don't have the "black cultural resources" to pass on to their children and may or may not have the black community ties.[31] Parents have been central to the formulation of discourses around multiraciality.[32] In the Multiracial Movement, this has taken the form of the overrepresentation of white mothers on the forefront of activism on behalf of their multiracial children.[33]

In interracial families in the Japanese American community, the mothers tend to be Japanese American, and this may have different implications in terms of racialized gender practices. In other words, it may be different for a girl to learn that she is a woman from a woman of color than from a white woman. Conversely, boys with Japanese American mothers may identify more with their white fathers, and with white masculinity. In each case, however, Japanese American mothers in interracial families maintain ties to their communities of origin. As a result, the children often attend and participate in Japanese American community events. The fact that these Japanese American mothers (and grandmothers) are "bringing along" their children to Japanese American cultural festivals such as the Cherry Blossom in San Francisco or Nisei Week in Los Angeles, or to Japanese American sporting events such as basketball tournaments may create connections and opportunities for multiracial Japanese American kids to better understand how they are Japanese American. At the same time, white fathers of Japanese/white kids tend to not be vocal on behalf of their children's ethnicity.[34]

Charles Gallagher found that white U.S. students view Asians as quiet, less threatening, harder working than blacks.[35] These perceptions of Asians as more culturally similar and less threatening than blacks to whites may have more to do with demonstrating how pervasive the model minority myth is, particularly in areas where there are few Asians, than in discussing racial options for people of Asian descent themselves. In addition, to view multiracial Asians as more similar to whites based on the perceptions of whites themselves reinscribes white racial entitlement regarding whom they see themselves as "close" to and whom they will allow to be honorary whites.[36] It is an entirely different matter to actually ask those who are being incorporated if indeed they feel white or not. It may be true that some Asians are honorary whites and that some Asian/white multiracial people may be able to take advantage of whiteness, but what about those that are not seen as or cannot pass for white? What about those that are mistaken for something else entirely such as Latino? Some Asian/white multiracials may refuse to identify as strictly white, even if whites accept them as white.[37] In fact, the case study here may show that the issues of being part Asian, and not the issues of being part white, are what led to the establishment of an Asian-focused multiracial group. Unlike broader multiracial groups, which have tended to default to black/white couples and children, Hapa Issues Forum has focused its dialogue and oriented its political action toward Asian

American communities on behalf of Asian Pacific Islander multiracial people. In this sense, the coming together of multiracial Asian/whites around their Asian ethnic side may be an illustration of more complex understandings of identity, wherein they can now be accepted as Asian and not just white.

The founders of Hapa Issues Forum, originally a multiracial Japanese American organization, realized during a Japanese American history course at UC Berkeley that they were fast becoming a majority in the Japanese American community and needed to develop their own voice in relation to it. Where white mothers are a strong voice in the multiracial movement, among Japanese American/white multiracial families the children, not the parents, are the voice in the formation of groups such as HIF. In this sense, Japanese American mothers brought their children into the community and the multiracial young people were able to work from the inside of the community. As an indication of the increasing number of multiracial people within the Japanese American community, I turn to the year-end issue of the *Pacific Citizen* (2001), the national newspaper of the JACL, which highlighted Japanese American families. In this issue of thirty articles about Japanese American families, roughly one-half (fourteen) were about or explicitly addressed multiraciality. In fact, multiraciality is so infused into the definition of what it means to have a Japanese American family now that multiracial presence and projects are seen to be part of the community within organizations like JACL.

STRUCTURAL DIFFERENCES AND MOBILIZATION PATTERNS

The unique historical racial patterns and demographic pressures of gender and class are important explanatory factors for the multiracial mobilization *within* the Japanese American community. Most multiracial groups concerned primarily with the black/white racial experience have framed their concerns as universal issues of multiraciality and focused their activism on the state. Hapa Issues Forum is focused on getting multiracial Japanese Americans accepted into the Japanese American community and has recently included the multiracial Asian Pacific Islander (API) experience. Today, HIF has grown into a national nonprofit organization with eight chapters including nonstudent chapters and one chapter overseas in Japan (founded by multiracial Japanese people who live in Japan).

HIF tries to expand racial definition pan-ethnically to include all multiracial Asian Americans without trying to either essentialize or dilute the meaning of that multiracial category. Many of the founders of HIF explained to me that they did not feel comfortable in multiracial organizations dominated by black/white multiracial family members and issues. This political position seems to recognize the differences in racial discourse and appreciate that the historical/structural and gender factors in the Asian Pacific Islander community are different than in the black community. Hapa Issues Forum writes, "Ultimately we hope to enhance the nation's respect for diverse cultures, build an inclusive community and to broaden the understanding of Asian Americans to include Hapas" (http://www.hapaissuesforum.org). They are trying to overcome existing rejectionism in the Asian Pacific Islander (API) community and to work from within the community to change racial meanings. Other, traditionally monoracial API groups are taking notice. For instance, Stewart Kwoh, president and executive director of the Asian Pacific American Legal Center of Southern California (APALC) stated, "[c]ommunity organizations like ours need to be able to reach out to all segments of our community, including those of mixed-race heritage."[38] Ted Wang, policy director for Chinese for Affirmative Action, has stated that "Hapas are becoming an increasingly larger part of the Asian Pacific Islander community," and thus, "[w]e need to think about ways to be more inclusive and to address Hapa issues as part of our larger goal of eliminating discrimination from society."[39]

Hapa Issues Forum is trying to diversify the existing community by claiming multiracial rights, while keeping in mind the original goals of traditional Asian Pacific Islander groups. Their work is based on a collective identity and understanding of working for multiracial reconciliation and rights from within an established group of color, the Asian American community. This focus on community rather than the state may come to characterize other racial projects in a post–civil rights era. Such a focus may be able to create a more flexible and malleable, context specific, understanding of race and multiracial identity in which Asian and white identities are not mutually exclusive because there is less political imperative to make Asian/white multiracials choose one identity over the other. In fact, the ability to have more flexible racial loyalties may be more dependent upon the small size of the Japanese American community than its middle-class status. A similar process is taking place in other, less well-off, Asian Pacific Islander communities, as indicated by the fact that HIF has more and more members who are part Vietnamese, Filipino, and representative of other Asian groups. Of course, HIF is a self-selected group of Asian descent individuals who identify with (or choose to highlight) the Asian part of their ethnic background. If all or even most Asian/whites could slide pleasantly into whiteness, there would be no need for and therefore no existing Asian-focused multiracial groups such as Hapa Issues Forum.

The founders of HIF recognize however, that not all racially mixed people are the same, the case of multiracial Japanese Americans may not be generalizable to all multiracial people or issues, and that this fact illustrates the hierarchy of race that still exists within our society. HIF knows that their position within the American racial hierarchy may be less marginal if they are part white and are seen by others, particularly whites, as kinder, gentler, people of color than black/white multiracials. HIF has a stronger voice within the Japanese American community and got cooperation from the JACL precisely because the Japanese American community is a small group relative to other racial/ethnic groups, particularly other Asian American groups, and multiracial people make up a bigger and bigger proportion of it. HIF did have some success within other Asian ethnic communities, but since their membership was predominantly of Japanese American descent, their largest success has been in dialogue with that particular community.

Secondly, HIF organizers who approached JACL for support addressed the fact that multiracial Japanese Americans may have experienced racism and rejection from *within* the Japanese American community. HIF organizers also had personal and familial ties to Japanese Americans. Perhaps most important, HIF introduced a racial ideology grounded in their multiracial experiences to replace the historical Japanese American ideologies of rejectionism. HIF asserted the right and ability to be accepted as full-fledged Japanese Americans even though many of them were half white.

Pushed by a growing number of educated, middle-class, and culturally aware multiracial Japanese Americans who were claiming membership within the traditional Japanese American community, JACL struggled with expanding community boundaries by theorizing race as flexible. In practical political terms, the Japanese American community offers one model of strategic constructionism—a situation where multiracial young people have worked to support existing communities and where the community in turn recognizes their multiracial identity and gives them "parity of esteem."

ACCESS OR ON-GOING RESTRICTION TO PARTICIPATION?

Increasing numbers of multiracial Japanese Americans have caused many inside and outside the Japanese American community to be critical of the use of "racial eligibility" rules to govern who can and who cannot participate in Japanese American activities such as basketball leagues and beauty pageants.[40] Nonetheless, almost all Japanese American leagues and pageants in California and Hawaii have racially based rules about who can participate. For example, in order to run for Cherry Blossom Queen in San Francisco or to play youth Japanese American basketball across the bay in Oakland, you must be at least 50 percent Japanese (racially) to participate. These racial rules clearly reinscribe "race" with biological meaning and power as they often use birth certificates with "race of mother" and "race of father" on them to determine eligibility. In this context they don't ask if race is "real" or not, but assume it has real importance to those who want to keep the leagues primarily for Japanese American use.

At the same time, newspaper articles within the Japanese American community seem to imply that issues of multiraciality must be addressed on a collective level.[41] For example, one of the oldest and most established Japanese American civil rights organizations, JACL, supported the push by multiracial people (particularly multiracial Japanese Americans) to have multiracial representation on the census in the year 2000. JACL was the only "traditional" racial civil rights organization that publicly supported the right of multiracial people to check more than one box on the race question on the census.[42] The Japanese American community needs multiracial support to maintain community strength. They also rely less on civil rights legislation because they don't have the same economic needs or face the same discrimination as other groups of color. In addition, many of the decision makers in the community have multiracial children and family members, and multiracial issues have hit home for them.

CONCLUSION

In this chapter, we have seen that racial constructionism, in the Japanese American case, offers an example of how a community can produce both exclusionary (i.e., racial eligibility rules) and inclusionary (i.e., entire community conferences based on multiracial issues) discourses toward multiraciality at the same time. Despite the historical background of Japanese American racial thought, under current demographic pressures there is a certain attempt to integrate multiracial Japanese Americans into the community. In addition, Japanese American mothers and grandmothers have brought their kids along to community events, despite rejection, and have allowed them to develop their own multiracial voice from within Japanese American community organizations. Therefore, the Japanese American community has a slightly different racial project than other groups of color, namely African Americans, which has interacted differently with multiracial projects, faced different demographic pressures, and produced different political outcomes.[43] There are trends that encourage the community to work with and accept multiracial Japanese Americans, but these exist alongside rules that do not allow those same multiracial Japanese Americans to participate in certain events at all.

In the end, Hapa Issues Forum's acceptance by the Japanese American community, which, clearly, still harbors some restriction and rejection, may indicate that some Japanese American/white multiracial people are trying to subvert whiteness by celebrating their Japanese American ethnic ties and working from within that community of color, collaboratively with other groups, to open up space for multiraciality to be recognized as fundamental to the Japanese American contemporary experience. Ultimately, working within the Japanese American community around the issue of multiraciality in the end will most likely affect whiteness and whites as well.

NOTES

1. For examples of constructionism see Stephen Cornell and Douglas Hartmann, *Ethnicity and Race: Making Identities in a Changing World* (Thousand Oaks, CA: Pine Forge Press, 1998).

2. Michael Omi, Davies Forum "Re-Orienting Asian America" Lecture (Spring 2000).

3. See Charles Gallagher, "Racial Redistricting: Expanding the Boundaries of Whiteness," this volume.

4. Originally defined as a Hawaiian word from "hapa haole" which meant half white foreigner. In California, where most HIF chapters are located, this term has come to mean anyone who is part Asian American. For more on the definition of the word *hapa* see the Hapa Issues Forum web page at *http://www.hapaissuesforum.org*.

5. Frank Dikkotter, ed., *The Construction of Racial Identities in China and Japan: Historical and Contemporary Perspectives* (Honolulu: University of Hawaii Press, 1998).

6. In my fieldwork in Japan (1990), some people that I interviewed told me that if you are a Japanese person who has lived abroad for a certain amount of time, you are not truly Japanese anymore so this test of authenticity may extend beyond blood connections to include cultural competence as a measure of authenticity and Japaneseness as well.

7. M. Hane. "The Outcaste in Japan," in *Peasants, Rebels, and Outcastes: The Underside of Modern Japan* (New York: Pantheon, 1982), 138–71.

8. Ronald Takaki. *Pau Hana: Plantation Life and Labor in Hawaii 1835–1930* (Honolulu: University of Hawaii Press, 1984).

9. Darrell Montero, *Japanese Americans: Changing Patterns of Ethnic Affiliation Over Three Generations* (Boulder: Westview, 1980).

10. Eileen Tamura, *Americanization, Acculturation, and Ethnic Identity: The Nisei Generation in Hawaii.* (Urbana: University of Illinois Press, 1994), 238.

11. Michi Weglyn, *Years of Infamy: The Untold Story of America's Concentration Camps* (New York: William Morrow, 1976), 77.

12. Jeffrey F. Burton, Mary M. Farrell, Florence B. Lord, and Richard W. Lord, *Confinement and Ethnicity: An Overview of World War II Japanese American Relocation Sites* (Tucson: Western Archaeological Conversation Center, National Park Service, U.S. Department of the Interior, Publications in Anthropology, 1999, v. 74), 34.

13. Carey McWilliams, *Prejudice: Japanese-Americans, Symbol of Racial Intolerance* (Boston: Little, Brown, 1944), 299.

14. Paul Spickard. *Japanese Americans: The Formation and Transformations of an Ethnic Group.* (New York: Twayne, 1996).

15. Frank Abe, "Conscience and Constitution" video recording; 2000. *http://www.pbs.org/conscience*.

16. Darrell Montero, *Japanese Americans*.

17. Kenji Taguma, "Historic JACL Ceremony Recognizing WWII Resisters Called a First Step in Reconciliation," *Nichi Bei Times*, May 14, 2002.

18. William Wei, *The Asian American Movement* (Philadelphia: Temple University Press, 1994).

19. Yen Espiritu, *Asian American Panethnicity: Bridging Institutions and Identities* (Philadelphia: Temple University Press, 1992).

20. Hapa Issues Forum Press Release, "Over One in Ten Asian Pacific Islanders in California are Multiracial New Census Data Show" (July 19, 2002).

21. Larry Hajime Shinagawa and Gin Yong Pang, "Asian American Panethnicity and Intermarriage," *Amerasia Journal* 22, no. 2 (1996): 127–52.

22. Census 2000:summary file 1. *www.census.gov.*

23. Jonathan Tilove. "Pandora's Box: The Pitfalls of the Census 2000," *The American Prospect*, April 24, 2000, 38–42.

24. Rebecca Chiyoko King, David Omori, Dean Osaki, and Jill Shiraki, "Charting Course and Shifting Direction for the Nikkei Community," in *Japanese American Consortium of Community Related Organizations* publication (2000).

25. Table 1 1980 Census. *www.census.gov.*

26. Darrell Hamamoto, *Monitored Peril: Asian Americans and the Politics of Television Representation* (Minneapolis: University of Minnesota Press, 1994).

27. Charles Gallagher, "Racial Redistricting: Expanding the Boundaries of Whiteness," this volume.

28. Rebecca Chiyoko King, David Omori, Dean Osaki and Jill Shiraki, "Charting Course and Shifting Direction for the Nikkei Community."

29. Karis, this volume.

30. Dalmage, "Introduction," this volume.

31. Hettie and Lisa Jones, "Mama's white," *Essence*, May 1994, 78–158.

32. DaCosta, this volume.

33. For more on white mothers in census activism see Susan Graham, "The Real World," in *The Multiracial Experience: Racial Borders as the New Frontier*, ed. Maria P. P. Root (Thousand Oaks, Ca: Sage, 1996), 37–48. For more on the family level see, Maureen Reddy, *Crossing the Colorline: Race, Parenting and Culture* (New Brunswick: Rutgers University Press, 1994).

34. Perhaps this can be explained by the fact that many Japanese/white kids can and do pass whereas many black/white kids may not be able to do so. For a fuller discussion, see Pearl Fuyo Gaskins. *What Are You?: Voices of Mixed Race Young People* (New York: Henry Holt, 1999).

35. Gallagher, this volume.

36. Mia Tuan, *Forever Foreigners or Honorary Whites? The Asian Ethnic Experience Today* (New Brunswick: Rutgers University Press, 1999).

37. Debbie Storrs, "Whiteness as Stigma: Essentialist Identity Work by Mixed-Race Women," *Symbolic Interaction* 22, no. 3 (1999): 187–212.

38. Hapa Issues Forum Press Release. July 19, 2002, at *www.hapaissuesforum.org.*

39. Ibid.

40. Rebecca Chiyoko King, "Eligible to be Japanese American: Counting on Multiraciality in Japanese American Basketball Leagues and Beauty Pageants," in

Contemporary Asian American Communities: Intersections and Divergences, ed. Linda Vo and Rick Bonus (Philadelphia: Temple University Press, 2002).

41. Annie Nakao, "A Quest for Identity: Japanese American Confront a Changing Future," *San Francisco Chronicle*, September 10, 2000, A1, A14, A15.

42. Rebecca Chiyoko King, "Racialization, Recognition, and Rights," *Journal of Asian American Studies* 3, no. 2 (Summer 2000).

43. Rebecca Chiyoko King and Kimberly McClain DaCosta, "Changing Face, Changing Race," in *The Multiracial Experience*, ed. Maria P. P. Root (Thousand Oaks, CA: Sage, 1996), 227–44.

TEN

TRANSRACIAL ADOPTION:
REFOCUSING UPSTREAM

Barbara Katz Rothman

I PROFIT FROM American racism. More than almost anybody I know, I am a beneficiary. I have Victoria.

Victoria is the child by birth of two high school kids, a father who wasn't ready to settle down and a mother who wanted to finish school and make something of her life. Had she been a white child, she'd have been a very hot commodity in the adoption market. As a child of African descent, born in the late 1980s, she was part of a stream that flooded the market.

I came to the decision to adopt out of my work as well as out of my personal life. I had had two children by birth, aged fifteen and eight by the time Victoria arrived. My early decision to have home births and my subsequent interest in midwifery brought me to my dissertation and my first book; my work in the area brought me to my work on prenatal diagnosis and genetic counseling, the subject of my second book. Moreover, that work, on reproductive technology more or less, had me on a lot of reporters' and television producers' rolodexes when the "Baby M" surrogacy case arose. I found myself part of the media circus. Arguing against surrogacy, arguing that every woman is the mother of the child in her belly unless and until she chooses otherwise, I found myself arguing alongside a sometimes strange assortment of colleagues. Priests and religious leaders of other denominations were on my side while, bizarrely, some feminists sat on the other side. Also next to me, time after time in television studios, chatting over stale coffee in greenrooms, were adoption advocates. The problem, they assured the public and me, was not a shortage of babies for adoption: it was a shortage of the kind of babies the people who were hiring surrogates were willing adopt.

The unadoptable children included African American children and, in the late 1980s when "crack babies" and "boarder babies" were in the nightly news alongside "surrogate mothers," it also included newborn black babies. My first two kids were growing up and I could see the end of my active parenting years approaching all too quickly. When my husband and I began this process of adoption, with our first tentative steps of interviews, checking around to be sure that there really were more babies than available homes, thinking about what this decision would mean for our life as a family, my youngest child was the age my oldest had been when the youngest was conceived. We felt ready, then more than ready, and then eager.

However, alongside the eagerness, there was also some hesitation. It was not a hesitation about a third child, and it was not a hesitation about becoming a mixed-race family. It was a hesitation to step into the politics of transracial adoption as a white family of some privilege. I particularly did not want to enter into a competitive situation with black women and families looking to adopt. Nor did I want to participate in what at least some black social workers have seen as a genocidal project. Transracial adoption has a charged history in America, as anything about race always does in this country, and I share some of the concerns that the black social workers have raised.

While occasional black children have been raised in white families since colonial days, a pattern of formal adoption of children of African descent by families of European descent did not develop until after the social changes of the 1960s. The "sexual revolution," which, with the availability of contraception and greater acceptability of women without husbands keeping their babies, made for a "shortage" of adoptable babies. White infertile families were encouraged to look farther afield: to other countries, and to the African- and Native-descent children of this country.

The other contribution of the sixties, the civil rights movement and the dramatic presentation of Southern-style segregation to Northern (television) audiences, made transracial adoption appealing. Far removed from the sturm und drang of the American South, white families welcoming little black children into their homes made sense. So, off in the calm of places like Minnesota, individual loving families in largely welcoming communities opened their arms to individual orphaned children. This was not in itself an evil thing at all, but an act of kindness. Acts of kindness, however, sound a lot like acts of charity, and that may not be the best grounding for a child. This is also an act, be it of kindness or of charity that is indelibly marked on the child in those communities: black children do not fade in, blend away, and disappear into their white families and schools. Their story is written on their skins, knotted into their hair. Every child needs a loving and supportive family—but is that all every child needs? What about community, a place and a people? Can a black child find that in an all-white community?

Then too, what of the community that has lost these children? Individual parents may falter and fail, may choose not to or not be able to raise their children. But what are the consequences for a community of people whose children are being shipped off to be adopted by others, children sent far, in as many senses, from home?

Meanwhile, into the late 1960s and 1970s, very pre–sexual revolution, prefeminist ideas continued to shape adoption policy. This was long, long before openly gay and lesbian families could adopt. This was an era in which "father knew best," and the "family" meant the mother-father-child family. At the same time that African American babies and children from our cities were being shipped off to white suburbia, an African American colleague of mine, a woman who had a Ph.D., was a college professor, who lived in a lovely home and earned a fine living, was turned down by adoption agencies because she wasn't married. Her home was not suitable for a black child; a white suburban family was preferable. Adoption agencies still expected adoptive mothers to be committed to full-time, stay-at-home mothering, and adoptive fathers to be full-time "breadwinners." This was an era in which a suitable home had a separate bedroom for the baby, a yard, a white picket fence, and cookies in the oven. Too many black families didn't make the grade, were put out of the running for these children.

Transracial adoptions reached a high of 2,500 by 1971[1] when the president of the National Association of Black Social Workers, William T. Merritt, made his famous pronouncement: "Black children should be placed only with Black families, whether in foster care or for adoption."[2] Saying that 'Black children belong physically, psychologically and culturally in Black families in order that they receive the total sense of themselves," and that cultural heritage is an important part of a child's socialization, the Association vowed to end transracial adoption: "We have committed ourselves to end this particular form of genocide."[3]

Did they overstate the case? Probably. Did they use unnecessarily inflammatory rhetoric? Certainly. Did they have to call it genocide?

Many of the "white" families adopting black children have been, as is my family, Jewish. We are people whose "whiteness" is a recent American invention[4] and people to whom, in the second half of the twentieth century, the idea of "genocide" carries special weight.

Victoria and I stood in the Ann Frank house in Amsterdam last month, and talked about human cruelty—in Bergen-Belsen and slave ships both. To call my relationship with Victoria—the child standing in that attic hideaway because I am a loving mother who can bring a child to see the world—and Ann Frank's relationship with the Nazis who forced her into hiding and ultimately to her death—to call those relationships both "genocide" is crushing.

And of course it is absurd. It is silly to think in terms of genocide at 11:00 on a Sunday night when my husband is out hunting all-night stores to find the right graph paper for an overdue math homework the kid "forgot" to mention before bedtime; when I'm up all night with a sick kid—or, worse yet, with her sick hamster. Genocide is pretty far from our minds and experiences when the entire family, grandmother, uncle, and older brother included, have had to take sick days to get her through one bout of chicken pox. If this is genocide, it is certainly a very labor-intensive way to go about it.

It is indeed absurd and hurtful to use the language of genocide when you look at the acts of individual loving white parents of black children. That language so inflamed and infuriated so many people that perhaps the point and the sense of what the black social workers were trying to say could not be heard.

Because it is not absurd to think in terms of genocide when you look at social policy. The very same years that the United States was placing black children in white families, Australia was still using adoption as a genocidal plan. In April 1937, while Hitler was on one genocidal path, A. O. Neville, the "Chief Protector of Aborigines in Western Australia," asked: "Are we going to have a population of 1,000,000 blacks in the Commonwealth, or are we going to merge them into our white community and eventually forget there were any Aborigines in Australia?"[5] The latter was his preference, and forcible removal of Aboriginal and "half caste" children from their homes and into the homes of white Australians was his policy. Adoption was a plan to "breed out the blackness" of the Aboriginal children.

One of the definitions of genocide, from the 1948 International Convention on the Prevention and Punishment of the Crime of Genocide, is "the forcible transferring of children of a group to another group." What constitutes forcible transfer? The police chasing down hidden Aboriginal children in the Australian bush certainly appears to be, but so too may be a minority group so burdened by its poverty that children are placed out for economic survival. That is what the black social workers were pointing out.

One cannot look at an individual loving family, the warmly welcoming arms of whatever color holding the baby of whatever other color, and talk about genocide. But one can look at a system in which black children are twice as likely to be placed into foster and adoptive homes as are white children, and a system in which white families are more "acceptable" as adoptive families than are black families, and ask questions about genocidal policy.

There is a story we tell in medical sociology that is useful here as well. A man is walking alongside a stream when a dead fish floats by. He reaches in with a stick and flips it out, so that the rotting fish not pollute down-stream. A moment later, another fish floats by and again he flips it out. Within minutes he is standing there, too busy to stop, look up, and wonder, "What the hell is going on up there?"

The moral of the story is that we have to refocus upstream. Some versions of the story have drowning people floating by and the rescuer doing artificial respiration on one after another, without time to stop and see who is pushing them in. Sometime the story, like the one I told, is about indus-trial pollution, the factory at the top of the stream that systemically produces dead fish. But always, as much as work needs to be done downstream, the problem basically needs to be solved upstream.

There are several streams that feed into transracial adoption, each of which is deeply problematic at its source. Adoption itself is one: why is there ever a child placed for adoption? Because adoption solves, in a wonderful and satisfying way, the problem of infertility for so many people, we tend to forget that adoption itself is a problem and not just a solution. I once led a doctoral student reading group on adoption. Half a dozen graduate students, touched one way or another by adoption, wanted to explore the issue together, as sociologists. We read widely, bringing in books and articles to share with each other. One evening a man brought in a table of international adoption statistics. Sweden, not utopia, but a place with good social services, readily available contraception as well as abortion, decent services for single moth-ers along with all mothers and children—Sweden had had twelve domestic, nonfamily adoptions that year. Twelve Swedish women found themselves in a situation where placing their babies for adoption was their best option. Twelve. That is what you are left with when you take away all of the social forces operating upstream that put women in that awful position, and are left largely with the personal, idiosyncratic reasons. Twelve.

The United States is bigger than Sweden; if we had the kind of social supports the Swedish have, we would still have more than twelve babies available. However, we would never, ever, have anywhere near the numbers of babies we now have placed, and we would never, ever, have enough to solve the problem of infertility. Adoption is the result of some very bad things going on upstream, policies that push women into having babies that they then cannot raise.

Racism is of course the other feeder stream: More women of color find themselves placed just there, placed willingly or very much against their will. Some make adoption plans and place their babies in waiting arms; some have their children wrenched away by a deeply neglectful state, which then finds neglect. A lot of what adoption is about is poverty; a lack of access to contraception and abortion; a lack of access to the resources to raise chil-dren. In addition, a lot of what poverty is about in America is racism.

Moreover, as much as the black community stands there with open arms, absorbing as many of those babies and children as it can, the same poverty that pushes all those babies and children into the adoption stream ensures that there won't be enough black homes to take them all.

In a better world, adoption would all but disappear, leaving infertility as a problem that still needed to be addressed on its own terms. Moreover, in a better world, race too would almost cease to exist, race as a system of power and domination would collapse. What would that mean for adoption?

I have had my children in a Quaker school for their elementary school years. I share the values Quakers bring to education, their respect for every child as a person. My middle child was eight when Victoria arrived. I brought the baby to school to meet the third grade class. It was, as private schools tend to be, a largely white class, but being a Quaker school with the Quaker commitment to diversity, it was not entirely white. The class sat around in a circle on the floor, for morning meeting, and the baby and I joined them. The children asked a million questions: they asked about babies—there aren't many new brothers and sisters by the time you get to third grade. What does she do all day? Can she understand anything? Moreover, they asked questions about adoption: Is there a big room with a lot of babies? Who picks? The questions went on for about a half an hour. The question they never asked, those bright, interested children, was "How come they gave a black kid to a white family?"

In that little, almost utopian social world of a Quaker school, in those early years before the rest of America forces itself upon them, that third grade class did not recognize race. Those mostly, but not all white children knew all about color, and history, but not about race as a system, race as a way of dividing people up against each other. They weren't so much color-blind, as a race blind, seeing difference but not oppression.

However, the world we live in is not such a utopian world. If it were, black children would be proportionately present in both private schools and adoption agencies. The even playing field we created in that classroom, in which color is only difference, not race and not hierarchy, doesn't exist right outside the door, does not exist in the street of Brooklyn where the school is placed. As a parent of a black child, I knew I could offer such utopian vision as reality for maybe a decade. Give the kid ten years of celebrating diversity without understanding or experiencing racism. That first decade is about psychology; nurturance and love and building a strong foundation. In that second decade—the one we now enter—the rest of the world needs to be dealt with, and race as a system enters our lives increasingly. Now I have to teach Victoria to be careful not to look like she might be shoplifting when she visits the stores near her school.

I recently published a book on genetics, *The Book of Life*.[6] I spent years thinking intensively about genetics, biology, culture—thinking about who and what we are, thinking about identity. I found myself fascinated by the way genes shape our bodies and how we use those shapes to construct community. Race is, of course, the obvious one. However, it is not always about race. I read about dwarfs and dwarfism. A single errant gene, a random mutation, and people are born with that distinctive body shape. It is a body shape associated with childhood, even babyhood; the large head, small limbs— in a way, rather endearing. But it is a shape not generally associated with adult sexual development, and so presents a sometimes comic juxtaposition with beards or breasts, other signs of adulthood and sexuality. Probably not an easy body to live with, surely a tough adolescence; growing up without growing up. That gene constructs a shared experience; that experience becomes the basis for constructing a community, a people connected across time and space, a tribe in Diaspora. Dwarves form a community—formally, in the organization of Little People of America, and informally, in networks and relationships. Dwarfism isn't just a variation, one of the ways people can be in the world, though. Dwarfism is labeled as a "condition," medicalized, a form of deviance. When the human genome is mapped, it is the "normal" and not the "dwarf" gene that is included as a reference point.

Similarly, whiteness in America has been constructed as the norm, and blackness as the other. This is most assuredly an arbitrary line; no amount of melanin production is the norm against which variation can be measured; no hair texture a standard to which others can be compared. Repeatedly, the geneticists, the anthropologists, and the scientists of all sorts assure us that there is no such thing as race. However, lines that are biologically, genetically arbitrary can be socially quite powerful. Just because race doesn't exist, it doesn't mean racism does not.

If my daughter Victoria's skin and hair and bones mark her as African, if the genes that shape her body mark her place in the race scheme of America, how different is that than the way the Achondroplastic dwarfism gene marks people's membership in the world? Being a little person in a big person's world is a shared experience, and one that shapes a community. The community is shaped as much by the stereotypes, prejudice, and discrimination of the larger world as by its own physical difference. We start with the physical, and move on to the creation of culture, a worldview, and a community. If I had a dwarf child, I'd want her to know dwarf adults, I'd want dwarf friends, I'd want her to learn that culture, be welcomed into that world.

Social worlds, communities, are always formed by some kind of binary thinking, some kind of us and them, or more pointedly, us and not-us. Without hierarchy, domination, power, binaries can be celebrated and enjoyed. Too often, though, those binaries become the basis for oppression, exclusion, and domination. That has certainly been the history of race in America; many of us work hard to keep it from being the future of race in American.

I knew, when I offered to raise Victoria, that I would be raising a child in one world for another; that there are separate worlds of black and white in America, and that however my life tries to straddle and blur the lines, the lines exist here, and it is a line she has to cross. That crossing is what Heather Dalmage calls "Tripping on the color line," tripping as in stumbling, and tripping as in playing, fantasizing, enjoying.[7]

Nevertheless, the truth is we raise all of our children for worlds we don't, won't, and can't inhabit. My niece is deaf; her parents frantically learn to sign as they raise their daughter to take her place in the deaf world. In addition, my son is gay. My world crosses that line too—I have many gay and lesbian friends (some of my best friends) but my world is on the other side of that line—the other side of a line my son crosses. Is that line written too in genetics, a "gene" for gayness? Does it matter? Call it a gene, call it a combination of biology and circumstances, call it life itself playing out anyway it chooses; I'm here; he's there. The world can make it hard, awful, and frightening to be gay and that community can close in on itself for protection. On the other hand, the world can make it okay to be gay, and that line becomes more permeable, that community becomes just one more place to belong in this world. I parent my son to be his own true self in his own place, and that includes his place as a member of the gay community, as surely as Victoria's place includes her place as a member of the black community does. In good times or in bad, I work for a world in which communities are places of comfort and celebration; I recognize that in this world communities can also be safe harbors in unsafe worlds.

Families will always find themselves made up of all kinds of people, overlapping all kinds of communities, straddling all kinds of lines. Hearing people will be raising deaf children, and deaf people hearing children; straight parents will be raising gay children, and gay parents straight children. And what of race? One way or another, by birth or by adoption, by accident or by design, as long as a color line exists, families will find themselves straddling it.

Moreover, what are we to do about it?

Transracial adoption—as a problem or as a solution—does not resolve at an individual level. Victoria and I are at the end of a long strange stream. There is the Eastern European anti-Semitism that brought my great-grandparents to New York, where their confrontation with American racism bleached out Semitic race and made my family "white." Victoria got to where she is via the slave trade to the American South and the Great Migration North. These larger historical streams landed us in Brooklyn—ensconced in a Caribbean neighborhood.

In addition, what are we to do about it?

If you want to understand families like ours—

If you want to help families like ours—

Or if you want to prevent families like ours—

the solution will not be found within our families. The solutions will not be found down here at the end of the stream where we are all doing the best we can. No, if you want to understand, help, or prevent transracial adoption, you're going to have to refocus upstream.

NOTES

1. Rita J. Simons, Howard Altstein, and Marygold S. Melli, *The Case for Transracial Adoption*, (Washington, DC: American University Press, 1994), 41.

2. Ibid., 40.

3. Ibid., 41.

4. Karen Brodkin Sacks, "How the Jews Became White Folks," in *Race*, ed. Stephen Gregory and Roger Sanjek (New Brunswick: Rutgers University Press, 1994).

5. Carmel Bird, ed., *The Stolen Children Tell Their Stories* (Sydney: Random House Australia Pty. Ltd., 1998), 138–39.

6. Barbara Katz Rothman, *The Book of Life: A Personal and Ethical Guide to Race, Normality, and the Implications of the Human Genome Project* (Boston: Beacon, 2001).

7. Heather M. Dalmage, *Tripping on the Color Line: Black-White Families in a Racially Divided World* (New Brunswick: Rutgers University Press, 2000).

ELEVEN

PROTECTING RACIAL COMFORT, PROTECTING WHITE PRIVILEGE

HEATHER M. DALMAGE

RESEARCH HAS SHOWN that multiracial organizations are disproportionately attended and directed by white parents, particularly white mothers, in multiracial families.[1] Based on open-ended, recorded, and transcribed interviews conducted with seventeen white members of black/white multiracial families, I explore the construction of racial identities among whites that join multiracial family organizations. Many whites join multiracial family organizations in the hopes of making connections with others who are "like them and their children." These connections are important in a society in which multiracial family members face discrimination from all sides. Moreover, when whites cross the color line in their family relationships, they lose some of the privileges of whiteness; they lose the control of some racial spaces, and then experience to varying degrees the terror of whiteness. The experiences shatter much of the psychological, if not the material comfort that whiteness had previously provided. These whites begin searching for ways to address racism and gain control of their racial space. The desire to once again feel comfortable and safe leads many of these whites to multiracial family organizations. I argue that these organizations become, in part, sites for whites to rearticulate their racial identities and develop connections and networks with others who share their racial space.[2] Unfortunately, the rearticulation of their white racial identities, for some, is based on ideologies of Americanness and rugged individualism and thus rather than a transformation, the rearticulation of identity becomes a redoubling and reinscribing of white privilege. By exploring the construction of racial identities of whites who join multiracial family organizations we can better understand the political ideologies that drive the Multiracial Movement and ultimately how to create a more progressive agenda.

ON BEING COMFORTABLE IN THE WORLD

While people of color experience, to vary degrees, the terror of whiteness and Americanness, whites (also to varying degrees) experience privilege and view whiteness and Americanness as representative of goodness. Richard Dyer suggests that because whites are socialized into a belief that whiteness is both superior and good "they do not imagine that the way whiteness makes its presence felt in black life, most often as terrorizing imposition, a power that wounds, hurts, tortures."[3] Following the attack on the World Trade Centers, the media interviewed a number of whites who expressed "shock," "surprise," and "disbelief" that anyone would hate or want to attack the United States. When that shock quickly turned to a broader fear, the government, along with the business community, proactively worked to return America to "normal." The threat had to be identified and contained. In short, they worked to reassure the citizenry that some level of safety could be achieved, even though that meant trampling on the civil liberties of perceived transgressors and anti-citizens, and committing to a war without spatial or temporal borders. Almost twenty years ago, James Baldwin poetically wrote about such a chain of events as the basis of white Americanness:

> Because they think they're white, they do not dare confront the ravage and the lie of their history. Because they are white, they cannot be tormented by the suspicion that all men are brothers. Because they are white, they are looking for, or bombing into existence, stable populations, cheerful natives, and cheap labor. Because they are white, they believe, as even no child believes, in the dream of safety.[4]

Whiteness as an institutionalized norm leads many whites to feel entitled to being safe and comfortable racially in the world. U.S. institutions intersect to ensure that racial ideology reproduces a context in which whites can continue to command and demand control of the racial spaces they occupy. Our political and legal system has been created through images and definitions of whiteness, white people, and white privilege.[5] Cheryl Harris writes:

The concept of whiteness was carefully protected because so much was contingent upon it. Whiteness conferred on its owners aspects of citizenship that were even more valued because they were denied to others. Indeed, the very fact of citizenship itself was linked to white racial identity. The Naturalization Act of 1790 restricted citizenship to persons who resided in the United States for two years, who could establish their good character in court, and who were "white."[6]

This process of racial formation and "citizen formation" defined whites as having the potential for goodness and value and created the material inequalities that continue to define the United States.[6] Evelyn Nakano Glenn points out that "imagining non-European 'others' as dependent and lacking the capacity for self-governance helped to rationalize the takeover of their lands, resources, and labor."[7] The housing market remains inextricably connected to injustices in the educational system through the processes of redlining, steering, and school funding based on property taxes.[8] The educational system is intimately linked to the economy. The media, in general, continue to spin stories in a way that facilitates whites' comfort with injustice. Robert Stam and Ella Shohat have written: "The residual traces of centuries of axiomatic European domination inform the general culture, the everyday language, and the media, engendering a fictitious sense of the innate superiority of European-driven cultures and people."[9] Taken together, the institutional and ideological practices create a house of mirrors in which injustice is distorted into an ahistorical question of individual morality and ability, white supremacy is distorted into normalcy, and in which whites "believe, as even no child believes, in the dream of safety."

Martha Mahoney has argued that one of the most prominent characteristics of whiteness is its separation from and lack of contact with people of color.[10] Contact that does occur between whites and people of color often takes place in arenas that are white controlled. The institutionally backed power that whites are able to exercise provides whites with a sense of safety and comfort. When social interaction occurs blacks are expected to make it palatable and comfortable for whites. At other times in history, blacks who misread, ignored, or challenged whites' assumption about their entitlement to comfort faced retribution that included psychological and physical violence, and death.[11] Today, the prison industrial complex provides the means for state sanctioned violence against people of color who threaten white American comfort.[12] On a day-to-day basis, blacks who do not "respect" or defer to white comfort are labeled troublemakers. In schools, they are sent(enced) to BD/LD classes and given harsher punishments than their white counterparts.[13] In the workplace they are accused of having "attitudes" and "not being team players."[14]

Based on my interviews, I found that for some white members of multiracial families, their interracial relationship remains their first and only close connection across the color line. These whites expressed a desire for more interaction with African Americans, but as one woman stated, "blacks seem out of reach." The desire for greater connectedness with blacks did not seem to outweigh the desire to avoid racial discomfort. In short, these whites were not willing to give up a crucial aspect of white privilege—comfort and control in interracial interactions—even when they and their multiracial family were victims of white racism.

For example, Theresa is a white woman who was raised in a wealthy white community and has had very little contact with people of color. Her black husband, Jason, is her sole close contact with African Americans. Now a mother, she is faced with decisions about how to raise her multiracial son. She outlines the dilemma:

> I am more aggressive about getting black culture into our lives than Jason is. To me our friends should represent the community. Jason works a lot and also his interests don't lead to the black community. He doesn't belong to a black church, so it's difficult to get in there. Socially, most of our friends are white.

Notice the way Theresa constructs the problem. She suggests that despite her aggressiveness she has been unable to connect with African Americans. The sentence, "I am more aggressive about getting black culture into our lives . . . ," suggests that her goal is to bring African American culture *into* her life rather than reaching out and becoming engaged in black communities. However, when speaking of her black husband's interaction with blacks she points to his failure to make connections in black communities. By default, then, most of their friends are white. In short, Theresa's framing of race suggests that black culture is something that should be brought to her, that in her mind she cannot and should not have to reach out to blacks. Recalling an African American festival she attended, Theresa questions, "Do I really belong here?" She describes herself as an "observer" and speculates it is because the black community is "very tight knit" with a "unique cultural feel." While she did not receive any negative or hostile reactions at this event, she thinks of herself as different from blacks and thus did not actively make connections. Instead, Theresa has joined a local multiracial family organization in her town. Like other multiracial family organizations, this one is disproportionately comprised of white mothers of multiracial children. This is the space in which she feels most comfortable, the people she looks to for advice on how to raise her son and negotiate her newly acquired uncomfortable whiteness.

Likewise, Evelyn, a twenty-nine-year-old white woman who has been in an interracial relationship for eight years bemoans that she "would like more contacts with black people but, I don't have many opportunities and my partner doesn't provide me with any." Similar to Karis's study,[15] I found that many whites defer matters of race to their partners. When the black partners fail to deliver, that is, make connections with other blacks, the white partners render themselves powerless. The desire/demand for racial comfort inhibits many whites from reaching out on their own and instead they place the onus of creating and maintaining their sense of white racial comfort on the backs of their black partners.

For instance, Theresa details the psychological pressure she feels when visiting her in-laws and being confronted with a situation in which she is outnumbered racially. In these incidences, she holds her husband (and his friend) responsible for her racial comfort and safety.

> I do have moments of uncomfortableness when I'm the only white person within a ten-block region. I would go to the corner store and wonder, "Oh God, what do they think of me?" No whites go into that store. I don't want to appear afraid or show the other stereotypical reactions they would expect from me. Jason is good friends with the woman in there. So once they see me talking with Eileen, it's fine, but it's that walking into the front door.

Theresa is fearful and uncomfortable around blacks. Her statement, "I don't want to appear afraid," indicates that she is in fact afraid. Rather than reflecting on the social context of segregation and the underlying racist images that feed her fears, Theresa explains what it is about blacks that cause her to feel uncomfortable. She constructs the scenario in which blacks have the power to make her uncomfortable; she is powerless. All she can do is negotiate the hostile stereotyping through impression management. Moreover, rather than reflecting about her own need for racial comfort, she clings to her husband's friend, Eileen, to provide her a sense of comfort.

Interestingly, much of the demand whites express for comfort is couched in a language of avoiding the perceived threats against them, that is, whites as victims of racial hostility. Thus, as we saw in the cases of Theresa and Evelyn, reaching out to blacks is beyond the realm of comfortable and safe possibilities. In circular fashion, then, separation and isolation allow whites to build their worldviews around their own projections (fed by a steady diet from the media and other mainstream institutions), and their own projections, in turn, cause them to want to avoid interaction. Without a critical reflection on the processes of whiteness, white members of multiracial families will continue to turn to and create multiracial family organizations as sites for racial comfort.

Unfortunately, given the isolation, projection, and demand for comfort many whites fail to grasp the connection between their deep desire for racial comfort and reproduction of whiteness.

ON BEING THE PUREBRED AMERICAN

Ruth Frankenberg has noted, "Whiteness and Americanness, though by no means coterminous, are profoundly shaped by one another."[16] Those unable or unwilling to conform to the norms of Americanness are viewed as transgressors, anti-citizens, and threats to the American way of life.[17] In short, these individuals and groups are judged, coerced, contained, and terrorized. Think historically about those who have been deemed threats to America and the resulting treatment: slavery; Trail of Tears; Chinese Immigration Acts; internment camps; Bracero Program; colonies and territories; Jim Crow Laws, redlining, racial profiling, and the antiterrorism campaign. According to Evelyn Nakano Glenn, "American citizenship has been defined, by those who have it and therefore speak for all citizens, as universal and inclusive (the so-called American Creed), yet it has been highly exclusionary in practice."[18] Those against whom white Americans define themselves may shift, but exclusionary practices remain.

Throughout most of U.S. history, interracial relationships and multiracial people have been stereotyped and scrutinized because they potentially challenge discrete hierarchical categorizing.[19] Without an awareness of the larger sociohistorical context of discrimination against multiracial family members, many whites in multiracial families defend their families and themselves against racial stereotyping by denying that race matters. So much time and energy is spent looking for and arguing about our "sameness" that many of these whites do not question their white identity or the material inequalities of race.[20] By articulating race in a color-blind manner they are, as Howard Winant states it, preserving "the legacy of a racial hierarchy far more effectively than its explicit defense."[21]

In this section, I will explore two interviews with members of a local multiracial family organization in Chicago: James is thirty-three years old, lives in Chicago and has some college. Gina is forty-three years old, lives in a suburb of Chicago, and has taken some graduate courses. Like many others in interracial relationships, James is concerned that people think that his relationship is based solely on sex. In his attempts to debunk the sexual stereotype of interracial couples, he dismisses the realities of race and racism. James argues:

> People can throw out their theories of this and that, but an American is an American is American. Your background is not American,

but when you came here you became American. You may be fresh off the boat from Viet Nam, but when you became an American citizen, you are as American as I am, even if you just got here yesterday. I just don't buy the argument that "I'm an African American, Mexican American, or a Polish American." No, you're an American, period.

James is implying that Americanness is expressed in a society governed by color-blind and meritocratic practices in which, miraculously, legal citizenship is the sole key to a level playing field. His definition of American assumes a system in which race, gender, and class hierarchies do not exist. While his statement, "you are as American as I am," implies that he epitomizes Americanness, his next statement, "you may be fresh off the boat," dismisses the relevance of history and global inequalities in the construction of Americanness and whiteness. On census forms James "always checks *other* and writes *American*" as his "little way of fighting it." The "it" is the process of categorization of people into racial groups. He denies that race matters in his life and his relationship, and thus avoids reflecting on his white identity and privileges. According to James we are all the same, therefore he has earned his status and the right to judge immigrants and people of color.

Similar to James, Gina refuses to acknowledge the importance of race. Interestingly, Gina grew up in what she describes as a very racist family and community. Disowned by her mother because of her marriage, Gina now keeps in touch with her family through her younger sister. Despite her willingness to articulate the pervasive racism she grew up learning and later being tormented by, she clings arrogantly and passionately to a meritocratic view of the world. When I asked her to define white culture she replied:

I don't know that I think of white culture because I recognize the ethnicity in our country when it comes to being white. I think of white just in terms of my skin color. But I think of me being as purebred American as you can get, and that is Irish German. So, I look more at the ethnicity. That's why I love Chicago. I see Berwyn not as white but as Bohemian, Rogers Park as Jewish, Chinatown not as Asian, but Chinese. In terms of white community? I don't think it exists. There is an American culture which is a mix of everything wonderful that everyone brought with them from other countries that we've been able to develop and then on top of that we've added music and all these other things like roller blading. Maybe if I hadn't left my community in Indiana I would have felt a white community, but not here. I don't know if I can think of anything that can typify white culture because nothing is white culture. What ethnicity are we talking about? I think of skin color as white and everything else in our country is plain old American or ethnic.

Several interesting (and troubling) points are raised by the Gina's analysis of white culture. First, like James, she sees herself as the epitome of an American by pointing out that she is "purebred American," a mixture of two groups of European descent. Second, her discussion of ethnicity extends only to whites and Asians and illustrates the "almost white" status sometimes assigned to Asians. Third, the notion that American culture is a wonderful melting pot ignores the genocide against and commodification of cultures, as well as the unending list of racist projects against various groups of people. In short, her construction of the American racial landscape fails to "confront the ravage and the lie of history." Finally, she notes that her community of origins in Indiana might typify a white community—the same community she notes is deeply racist. Here she implies that racism is a characteristic of white communities that exist outside the center. She of course, is situated at the center. Gina finishes her thought by restating that to be white means to have white skin. When asked directly, "What does it mean to have white skin in society?" She responded:

It means that I burn more easily, I am more susceptible to skin cancer. I don't see it as better or worse. I have taken classes with female teachers who felt that they were discriminated against because they were women. I have gotten everything I've ever wanted, the jobs, promotions. I have never felt discriminated against because I am a woman and I feel the same way here. I don't know that I've ever gotten any benefits because I am white . . . I can't think of a time when I felt that white skin mattered.

Despite the very personal experience of being disowned by her mother and recognizing her childhood environment as racist, Gina still clings to a color-blind perspective. Moreover, she draws on a gender-blind argument in an attempt to legitimize her point. Perhaps Gina believes that as a woman her statement against the existence of gender inequality carries greater weight and can transfer legitimacy to her argument against the existence of racism in society. In circular fashion, this ahistorical, self-proclaimed legitimacy is used to defend a system of whiteness. History is ignored or refashioned to legitimize the injustices and unearned privileges.

While Gina struggles to deny whiteness, she expresses an "appreciation of black culture" and names black culture as visible in the areas of music, fashion, cooking, and religion. Yet, Gina has little to no connection with blacks outside of her immediate relationship. She expresses a desire to "reach out to the black community" but "feels threatened" when she attempts to do so. Among her white coworkers and friends, she is often looked to as having insights about African Americans because of her marriage. In her construction of a meritocratic world in which race does not matter the oppression faced by blacks is a problem caused by blacks—inequality is an outcome of blacks not using their bootstraps. She assumes the role of expert and harshly criticizes blacks, stating that "it's frustrating to me because I can't do it for them." In her racial isolation, she speaks about others, but refuses to interrogate her own racial identity.

After dismissing race as an issue in her life and in the larger society, Gina laughs off a racist incident directed at her husband.

> The funniest thing that ever happened to me in my whole life. We were at Denny's and this little blond girl, cute girl, leaned over to our booth and said, "Dad, there's a nigger." I bet it wasn't a minute later, that family was out of there.

Gina laughed as she characterized this tragic, hostile, and hurtful event as funny. Perhaps Gina does not know how to express the pain she may have felt for her husband, yet based on her other comments it appears more likely that Gina has not reflected on the importance and centrality of race in society. By defining this event as the "funniest thing that ever happened," Gina dismisses the pain, terror, and material injustices of racism. Moreover, the description of the girl as a "little blond, cute girl" connotes an innocence and naiveté. In their recent book *The First R: How Children Learn Race and Racism*, Debra Van Ausdale and Joe R. Feagin point out that children are neither naive nor innocent in matters of race. For instance, upon observing a three-year-old girl, Carla, who stated, "Niggers are stinky," Ausdale and Feagin write:

> Like most of the children we observed, Carla is not the unsophisticated, innocent child of many adult imaginations. This three-year-old knows how to use racial material, such as the hurtful epithet, which she has learned from other sources.[22]

James and Gina are members of a local multiracial family organization and look for ways to debunk myths about interracial couples and families. However, the defenses they use perpetuate whiteness through the unquestioned, uninterrogated white identity. By clinging to ideas of color-blindness and meritocracy, neither has to place themselves as racialized beings who interact with and receive privileges from a system of whiteness. They each claim a right to speak about and for African Americans and other people of color, although neither has a sense of connection to blackness. Like Theresa and Evelyn, each works to maintain their sense of racial comfort.

ON BEING THE RUGGED INDIVIDUAL

By erasing the importance of whiteness, these whites are able to establish themselves as rugged individuals who travel through the world free from categorization and community demands. Interestingly, several white men and women used the phrase "lone ranger" to described themselves, others explained that they follow the path least traveled. The rugged individual has a long romantic history in the United States; it is a central defining aspect of Americanness. The rugged individual does not count on others and owes nothing to others. She or he is a fearless person who is freed of community obligation and willing to risk it all to prove a point and maintain a sense of integrity. William Aal has pointedly stated, "Those who can afford individualism are exactly those who have power."[23] These individuals can generally risk it all because systems are in place to assure more opportunities are on the horizon. Instead of community, the lone ranger makes claims to his or her internal strengths—strengths that are perfectly matched to the central tenets of whiteness, masculinity, and Americanness.

As proof of his rugged individualism, James explains that he does not care what other people think about him. "I don't try to fit into somebody's category. I'm just going to keep doing what I'm doing and be successful at what I'm going to be based on me and me alone." The invisibility of whiteness and the ideals of Americanness and masculinity provide James a relief from being forced to name (or claim) a racial community. Moreover, individualism strengthens a system of whiteness by translating racism into an individual problem rather than a pervasive institutional arrangement. Within this ideological context, the only way to fight racism is to address individual pathologies. For instance, when people stare at James and his wife he defines the stare as a sign of individual pathology:

> If you want to stare, then stare. I'm going to put it right back in your face. You gotta deal with it, it's not my problem. You have the problem.

Because the problem is at the level of the individual James need not explain the inconsistency between the fact that people stare because race matters and his claims to a color-blind meritocracy. In short, according to James, the system is color-blind, fair, and just. The problem occurs at the level of individuals in that system.

Similarly, Gina portrays herself as a rugged individual. Gina has stood up to her mother who has disowned her, and takes pride in her interracial marriage despite her repeated claims that race does not matter.

> I was proud that I could be the first in the group that I hung out with in college to be in an interracial marriage. I went to this really progressive college and I was progressive enough to have a black husband. That's not what I was trying to do, but I was just glad to show off.

The obvious question raised here is, what is she showing off if race doesn't matter? Clearly, race matters and she uses her interracial marriage to prove her "progressiveness" and individual strength. Her black husband becomes her outward badge—the proof—of her progressiveness. She goes one step farther and indicates what she sees as the ultimate display of strength and daring: "We like to travel south. We aren't going to be careless, but were not going to let anything keep us from doing what we want." In short, Gina describes herself as an independent individual who gallantly challenges society by her life choices.

Whiteness is built around a demand for social comfort and the myth of a level playing field as the backdrop for the lone ranger adventures. Many white members of multiracial families may desire a connection to blackness and yet find it easier to remain physically and socially isolated in white worlds and multiracial organizations. Instead of exploring the underlying cause of their discomfort, they retreat to comfortable spaces, make claims to a color-blind world (or a level playing field in which blacks and whites are equal opportunity discriminators against multiracial families) and in which blacks are "out of reach." These individuals then point to their choice of partner as proof of their rugged individualism. The contradictions become apparent. In a truly color-blind society, interracial marriage would be nothing more than marriage and these individuals would not look to multiracial family organizations to help them feel comfortable with their new racial location.

TRANSFORMING WHITE IDENTITIES

Several of the white partners/parents interviewed expressed some form of critique of whiteness. Interracially married whites who recognized their privilege as whites have begun to struggle to create antiracist identities. For these individuals whiteness was visible both as an identity and as a system of racist oppression, which they felt compelled to struggle against. In addition to joining multiracial family organizations, these individuals were likely to have many connections with people of color. Neil Gotanda points out that "[u]nder the American system of racial classification, claiming a white racial identity is a declaration of racial purity and an implicit assertion of racial domination."[24] The individuals I interviewed expressed a similar view of white racial identities and thus several rejected white identities while acknowledging white privilege. This rejection was expressed in self-identifying phrases such as *apart from the white community, antiwhite, black, not totally white,* and *passing for white.* These individuals also spoke of being outraged by racist comments, feeling a lack of connectedness or comfort around whites, and feeling a sense of solidarity with people struggling for liberation on all kinds of fronts.

As parents, many of these whites saw the struggle against whiteness as essential to parenting in a society that identifies multiracial children as black. In this section, I will highlight the interviews of Donna and Shelly. Each of these women belonged to a multiracial family organization in Montclair, N.J. Donna, an Irish American woman, has been interracially married for more than five years and has two children. She speaks to the sense of being a spy around whites and struggles to find the words to describe her shifting racial identity. Donna recalls a conversation that took place at an event with other social workers in the New York public school system:

> I was at a table of all whites. One woman said, "The school I'm in is ninety-nine percent white." Another social worker said, "You're so lucky, I don't see a white face all day long." Now they said that and I'm there and it's like, "You think I'm just like you because I'm white, but I'm not like you at all and now I know how you really think." I'm allowed in like I am one of them. I can listen in and can use that information against them as well. I feel like a spy, they really don't know what I am. I may look white, but I'm not. It's like I'm not really white, you know? I'm white, but I'm not really one of them.

While Donna speaks to being "not really white," she does not speak out against the racist conversation between her colleagues. When I asked Donna how she would "use that information against them" she said she would inform her black colleagues about the stated perspectives. In doing so, Donna acts in solidarity with African Americans, rather than standing outside black communities and passing judgment, as in the cases of Gina and Raymond. However, her silence during her white colleague's conversation can be construed as tacit approval of the conversation and allows her colleagues to continue seeing her as white. Moreover, her black colleagues do not need yet another confirmation that racism exists. More to the point, the strategy of remaining silent and informing her black colleagues later indicates that Donna is still grappling with transforming her own white racial identity. The hope for an antiracist transformation lies in the fact that Donna is consciously struggling with her white racial identity and has many friendships and collegial ties with African Americans.

Like Donna, Shelly has many connections with African Americans. She has been divorced for several years and is currently raising her multiracial sons as a single parent. Since her town and its organizations are segregated, she has chosen to put her time and energy into African American organizations.

> They don't need me, but I need them. I am still pretty much an outsider looking in, but at least the little bit that I am involved and can do, I can feel the pulse of what's going on. And when you're raising African American males in a country that pretty much hates them and is afraid of them, you need to be a part of that, so it helps me. I wouldn't say I'm a big asset to them [African Americans], and I'm sure they don't see it that way, but I'm grateful that I am able to be a part of it, particularly for my children.

Shelly recognizes and is grateful for the organizational support. Juxtapose Shelly's gratitude to Gina's "frustration" that she "can't do it for them" and Theresa's fear of being the only white person.

As a current member of a local multiracial family organization, Shelly suggests that other whites in multiracial families do not reach out to blacks because

> [t]hey feel they are not welcome, so they don't want to go someplace where they're not wanted. I don't know what they think will happen if they go, but my feeling is that we have expected black people to do this forever; to put themselves in awkward positions to make them prove that they want to be our friends. I mean how uncomfortable can that be?

Individuals such as Shelly do not presume to be experts, spokespersons, or saviors. Instead they used statements like, "I'm still learning" or "I can never fully understand." These statements are not used as excuses for not becoming involved in black communities. Nor are they used as evidence that there is some essential difference between blacks and whites that prevent understanding, acceptance, and appreciation. Instead, these individuals use such statements to express gratitude, humility, and solidarity toward and with African Americans who helped them in the struggle to counter the often terrifying and punitive measures of whiteness.

Antiracist whites related incidences in which their whiteness caused them humility, embarrassment, anger, and frustration. As they transformed their white identity they spoke of losing or dropping white friends that did not understand or were not willing to consciously explore whiteness. They spoke of eventually finding new friends who were committed to being antiracist, many of whom were people of color.

The transformation of racial identities is complex and messy. While identities can be written about in discrete groupings, the lived reality is not so clear-cut. For some the transformation of their white identities meant vilifying all whites as bad and naming all blacks as good—a difficult essentialist trap. Nonetheless, those individuals who were willing to question racial identities and reach across the color line for connection and understanding were less likely to advocate for a multiracial category, and spent more time in black organizations and communities than multiracial organizations. The voices of white multiracial family members who are struggling from *within* communities of color are often silenced, marginalized, and dismissed by the more vocal advocates for a multiracial category and color-blind agendas.[25]

Understanding the centrality of "comfort" in the creation and maintenance of white racial identities can help us better understand the way whiteness and white privilege are reproduced in society. In other words, if whites who live with a black partner and/or children and thus face to some extent the terror of whiteness and are still unwilling to explore their own racial identities, then what of those who have no intimate connection to blackness? Moreover, because the search for racial comfort is at the heart of most multiracial family organizations it becomes clearer why whites are disproportionately represented. Finally, many whites who are parenting black and multiracial children as a result of adoption or birth seek multiracial family organizations as places for comfort, support, and advise. Instead of exploring their own white racial identities, these white parents seek comfort with other white parents, and the onus of race and white supremacy remains on the shoulders of their children and all people of color.

NOTES

1. See Kim Williams, "Linking the Civil Rights and Multiracial Movements," this volume.

2. Virtual communities serve a similar purpose, although that is beyond the scope of this study. For an in-depth analysis of online multiracial communities, see Erica Chito Childs, "Multirace.com," this volume.

3. Richard Dyer, *White* (New York: Routledge, 1997).

4. James Baldwin, "On Being White . . . and Other Lies," in *Black on White: Black Writers on What it Means to be White*, ed. David Roediger (New York: Schocken, 1999), 180.

5. Ian Haney Lopez, *White By Law: The Legal Construction of Race* (New York: New York University Press, 1994).

6. Racial formation is the term used by Omi and Winant to describe the ever-changing racial landscape played out in an ideological, political, social, and cultural context that advantages whites. I borrow from their term when I talk about "citizen formation" as that process of defining U.S. citizenship.

7. Evelyn Nakano Glenn, "Race, Gender, and Unequal Citizenship in the United States," paper delivered at *The Changing Terrain of Race and Ethnicity: Theory, Methods, and Public Policy* (University of Illinois at Chicago), October 26, 2001.

8. Joel Spring, *American Education*, 6th ed. (New York: McGraw-Hill, 2001).

9. Quoted in Nelson M. Rodriguez, "Emptying the Content of Whiteness," in *White Reign Deploying Whiteness in America*, ed. Joe Kincheloe, Shirley Steinberg, Nelson Rodriguez, Ronald Chenault (New York: St. Martin's Griffin): 1998.

10. Martha Mahoney, "Social Construction of Whiteness," in *Critical White Studies: Looking Behind the Mirror*, ed. Richard Delgado and Jean Stefancic (Philadelphia: Temple University Press, 1997).

11. Grace Elizabeth Hale, *The Making of Whiteness: The Culture of Segregation in the South 1890–1940* (New York: Vintage, 1998).

12. Angela Davis, "Race and Criminalization: Black Americans and the Punishment Industry," in *The House That Race Built*, ed. Wahneema Lubiano (New York: Vintage Books, 1998), 264–79.

13. Joel Spring, *American Education*.

14. Kathryn Neckerman and Joleen Kirschenman " 'We'd Love to Hire Them But . . . ': The Meaning of Race for Employers," reprinted in *Rethinking the Color Line: Readings in Race and Ethnicity* (Mountain View, CA: Mayfield, 1999), 276–87.

15. Terri Karis, " 'I Prefer to Speak of Culture': White Mothers of Multiracial Children," this volume.

16. Ruth Frankenberg, *White Women, Race Matters: The Social Construction of Whiteness* (Minneapolis: University of Minnesota Press, 1993), 233.

17. See Barbara Ransby, paper delivered at *The Changing Terrain of Race and Ethnicity: Theory, Methods, and Public Policy*, University of Illinois at Chicago, October 26, 2001.

18. Evelyn Nakano Glenn, "Race, Gender, and Unequal Citizenship in the United States: Historical Roots and Development," paper delivered at *The Changing Terrain of Race and Ethnicity: Theory, Methods, and Public Policy*, University of Illinois at Chicago, October 26, 2001.

19. See for instance, Werner Sollers, *Interracialism: Black-White Intermarriage in American History, Literature and Law* (London: Oxford Press, 2001); Abby Ferber, *White Man Falling: Race, Gender, and White Supremacy* (Lanham, MD: Rowman and Littlefield, 1998); and Martha Hodes, *Sex, Love, Race: Crossing the Boundaries in North American History* (New York: New York University Press, 1999).

20. Heather Dalmage, *Tripping on the Color Line: Black-White Multiracial Families in a Racially Divided World* (New Brunswick: Rutgers University Press, 2000); Ruth Frankenberg, *White Women, Race Matters: The Social Construction of Whiteness* (Minneapolis: University of Minnesota Press, 1993).

21. Howard Winant, *The World is a Ghetto: Race and Democracy Since WWII* (New York: Basic Books, 2001), 35.

22. Debra Van Ausdale and Joe R. Feagin, *The First R: How Children Learn Race and Racism* (Lanham, MD: Rowman and Littlefield, 2001), 1.

23. William Aal. *The Making and Unmaking of Whiteness*, ed. Brigit Brander Rasmussen, Irene J. Nexica, Eric Klinenberg, and Matt Wray (Durham: Duke University Press, 2001), 307.

24. Neil Gotanda "A Critique of 'Our Constitution is Color-Blind,' " in *Critical Race Theory: The Key Writings That Formed the Movement* (New York: The New Press, 1995), 259.

25. Dalmage, *Tripping on the Color Line*.

TWELVE

IDEOLOGY OF THE MULTIRACIAL MOVEMENT:

DISMANTLING THE COLOR LINE

AND DISGUISING WHITE SUPREMACY?

EILEEN T. WALSH

THE MULTIRACIAL MOVEMENT stands at the crossroads: will its identity politics take the path that encourages individuation to the exclusion of collective political action? Will it seek refuge in the promotion of hybrid identities that distance mixed-race persons from forging political alliances with blacks and other disenfranchised groups? Alternatively, will it coalesce around a group identity that challenges whiteness as the quintessential trope of privilege?

Despite the significant gains of the civil rights movement, racial disparities exist today in every major arena: criminal justice, education, health care, housing, and wealth accumulation.[1] The dismantling of these racial hierarchies cannot be accomplished by intellectually agreeing that social constructions of race are fiction; nor can that dismantling be accomplished by the promotion of individual rights. It is worth noting, however, that all of the rationales put forth by the following agents of change have been rooted in the rhetoric of individual rights. Jurisprudence depended on arguments regarding an individual's right to choose a partner in decriminalization of marriages across the color line.[2] Proponents of transracial adoption depended on arguments about the child's right for a loving home.[3] Multiracial people have argued for a bill of rights and recognition of microdiversity and diverse heritage.[4] These hard-won battles that focused on individual rights, however significant, cannot achieve the systemic elimination of racial hierarchies. An elimination of those inequalities requires a focus both on group rights as well as on the complex connections between racial hierarchies, gender, and social class structures. The Multiracial Movement's goal to redefine racial identity is quite likely to change not only the nature of racial classifications but also the identities and group allegiances of those who identify as multiracial. Unless the Multiracial Movement shifts its attention away from asserting the rights of individuals, however, its enduring legacy will be to sustain existing hierarchies, albeit along a color continuum instead of through a fictional racial dichotomy. If the Multiracial Movement is to succeed in eliminating race and the racial hierarchy, it must adopt and promote an antiracist, social justice agenda. Disappearing race from the vocabularies and consciousness of academics, policy makers, and the citizenry prior to dismantling the structures of inequality that persist not only puts the cart before the horse, it also serves to render white privilege invisible—a most dangerous proposition with a long legacy. Ignoring the ways in which race has been constructed as an essence, as well as marker for white group privilege, allows the mischief of race to remain hidden insidiously in our institutions while individuals, distracted from ferreting out injustice, delight in the belief that color no longer matters.

CONSTRUCTING A CATEGORY FOR HYBRID IDENTITIES CAMOUFLAGES MULTIRACIAL HERITAGE

The last decade has seen the coming of age of the first generation of children born after the U.S. Supreme Court decriminalized marriages across the color line.[5] Although such crossings have been present since colonial times, the one-drop rule of hypodescent has masked their prevalence. On both sides of the Atlantic Ocean, the one-drop rule of the United States is being questioned. Not only have children and parents of racially mixed families asserted their voices, but they also have created social pressure to rethink multiracial heritage.[6] Volumes documenting the alleged increasing number of racially mixed youngsters challenge notions about marriage and family formation across the color line.[7] Danzy Senna has declared the onset of the "Mulatto Millennium" in which "Pure breeds (at least the black ones) are out and hybridity is in. America loves us."[8]

Struggling against monoracial categories, the Multiracial Movement has staked out important territory and demanded recognition of multiracial heritages and diverse racial/ethnic identities.[9] The Multiracial Movement sought to reject the rigid racial categories that have been constructed over time to simultaneously create the fiction of both race and its corollary, racial purity, which form the basis of white supremacy. It demanded acknowledgment of hybrid identity and questioned the commonsense understandings of race in the twentieth century. Although the movement successfully has brought attention to the fiction that created existing racial categories, there is an ominous potential for the Multiracial Movement to become a pawn of the policy agendas on both sides of the political spectrum that threaten people of color.[10] The neoconservative contingent waves the "color-blind" banner over its thinly disguised policies to prop up and promote the existing racial hierarchies in which whites retain a disproportionate share of property, power, privilege, and prestige.[11] Likewise, the neoliberal contingent eschews a frontal attack on racial injustices with the hope that economic reform will benefit all disenfranchised groups without the derisive rhetoric of race—in other words, fearful of backlash from white voters, the New Left conflates social class inequality with racial inequality.[12]

AT THE ROOTS OF RACIAL CATEGORIES: GENDER AND SOCIAL CLASS

Thinking of race as one of the distinctive threads woven into the fabric of American social structure and consciousness distorts the historical evidence about the ways that race was constructed and reconstructed as a fiber inextricably intertwined with the threads of power relations known as gender and social class. Clinging to the popular idea that race is a distinctive thread oversimplifies strategies for unraveling remaining racial hierarchies.

At various points in the United States, different criteria have been used to construct the boundaries around the racial categories of white, nonwhite, black, and other.[13] Although racial categories have changed with shifting political and economic conditions, the "history of racial categories is often a history of sexuality as well, for it is partly as a result of the taboos against boundary crossing that such categories are invented."[14] In the United States, racial classifications used to construct and maintain the racial hierarchy have been unique and contradictory. For instance, to classify the offspring of blacks and whites, the colonies broke with British tradition of patrilineal descent and created a series of inheritance laws concerning the transmission of slavery status. Laws of "partus sequitur ventrem," stated that offspring, or issue, followed the mother; this "law of the womb" determined that the child's status as free, indentured, or slave resulted from the mother's status.[15] As a consequence, a child from a union of a free white women and a black man (free or not) was granted status as a free white; conversely, the offspring of a black woman slave and a free white male was destined to the status of a black slave. The obvious inconsistency of this classification system threatened to undermine the presumed biological basis of inferiority that formed the ideological lynchpin for the enslavement of African descendants. Further complications of this classification system became apparent with the growth in numbers of offspring whose status as free or slave could not be "read" from looking at their bodies.

Extensive, recent scholarship documents the regional responses that resulted in a hodgepodge of rules for constructing racial categories and for the evolving prohibitions against crossing the color line. One consistent purpose of the laws on adultery, bastardry, and marriages across the color line, however, is the attempt to regulate white women.[16] Despite the significant regional variation and inconsistent zigzags over time in racial definitions, the intent and consequence of the diverse rules evolving between the colonial period and the Civil War consistently accomplished three outcomes. First, the rules privileged whiteness by preserving the individual rights of the children born to white women while simultaneously oppressing black women by committing all of their children to slavery—a group status. Second, the rules asserted the power of white men over all women and over black men.[17] Third, the rules privileged social class: the toleration of sexual liaisons between white women and black men in the antebellum period reflected dominant beliefs that black women seduced white men and that only *poor* white women associated with black men; this powerful ideology that conflated whiteness with feminine purity gave planter-class women a great stake in patriarchy, while at the same time it provided some of those women who had children as the result of illicit liaisons the resources and opportunity to conceal their children's paternity.[18]

During the nineteenth century many states developed racial categories based on a combination of two variables: social class standing and known ancestry that assigned persons to racial categories according to complicated assessments of the presence of a grandparent or great-grandparent of African descent.[19] Most scholars agree that with the end of the slavery as a system, fluidity and inconsistency of racial categories solidified into a rigid caste system based on the fictional binary of black and white.

In sum, as the rigid binary color line evolved in this country, it reflected regional differences and frequent renegotiation of racial categories based on the interaction between gender and social class. In addition, the "law of the womb" where the status of child followed that of the mother proved problematic and gave way gradually to a set of rules based on hypodescent— ancestry with any known Negro blood precluded categorization on the "white" side of the color line.

The racial identities and consciousness prevalent in this country rely in large part on the projection of the rather recent binary racial thinking into our distant history. As a result of the shifting meanings of racial categories, it is difficult to animate and capture a sense of our long, elusive past of multiracialism in the United States. Losing sight of that historical vision, however, may create a mirage of multiracialism—an illusion of integration and equality that provides an undeserved hubris about how far we have come and blinds us to the difference between a masked multiracial heritage and an acknowledged multiracial heritage. The evidence tells us that there is a long history of individual rights that afforded some children of diverse heritages an escape from the harsh realities of membership in a group subject to discrimination and status as noncitizens or second-class citizens while other children of diverse racial heritage were consigned to group standing as blacks. The evidence suggests that the use of individual rights as a continued escape valve does not guarantee the elimination of racial hierarchies.

The construction and evolution of the color line in the United States required social processes that depended as much upon the interlinking systems of patriarchy and social class stratification that are embedded in our institutions as upon white supremacy. Gender, race, and social class have mutually constructed and supported the racial hierarchies apparent in our country today. Understanding the historical and political evolution of the color line highlights how the socially constructed categories of gender and social class were and remain as important in the creation and recreation of racial disparities as is the ideology of white supremacy that enforces and patrols the boundary between so-called whites and historically racialized peoples.

ENCOURAGING INDIVIDUATION TO THE EXCLUSION OF COLLECTIVE ACTION

Many arguments of the Multiracial Movement rest on the idea that the right to an individual identity is not possible within the racial classification system that existed in the second half of the twentieth century. The idea that the individual has a right to select a unique identity and that such a selection results from experience that is entirely individualistic parallels many of the arguments of the postmodern writers. Postmodern writers and some feminist theorists use the concept of the intersection of race, class, gender, and sexuality as a particularistic and unique location in the social structure. However, the "intersection of race, class, and gender" is a concept that is not used uniformly by all sociologists to refer to the interplay of structures affecting different groups. Used by Patricia Hill Collins and other black feminist writers, the term represents a concept that is a departure from the tradition in American sociology: it considers that race, gender, and social class (and, to a degree, age) are mutually constructing systems that shape group experience, knowledge, and praxis.

Until the last decade, within the discipline of sociology, race, class, and gender were discussed and conceptualized as variables distinct and separate from the confluence of their interactions in determining social position; much of the literature sought to weigh the relative "effects" of what were viewed as distinct, independent variables. In the positivist tradition, however, there was no recognition that race, class, and gender are experientially inseparable. Agents of knowledge cannot disaggregate their feeling experiences into distinct influences from race, gender, and social class.

Some feminist and postmodern theorists used the concept of intersections to promote an individualist approach to understanding identity and social position. Despite the practice by some authors of using the concept to locate a particular vantage point of an individual, the concept has broader theoretical use that explains both the nexus between social structure and groups and the complex interaction of structure and everyday experiences mediated through groups. The concept of intersection, as a heuristic device and a theoretical tool, can lead to understanding how members of groups come to know what they know. The concept also provides strategic insights that can empower groups to deploy situated knowledge in challenging the oppression of existing power hierarchies.

Many postmodernist writings decenter and deconstruct experience as entirely individualistic. As a result, postmodern writings emphasize difference rather than the potentials for collective action. For example, by focusing on the discourse of decentering and deconstruction, it is more likely that the situated knowledge of a homosexual black man will appear starkly in contrast to the situated knowledge of either an aging, white homosexual of the privileged class or a poor, black single mother. Difference and uniqueness are emphasized by a focus on the individual's unique positions on the axes of gender, race, and social class, which, in turn, situate the individual's knowledge, or standpoint. Such constructions of how identity affects consciousness are unlikely to promote a sense of shared oppression or a call to collective action. In fact, extreme individual analyses often critique the concept of "shared" group consciousness as a remnant of essentialist thinking—one that puts too much emphasis on the commonality of a group, as if the "essence" of being a woman or being black is somehow shared by all those with a similar status. On the other hand, black feminist writers, such as Patricia Hill Collins, warn exploited or oppressed persons to recognize their group affiliations, since, "for oppressed groups, diluting difference to the point of meaninglessness comes with real political danger."[20] Collins has noted further that "[b]ecause groups respond to the actual social conditions they confront, it stands to reason that groups constructed by different social realities will develop equally different analyses and political strategies."[21] Both truth and knowledge are largely dependent on social location of the group. Knowledge consists of the experiential information we store as well as the way we make "sense" of experience through interpersonal construction of meaning.

The postmodern conceptual tools of decentering and deconstruction can be useful to analyze power and knowledge. Yet, in terms of political action, a postmodern analysis is more likely to result in a sense of hopelessness and despair than in a realization of the possibilities for forming alliances. Rainier Spencer discusses how the "multiracial" is not based on what its members have in common backgrounds, but rather is rooted in what they are not—monoracial.[22] This raises an important issue in terms of how those who select a "multiracial" identity feel connected to various groups. Use of an individual lens on the intersections of race, gender, and social class removes the leverage that could serve to dislodge the hierarchical power structure from a potentially insightful analysis or call to action.

How then should the Multiracial Movement conceptualize the link between individual identity and strategic action with group location? Societies are constituted, reproduced, and changed by individuals behaving in structures. Emotion, intention, rationalities, and meaning are the result of how people interpret the world around them. In describing the connection between an individual's way of knowing and the dependence on a group for processing meaning and interpretations, Darnell Hunt states:

> [H]umans do not exist in a social vacuum; they are linked by various network ties to important others whose affection, approval and or respect they need and seek. Through social network discussions, individual audience members (re) negotiate their initial decodings of texts in ways they consider socially acceptable. Often this acceptability depends upon the social location of network members, upon the imprints that race, class, gender and sexuality have made on their life chances and subjectivities.[23]

Like all of us, those who identify as multiracial belong to multiple groups. If a multiracial identity results, however, in the formation of social networks that exclude discussions with blacks and other so-called minorities in favor of networks that emphasize differences between those minorities and those of so-called diverse racial heritages, it is likely that the gaps in understandings of social situations will increase. Without ties to important others for whom race has affected life chances and shaped day-to-day experiences, multiracial identities may come at a cost of further dividing the interpretations, commitments to justice, and ability to make sense of social texts.

It is significant that this notion of knowing acknowledges the importance of affection, a moderate feeling or emotion, in making social "sense" of experiences. Taking what an individual knows and putting it into action for gaining or using power depends on emotion, an important impetus to action. The following section describes how my location on the various axes of gender, race, and social class led me from a very individualistic way of knowing to an emotional, group-based consciousness that has resulted in a commitment to social justice for all oppressed groups.

CHALLENGING WHITENESS AS PRIVILEGE
THROUGH GROUP IDENTITY

As a woman, my whiteness as well as the social class trajectory I have traveled poised me to accept certain versions of how the world works and to interpret life events by accepting narratives, stories, and accounts that reso- nated with what I "knew" to be so. Other accounts, I discarded as flawed. Largely through a refraction of those culturally mediated accounts with my own "gut feeling," based in values and beliefs, some accounts "fit" and others did not. Openings to listen to other accounts only occurred when I was confronted with a bizarre experience or a serious injustice that did not fit either my knowledge or the accounts in circulation around me.

As one of the few students from a working-class family at an expensive, private, undergraduate university and later as one of the only women in a predominantly male workplace, I occupied outsider-within positions. From my vantage point, I was aware of the disconnections between my actual, lived experience and the cultural stories and explanations circulating around me. Throughout that time, I functioned as an individual with an awareness of my unique social location, but I did not feel any group consciousness.

Only when I came to raise a black daughter in a world befuddled by, or alternatively hostile to us, did I begin to form a sense of connectedness to an imagined community of persons categorized as black.[24] Through my intense love and caring for her, her father, and his family, and my nascent realization of the significance of race for them in this society, I began to feel like an outsider within the white world I had previously inhabited. Although it was no longer an option to remain ignorant and in denial of the true meaning and extent of white skin privilege, I might have engaged actively in attempts to extend my privilege to the two people I loved. On the other hand, I could choose a commitment to fight an all-out battle to change the oppression experienced by all people of color. The writings of black feminists resonated strongly with me: they talk of "the power of intense connectedness and of the way that caring deeply for someone can foster a revolutionary politics."[25] My love for my family motivated a sense of connection to a broader collectivity, but it was not sufficient to sustain the more difficult choices. It was anger and rage at the endless experiences of injustices I witnessed that created a reservoir of strength to take on necessary political battles. When I read Audre Lorde and bell hooks, I began to understand how my emotionally debilitating experiences with social injustice could be put to productive use:

Every woman has a well-stocked arsenal of anger potentially useful against those oppressions, personal and institutional, which brought that anger into being. Focused with precision it can become a powerful source of energy serving progress and change. . . . But anger expressed and translated into action in the service of our vision and our future is a liberating and strengthening act of clarification, for it is in the painful process of this translation that we identify who are our allies with whom we have grave differences and who are our genuine enemies. . . . Anger is an appropriate reaction to racist attitudes, as is fury when the actions arising from those attitudes do not change.[26]

I will never be part of the group that identifies as black. Race doesn't work that way. Nor do I feel a sense of connectedness anymore to any perceived or imagined group of whites. I have discovered too much hostility and too dense a denial there. Certainly, I have retained my white family and some of my white friends. In other cases, I have withdrawn from many who have exposed deeply held commitments to a sense of unearned superiority.

Like other white women who cross the color line, I often sense myself in disguise among other white-skinned persons to whom I have not "outed" myself. [27] Too often, in an all-white group a remark is made that reminds me that I am a complete outsider. School authorities, in particular, and others who view my family as "racially diverse," discount my interpretations of racial experiences for not being as "objective" as their white view. Although they have not been on the receiving end of racial discrimination, they are quick to position themselves as more qualified than I am to assess the motives and determine the intent of blatantly racist remarks made about people of color. Repeatedly my lived experience with racial issues has been dismissed as "a personal issue." In the world of whiteness that I once inhabited as a native, a most mystifying transformation has taken place: when my relationship to family members of color is known, my testimony as a witness to what I see and hear is discounted or dismissed. [28]

My daughter, a young woman now, self-identifies as black. I feel that I have far more at stake in the collective future of black women than I ever will with any other group. My grandchildren will be viewed as multiracial or black (depending in large part on where they live) and their future depends on our collective efforts to make this a better place. Ironically, however, it was not until I connected with a group of black women writers with whom I felt a strong affinity—connected and experienced their consciousness and commitments to social justice—that I began to understand the implications of patriarchy as another system closely linked to white supremacy. From the standpoint of black feminists, I finally got a window that allowed me to see and "get" feminism. This awareness opened my consciousness to the importance of recognizing and combating social injustice on all fronts through strategic alliances with other groups. In those ways, intersections of race, gender, and social class as a group experience, not an individual experience, bridged gaps in my knowledge and motivated political action.

Each and every person of a so-called multiracial heritage as well as their family members have choices about selecting an identity, accepting an externally derived identity, or resisting any identities imposed by others. In so doing, how one comes to feel part of the collectivity either has the potential to shift existing power relations or the potential to support existing hierarchies of domination. The path of increased sense of individual rights absent a stake in the well-being of groups who have not shared equally in the resources of our society, is a road that does not challenge white supremacy. Equally available is the path toward destabilizing the current systems of inequality by changing our group allegiances.

By its very nature the concept of intersections creates a potential instability in the power relationships: due to the multiple planes coalescing into group locations in the social structure, and the diversity of allegiances that result from those intersections, people can form alliances to support and maintain the existing power structure or to resist it and promote their own interests.

THE DANGEROUS (MIS)APPROPRIATION
OF MULTIRACIAL IDEOLOGY

Every day, in every corner of America, we are redrawing the color lines and redefining what race really means. It's not just a matter of black and white anymore; the nuances of brown and yellow and red mean more—and less— than ever: the promise and perils ahead.

The captioned *Newsweek* cover story makes headlines of the "Redefining of Race in America." The article, called "The New Face of Race," features more pictures than text.[29] Its "Gallery of Native-Born Americans" features pictures of beautiful, brown faces with straight white teeth in appealing, friendly poses. Under each picture is a list of the ethnicities of the person. One little girl is identified as "Nigerian, Irish, African-American, Native American, Russian Jewish, and Polish Jewish."[29] This litany of ethnicities defies the longstanding racial binary of black/white, renders racial categorization impossible, implies the disappearance of race as an important or salient feature of our society, and ushers in the emergence of ethnicity paradigms that gloss over the difference between the experience of racialized groups and ethnic white experience.

Such public celebrations of diversity seem aimed at calming anxiety over the shifting demographics that find whites no longer a majority in states such as California, Texas, and New York. The editors send us the message that the hybrid combines many races—happily, with no sign of conflict. The net result, of course, is an image that approximates the voluntary, symbolic ethnicity familiar to whites.

What role does ethnic identity play in the lives of white Americans? Mary Waters has concluded that it provides a sense of imagined community—because it is symbolic and somewhat arbitrary—at the same time that it provides a sense of uniqueness, for it distinguishes the individual who selects it as distinct.[30] In an attempt to understand the 1980 census data on ancestry, Waters conducted interviews in upper-middle-class, white suburbs of San Jose and Philadelphia. She interviewed Roman Catholics to determine what ancestry they would cite in response to the ethnicity census question and what it meant to them. She found a fluidity and lack of consistency within families about their ethnic identity.

> For the ways in which ethnicity is flexible and symbolic and voluntary for white middle-class Americans are the very ways in which it is not so for non-white and Hispanic Americans. The social and political consequences of being Asian or Hispanic or Black are not symbolic for the most part, or voluntary. They are real and often hurtful.[31]

Moreover, Waters found that family histories of Americans of European descent often emphasize discrimination in the past that their forbearers had overcome. In fact, most of the respondents could tell family stories about how difficult the early years were in the United States due to discrimination. "All of my respondents were sure that their ancestors had faced discrimination when they first came to the United States."[32] Likewise, Stein and Hill have argued that Americans of later generations have a "dime store ethnicity."[33] That is, the choice of a grandparent to identify with narrows down for the "identity shopper" the range of groups with whom to symbolically identify; the process is similar to the way one might shop for a product in a dime store. This ethnic "identity" is not authentic, because it is chosen, brought out to display in public by the "shopper's" volition and is not externally imposed.

The best part of the story presented by the *Newsweek* article and other media sources about both increased diversity and increased racial "mixing" is not only that race no longer matters and has no meaning, but that America has arrived at this multiracial, hybrid reality with no apparent strife. Certainly none of the white readers of *Time* or *Newsweek* has had to question white privilege; there will even less possibility of a demand for "group rights," a fundamental premise of identity politics. The Multiracial Movement's focus on recognition of racially "mixed" persons in census revisions and the popular discourse play into an image that the racial hierarchy of this country has transformed into a multiracial democracy. Often, there is an implicit assumption that racism is on the wane due to this alleged increased mating across the color line. It would be well to point out that the evolution of a multiracial classification system in Brazil actually undermined civil rights by eliminating group identification with the oppressed. The mulatto class in Brazil did not feel allegiance to or identification with the *negritude* liberation movement blacks, the *preto* class. The black struggles did not have as many supporters as civil rights struggles as did those in the United States where all those of color, defined by the rigid binary racial system, recognized their own stake.[34]

CONCLUSIONS: COMMITMENTS TO SOCIAL JUSTICE

We don't choose our color, but we can choose our commitments. We do not choose our parents, but we do choose our politics. Yes, we do not make these decisions in a vacuum; they occur within a social structure that gives value to whiteness and offers rewards for racism.[35]

To what degree are interracial couples and multiracial families sites where individuals discover the tools to dismantle the oppression of racial legacies? To what degree, if any, are interracial couples and multiracial families committed to social justice? Unless these families are sites for the systematic resistance to the structured ways that race matters in our society, we cannot assume that multiracialism is a force that works to challenge the encoded white supremacy that pervades our institutions. An aim of the Multiracial Movement must include a clear focus on the ways that whiteness, although an imaginary myth, accrues power and privilege through use of certain racial discourses. In his examination of the ways popular racial discourse is circulated by the media, John Fiske observes:

> Whiteness survives only because of its ability to define, monitor and police the boundary between itself and others and to control any movement across it. Because its space is strategic and not essential, there is movement into and out of whiteness. While arguing that whiteness is better identified by what it does than by what it is, and by defining it as a flexible positionality from which power operates, we must not forget that people with white skins have massively disproportionate access to that power base. While not essentializing whiteness into white skins or Blackness into black ones, we must recognize that whiteness uses skin color as an identity card by which to see where its interests may best be promoted and its rewards distributed.[36]

When the rhetoric about the changing face of race is put in the service of maintaining existing hierarchies by conflating the historically different experience of ethnic whites with that of nonwhites, the Multiracial Movement's accomplishments can set the stage for a replay of some of the tired old tropes used to deny that race matters.

The very processes that perpetuate racial inequalities in our society depend upon putting backstage and out of sight the ongoing legacy of white supremacy that pervades the media representations, the public school curricula, legislation, and jurisdiction that continue to disadvantage oppressed groups. And, addressing racial domination as if it has been uncoupled from the socially constructed categories of gender and social class leaves intact the forces of oppression that support the current racial hegemony.

Although the movement's contributions are laudable, an unintended consequence of the multiracial project to bend the color line in this country may be the further disenfranchisement of those people of color who do not fit the newly evolving "multiracial" racial category. The Multiracial Movement's successes can be seized and appropriated to support the backlash against civil rights. Its rhetoric about the changing face of race provides a front about the disappearance of racial prejudice and discrimination. Behind the optimistic facade of interracial harmony, the hegemonic process of white supremacy is rendered invisible. The Multiracial Movement unwittingly provides "plausible" deniability to those in power who use the image of increased diversity and the "changing face of race" to promote policies that advance the interest of the "haves" while insisting that any call for group rights for the "have nots" is a throwback to the "separate but equal" era of American life. The literature about multiracial families often confuses the possible transcendence of prejudice that allows intimacy to develop between two people and within a family, with both a loosening of the societal taboo associated with crossing the color line and with optimism about eradication of racial hierarchies. In the tradition of liberalism, it puts all of the emphasis on the individuals with no attention to the structural ways in which society continues to be organized by race. In so doing, it puts little, if any, attention on the complex workings of white supremacy, gender, and social class. A new racial order of equality is not possible without understanding those links and committing to break down the interlocking infrastructures of oppression.

NOTES

1. See Douglas Massey and Nancy Denton, *American Apartheid: Segregation and the Making of the Underclass* (Cambridge: Harvard University Press, 1994). For a thorough discussion on the state's involvement in policies that have created persisting racial

gaps in wealth and income, see Melvin Oliver and Thomas Shapiro, *Black Wealth/White Wealth* (New York: Routledge, 1997).

2. See Peggy Pascoe, "Miscegenation Law, Court Cases, and Ideologies of 'Race' in Twentieth Century America," in *Interracialism: Black-White Intermarriage in American History, Literature, and Law*, ed. Werner Sollors (London: Oxford University Press, 2001). Her analysis of discourse in court decisions demonstrates that justifications for antimiscegenation has a long tradition of ignoring issues about the equality of racial groups in favor of promoting the individual's right to choose a partner from another group. Her analysis includes a critique of wording in the U.S. Supreme Court's landmark decision, *Loving v. Commonwealth of Virginia*, 388 U.S. at 12.

3. Maria P. Root, *Racially Mixed People in America* (Newbury Park, CA: Sage, 1992).

4. Maria P. Root, *The Multiracial Experience: Racial Borders as the New Frontier* (Thousand Oaks, CA: Sage, 1996). Also see Naomi Zack, *Race and Mixed Race* (Philadelphia: Temple University Press, 1996) and Naomi Zack, ed., *American Mixed Race: The Culture of Microdiversity* (Lanham, MD: Rowman and Littlefield, 1995).

5. *Loving v. Commonwealth of Virginia*, 388 U.S. at 12.

6. For instance, the revision of the 2000 census to allow individuals to check more than one ethnic box is a significant change resulting from the project of the multiracial movement. This historical project is outlined by Rainier Spencer, *Spurious Issues Race and Multiracial Identity Politics in the United States* (Boulder: Westview, 1999). Also see Marion Kilson, *Biracial Young Adults of the Post-Civil Rights Era* (Westport, Connecticut: Bergin and Garvey, 2000).

7. Maria P. Root, *The Multiracial Experience*.

8. Danzy Senna, "The Mulatto Millennium," in *Half and Half: Writers on Growing Up Biracial and Bicultural*, ed. Claudine Chiawei O'Hearn (New York: Pantheon, 1998). Also refer to Barbara Tizard and Anne Phoenix, *Black, White or Mixed Race? Race and Racism in the Lives of Young People of Mixed Parentage* (London: Routledge, 1993). A compilation of essays on so-called mixed bloods can be found in William Penn, ed., *As We Are Now: Mixblood Essays on Race and Identity* (Berkeley: University of California Press, 1997).

9. As Rainier Spencer points out in *Spurious Issues*, the Multiracial Movement has demanded recognition of those recently born to parents categorized as different races while simultaneously ignoring that for the past three centuries persons of mixed African and European heritage in the United States have been forced into a monoracial category of "black." Denying the multiracial heritage and heterogeneity of the majority of those categorized as "black," while advocating for the importance of declared multiracial identity for those born recently is one of ironic ways that racial hierarchies continue to get reinscribed.

10. In this regard, I rely on discussions of racial hegemony and view the Multiracial Movement as one of several competing racial projects. "A racial project is simultaneously an interpretation, representation, or explanation of racial dynamics, and an effort to reorganize and redistribute resources along particular racial lines. Racial projects connect what race means in a particular discursive practice and the ways in which both social structure and everyday experiences are racially organized." Michael Omi and Howard Winant, *Racial Formations in the United States from the*

1960's to the 1990's (New York: Routledge, 1994), 56. The Multiracial Movement's achievement in disrupting existing racial categories is one example of how racial categories shift and slide. For a critique of the movement's failure to contest the meaning of race, see Rachael F. Moran, *Interracial Intimacy: The Regulation of Race and Romance* (Chicago: University of Chicago Press, 2001), 154–78.

11. Omi and Winant, *Racial Formations in the United States from the 1960's to the 1990's*. The authors present a discussion that exposes neoconservatism as a racial project that served to erode the progress of the civil rights movement while it simultaneously masqueraded the white supremacist agenda by creating a "commonsense" understanding of a "color-blind" rhetoric where meritocracy is allegedly the driving force. Also, see Robin D. G. Kelley, *Yo Mama's Disfunktional! : Fighting the culture wars in urban America* (Boston: Beacon Press, 1997). For a review and critique of Ronald Reagan's and California governor Pete Wilson's use of the media and codes to reestablish patriarchal, white supremacy, see George Lipsitz, *The Possessive Investment in Whiteness: How White People Profit from Identity Politics* (Philadelphia: Temple University Press, 1998).

12. The seminal works that shift the rhetorical from race to class are William J. Wilson, *The Declining Significance of Race: Blacks and Changing American Institutions* (Chicago: University of Chicago Press, 1976) and William Julius Wilson, *When Work Disappears. The World of the New Urban Poor* (New York: Vintage Books, 1996). A discussion of the New Left and its conflation of class-based issues with race can be found in chapter 5 in Stephen Steinberg, *Turning Back. The Retreat from Racial Justice in American Thought and Policy* (Boston: Beacon Press, 1995) and also in Orlando Patterson, *The Ordeal of Integration: Progress and Resentment in America's Racial Crisis* (Washington, DC: Civitas, 1997). For a critique refer to Cornel West, *Race Matters* (New York: Vintage Books, 1994).

13. Ian Haney-López, *White by Law: the Legal Construction of Race* (New York: New York University Press, 1996); David R. Roediger, *Wages of Whiteness: Race and the Making of the American Working Class* (London: Verso, 1991); Alexander Saxton, *Rise and the Fall of the White Republic: Class Politics and Mass Culture in Nineteenth Century America* (New York: Verso, 1990).

14. Martha Hodes, ed., *Sex, Love, Race: Crossing the Boundaries in North American History* (New York: New York University Press, 1999), 1.

15. Martha Hodes, *White Women, Black Men: Illicit Love in 19th Century South* (New Haven: Yale University Press, 1997); Kathleen Brown, *Good Wives, Nasty Wenches, and Anxious Patriarchs. Gender, Race, and Power in Colonial Virginia* (Chapel Hill: University of North Carolina Press, 1996); and Orlando Patterson, *Slavery and Social Death: A Comparative Study* (Cambridge: Harvard University Press, 1986).

16. Kathleen Brown, *Good Wives, Nasty Wenches, and Anxious Patriarchs*, See also Nancy F. Cott, *Public Vows: A History of Marriage and the Nation* (Cambridge: Harvard University Press, 2000) An important discussion about impact on the construction of white femininity is found in A. Leon Higgenbotham and Barbara Kopytoff, "Racial Purity and Interracial Sex in the Law of Colonial and Antebellum Virginia," in *Interracialism: Black-White Intermarriage in American History, Literature and Law*, ed. Werner Sollers (London: Oxford University Press, 2001). See also Gary B. Nash, "Hidden History of Mestizo America," in *Sex, Love, Race: Crossing the Boundaries*.

17. It should be noted that contrary to the widespread belief that black men were routinely lynched as punishment for alleged sexual relations with white women throughout colonial and antebellum periods, the preponderance of evidence is that such violent action against black men began after Emancipation with the elimination of slavery and increased white sexual anxiety directed at black men. Frederick Douglass and Ida B. Wells and W. E. B. DuBois all note the prevalence of such lynching as a post–Civil War phenomenon. A thorough illustration of the illicit liaisons across the color line is in Martha Hodes, *White Women, Black Men.*

18. Peter W. Bardaglio, " 'Shameful Matches': The Regulation of Interracial Sex and Marriage in the South before 1900," in *Sex, Love, Race: Crossing Boundaries* and Eva Sack, "Representing Miscegenation Law," in *Interracialism.*

19. See Joel Williamson, *New People: Miscegenation and Mulattoes in the United States* (New York: Free Press, 1980).

20. Patricia Hill Collins, *Fighting Words. Black Women and the Search for Justice* (Minneapolis: University of Minnesota Press, 1998), 149.

21. Patricia Hill Collins, *Fighting Words,* 223.

22. Rainier Spencer, *Spurious Issues.*

23. Darnell M. Hunt, *O. J. Simpson Facts & Fictions. News Rituals in the Construction of Reality* (New York: Cambridge University Press, 1999), 48.

24. In describing my daughter I deliberately choose the designator "black" rather than biracial or "mixed," for three reasons. First, it was an identity externally imposed upon her by others at school and in our social settings based on her physical appearance in a milieu that was predominantly white. Second, I prefer "black" for political reasons over a hyphenated designator such as African-American, because it is primarily people of color whose identities are qualified as "Americans" by virtue of a hyphenated modifier (African/American, Chinese American, Japanese American, Mexican-American, etc.) Few, if any whites, identify primarily by country of origin of distant ancestors. Third, I avoid terms such as biracial, multiracial, and mixed race because they appear to reify race giving it more validity as a biological concept than is deserved.

25. Patricia Hill Collins, *Fighting Words,* 200.

26. Audre Lorde, *Sister Outsider Essays and Speeches* (Freedom, CA: The Crossing Press, 1984), 127.

27. Maureen Reddy, *Crossing the Color Line: Race, Parenting, and Culture* (New Brunswick: Rutgers University Press, 1994), discusses this common experience among white women married to black men.

28. There are a number of ways this has been expressed and articulated. At one extreme are those who challenge my continued membership in the exclusive circle of whiteness: as one student in one of my courses announced upon hearing I had a black child, "You are a traitor to the race. How could you? And, how could you expect any of us to take you seriously when you don't even think right like a white person?" More common are the reactions when I express my view that one of the whites who knows my family will address one of the others and say, "You know Eileen feels strongly about this. Because of her family, she sees race when it isn't even there." By virtue of my "contamination" by relations with black family members, my interpretations are dismissed. At the other extreme are whites who call upon me to speak

for blacks, which I, of course, demur. This theme is developed in my dissertation in progress, "The Edge of the Color Line: How Whites Married to Blacks Understand Race, Experience Whiteness, and Negotiate Identity through the Prism of Gender."

29. Jon Meacham, "The New Face of Race," *Newsweek*, September 18, 2000.

30. Mary C. Waters, *Ethnic Options. Choosing Identities in America* (Berkeley: University of California Press, 1990).

31. Ibid., 156.

32. Ibid., 161.

33. Howard F. Stein and Robert F. Hill, *The Ethnic Imperative: Examining the New White Ethnic Movement* (University Park: Pennsylvania State University Press, 1977).

34. See Darien J. Davis, *Avoiding the Dark: Race and the Forging of National Culture in Modern Brazil* (Brookfield: Ashgate, 1999). Also refer to Robert B. Toplin, *Freedom and Prejudice: the Legacy of Slavery in the United States and Brazil* (Westport, Connecticut: Greenwood Press, 1981). Thomas E. Skidmore *Black into White: Race and Nationality in Brazilian Thought* (New York: Oxford University Press, 1974), 70, notes:

> No slave society in the Americas failed to produce a large mulatto population. It was not the fact of miscegenation, but the recognition or non-recognition of the mixed bloods as a separate group, that made the difference.

35. George Lipsitz, *The Possessive Investment in Whiteness: How White People Profit from Identity Politics* (Philadelphia: Temple University Press, 1998), vii.

36. John Fiske, *Media Matters: Race and Gender in the U.S. Politics* (Minneapolis: University of Minnesota Press, 1994).

CONTRIBUTORS

ERICA CHITO CHILDS is Assistant Professor of Sociology at Eastern Connecticut State University. Her main areas of research explore issues of racial identity, interracial marriage, and family diversity. She is currently completing a book manuscript on the images and discourses surrounding black/white couples in America.

KIMBERLY MCCLAIN DACOSTA is Assistant Professor of African and African American Studies and Social Studies at Harvard University. She received her Ph.D. in sociology from the University of California, Berkeley.

HEATHER M. DALMAGE, Director of the Mansfield Institute for Social Justice, is Associate Professor of Sociology at Roosevelt University in Chicago. She has published and presented broadly in the area of race and multiracialism. Dalmage is the author of *Tripping on the Color Line: Black-White Multiracial Families in a Racially Divided World* (Rutgers University Press, 2000). She is on the board of the Chicago Council on Urban Affairs and is currently a fellow at the St. Clair Drake Center for African American Studies.

ABBY L. FERBER is Associate Professor of Sociology and Director of Women's Studies at the University of Colorado at Colorado Springs. Ferber is the author of *White Man Falling: Race, Gender and White Supremacy* (Rowman and Littlefield 1998), co-author of *Making A Difference: University Students of Color Speak Out* (Rowman and Littlefield, 2001) *and Hate Crimes in America: What Do We Know?* (American Sociological Association, 2000), and co-editor of *Privilege: A Reader* (Westview, 2003). She is also editor of the forthcoming volume, *Home Grown Hate: Gender and Organized Racism* (Routledge, 2004). She teaches in the areas of race, gender, and social theory, and has published in a wide range of journals, as well as *The Chronicle of Higher Education*.

CHARLES A. GALLAGHER is Assistant Professor at Georgia State University in Atlanta. His research focuses on the political and cultural meaning whites attach to their race and the rhetorical strategies whites use to explain racial inequality. He has written on the sociological functions of color-blind political narratives, the sociological implications of racial innumeracy, and has examined how ethnic history shapes perceptions of privilege in the United States. He is currently writing a book on race relations based on interviews with 150 whites from around the country. He is the editor of *Rethinking the Color Line: Readings in Race and Ethnicity.*

TERRI A. KARIS is a psychologist and Assistant Professor of Marriage and Family Therapy at the University of Wisconsin-Stout. She is a co-author of the book *Multiracial Couples: Black and White Voices*, and is co-editor of *Clinical Issues With Multiracial Couples: Theory and Research.* Karis has been the recipient of many awards including the Jessie Bernard Award for Outstanding Research Proposal from a Feminist Perspective and the Bush Leadership Fellowship. She is currently editing a book on cross-cultural couple relationships.

REBECCA CHIYOKO KING-O'RIAIN is currently a Government of Ireland Post Doctoral Fellow at Trinity College Dublin, pursuing research on the possible addition of a race/ethnicity question to the Irish Census. While at the University of San Francisco, she has researched the changing demographics of the Japanese American community in California and Hawaii through a case study of community beauty pageants, on which she is completing a book manuscript. She has also written about the impact of the 2000 Census on the Asian and Pacific Islander communities.

KERRY ANN ROCKQUEMORE is Associate Professor of African American Studies and Sociology at the University of Illinois at Chicago. She is co-author of *Beyond Black: Biracial Identity in America* (Sage, 2001). Her research focuses on racial socialization in interracial families and she is currently completing her next book, *Raising the Biracial Child: From Theory to Practice* (Altamira, forthcoming).

BARBARA KATZ ROTHMAN is Professor of Sociology at the City University of New York. Her books, published in the United States, Great Britain, Finland, Germany, and Japan, include: *In Labor; The Tentative Pregnancy; Recreating Motherhood;* with Wendy Simonds, *Centuries Of Solace;* editorship of *The Encyclopedia Of Childbearing;* and most recently, *The Book Of Life.* She is widely published in both popular and scholarly sources, and has lectured throughout the United States, England, Australia, New Zealand, Germany, Switzerland, and the Netherlands, where she was a Fulbright Scholar. She was a visiting professor at the Universität Osnabrück and a Leverhulme Professor at the University of Plymouth in the UK. Katz Rothman is past president of two national sociological professional associations, Sociologists for Women in Society and the Society for the Study of Social Problems.

RAINIER SPENCER is Associate Dean of the College of Liberal Arts at the University of Nevada, Las Vegas, and is the director of the Afro-American Studies Program there. He is the author of *Spurious Issues: Race and Multiracial Identity Politics in the United States*. Focusing on the ways that constructions of race are continually reified in the United States, Dr. Spencer is particularly interested in the deployment of biological race by multiracial identity advocates and by the popular media.

EILEEN T. WALSH, a graduate student in the Department of Sociology at the University of Southern California, is completing her dissertation on the gendered nature of whiteness. She directs the evaluation research (funded by the Department of Justice, Office of Juvenile Justice Delinquency Prevention) for The Family Violence Project, a nonprofit organization. As past president of the Laguna Beach Unified School District and the Capistrano-Laguna Regional Occupation Program, Ms. Walsh is a community activist in educational reform. Ms. Walsh teaches undergraduate courses at California State Polytechnic University (Pomona), Chapman University, and CSULA on race, gender, sexuality, and social class.

KIM M. WILLIAMS is Assistant Professor of Public Policy at the Kennedy School. Her research focuses on racial change, race-ethnic politics and political movements. She is currently finishing a book, *The Next Step in Civil Rights? The American Multiracial Movement*, and has contributed to a number of edited volumes. She received her Ph.D. from Cornell University.

INDEX

One-drop rule, 25, 37n20, 37n21, 37n22, 73, 128, 154, 222; basis in white supremacy, 115; challenges to, 220; as classification rule, 128; creation of black bodies by, 30; as cultural norm, 127; de facto application of, 127; hegemonic power of, 114; interracial sexuality and, 48; kinship rules and, 30; legal codification, 126; as mechanism for maintenance of control, 25; persistence of, 128; prevention of formation of family ties across racial boundaries and, 25; production of racial groups and, 29; racial categories and, 113; racialization of kinship and, 29; as racist implement, 121n14; relegation of persons to black group by, 113; reproduction of race fallacy by, 114; as social instrument, 114; social stratification and, 121n14; specific reference to blacks, 37n23; support for, 47, 105; understanding multiracial experience and, 11

Organizations, multiracial, 95n37, 151. See also Multiracial Movement; construction of racial identities of whites in, 203–216; disproportionate representation of white parents in, 203; growth of, 1, 5; I-Pride, 2; local, 5; need for, 213; political climate during development of, 3; protection of white privilege and, 203–216; racial comfort and, 203–216; reasons for joining, 19

Organizations, white supremacist, 9

Pacific Citizen (periodical), 185
Parham, Thomas, 104, 105
Pathology trope, 103–106
Patriarchy, 11, 40n55, 75n11, 159n30, 223
Patterson, Orlando, 74
Peller, Gary, 45
Petri, Tom, 133

Pierce, William, 55
A Place for Us (APFU), 88
A Place For Us Ministry for Interracial Couples, 4
Policies: group-based, 4; to maintain white control, 37n22; race-based, 3; social, 19, 20, 196; welfare state, 40n62
Politics: group, 106; identity, 4, 29, 66, 67, 229; multiracial, 19, 20–21; progressive, 12; racial, 2, 64, 72; of recognition, 89
Postmodernism: concept of intersection and, 223–226; decentering/deconstruction and, 225; fragmentation and, 12
Poststructuralism: centrality of borders in constructing identity, 45
Poverty: adoption and, 13, 197; racism and, 13; War on Poverty, 79
Powell, A.D., 153, 154
Privilege: afforded by racial categorization, 30; color-blindness and, 13; preservation of, 48; protecting, 203–216; racial, 44, 162, 163; recognition of, 213; reinscription of, 204; white, 13, 44, 55, 60, 72, 162, 163, 167, 168, 173n12, 203–216, 222; white supremacy and, 55
Project RACE, 87, 88, 102, 103, 135, 144
Pryor, Rain, 127

Race: access to amenities and, 73; adoption and, 2; American notions of, 20; assignment of, 36n18; awareness of impacts of, 12; as biological construct, 6, 10, 11, 47, 49, 99, 108, 109, 110–120, 112, 115, 117, 118, 123n47; centrality in society, 211; centrality of power to construction of, 7; "changing," 9; color-blind constructions of, 12; comfort, 14; complexity of, 13; connections to family and, 20; construction of, 45; construction

Race, 52; myth of purity of, 10, 14n1; privilege, 72; retention of disproportionate share of property, 221; self-identification as, 61; separatism, 54; superiority of, 52; as victims of racial oppression, 44; as victims of racism, 207–208

"Whitespeak," 169

White supremacy, 1; defense of white racial identity/privilege, 55; disguising, 219–231; entrenchment of, 6; family and, 8; hatred and, 43; interracial sexuality and, 43–56; Jews and, 50, 51; maintaining, 117; maintenance through antimiscegenation laws, 25, 26; multiracialism and, 8; one-drop rule and, 115; organizations of, 9; publications on, 43, 44, 45, 50, 51, 52, 53, 54; racial purity and, 221; reinforcement of, 7, 9, 14n1; reproduction on websites, 11; role in construction of Multiracial Movement, 9; struggles against, 5; upholding, 17

Wiegman, Robyn, 112–113

Wilberforce University (Ohio), 27

Williams, Gregory, 128

Williams, Kim, 9–10, 77–93

Winant, Howard, 3, 17, 75n3, 208, 217n6, 232n10, 233n11

Women: awareness of political implications of relationships, 162; color-blindness and, 11, 162; defining selves in multiracial families, 12; distancing from whiteness, 165–172; downplaying significance of race, 12; fluid racial constructions of, 162; focus on cultural rather than race, 165–170; middle-class respectability and, 12; public/private identities, 163, 170–172; racial border crossing and, 162; in racist societies, 11; regulation of, 222; support for interracial children, 164–165; white mothers in multiracial families, 11, 161–172

Woods, Tiger, 2, 5, 11, 104, 131–139

Young, Robert J.C., 46, 47

Zack, Naomi, 115

Zoeller, Fuzzy, 137, 138